Josh Widdicombe has been touring as a stand-up comedian for over a decade. He co-hosts *The Last Leg* on Channel 4 and *Hypothetical* on Dave and has appeared on everything from *Have I Got News For You* to *A League of Their Own* to *Blankety Blank*. More importantly in this post-TV age, he hosts one of the country's most popular podcasts – *Parenting Hell* – with fellow comedian Rob Beckett, as well as cult '90s football podcast *Quickly Kevin, Will He Score?*

JOSH WIDDICOMBE

Watching Neighbours Twice a Day ...

BLINK
bringing you closer

First published in the UK by Blink Publishing
an imprint of Bonnier Books UK
4th Floor, Victoria House
Bloomsbury Square
London WC1B 4DA
England

Owned by Bonnier Books
Sveavägen 56, Stockholm, Sweden

facebook.com/blinkpublishing
twitter.com/blinkpublishing

Hardback – 9781788704359
Paperback – 9781788704366
Trade Paperback – 9781788704694
Ebook – 9781788704373
Audio Digital Download – 9781788704380

A CIP catalogue of this book is available from the British Library.

Typeset by IDSUK (Data Connection) Ltd
Printed and bound by Clays Ltd, Elcograf S.p.A

13 5 7 9 10 8 6 4 2

First published in hardback by Blink Publishing in 2021.
This edition published in paperback by Blink Publishing in 2022.

Every reasonable effort has been made to trace copyright holders of material
reproduced in this book, but if any have been inadvertently overlooked the
publishers would be glad to hear from them.

Blink Publishing is an imprint of Bonnier Books UK
www.bonnierbooks.co.uk

To Pearl and Cassius,
I hope your childhoods contain something
as life affirming as *Neighbours*

And to Rose,
who would have thought this at the start of series 3?

CONTENTS

'To inform, educate and entertain'

Lord Reith, Director-General of the BBC, 1927–38,
summarising the purpose of the Corporation

'Television, the drug of the nation,
Breeding ignorance and feeding radiation'

'Television, the Drug of the Nation' by The Disposable
Heroes of Hiphoprisy, 1992

'Number 3 . . . It's a girl who can cry milk!'

Chris Evans, TFI Friday, *1997*

'Auntie Stella is having a party'
Gus Honeybun's Magic Birthdays
ITV, 5:10pm, 1 January 1990

I'd like to start this book by discussing the puppet and rabbit Gus Honeybun. I am fairly confident this is the first book in the history of literature to do such a thing, although I must admit I haven't read any Charlotte Brontë.

Until I left home to go to university at the age of 18, I assumed Gus Honeybun was a big deal. Not mega-famous – if I'd been asked for a list of '90s icons I wouldn't have plumped for Gascoigne, Blair and Honeybun – but a household name, like Des Lynam or Maureen from *Driving School*. Sadly, as I found out when throwing out a few Honeybun-based jokes to unimpressed girls in freshers' week, his fame actually stopped just north of Yeovil.

For those not raised in Cullompton or Great Torrington I should briefly explain the tale of Gus Honeybun. Augustus Jeremiah Honeybun (to give him his full name) was a shoddily made rabbit puppet who co-hosted *Gus Honeybun's Magic Birthdays* on Television South West (local ITV in the West Country). *Gus Honeybun's Magic Birthdays* would last ten minutes and consisted entirely of the host reading out children's birthday cards with Honeybun matching their age in years with the amount of times he would bunny-hop up and down. Naturally.

If the birthdays and bouncing up and down weren't enough for you, behind Honeybun and his human sidekick – and, to be clear, as with all great puppets, the human was the sidekick – a green screen would show different drawings of generic countryside scenes. Maybe a stile going over a fence in a field or a church in the snow, the kind of things you would get on a disappointing 1,000-piece jigsaw given to you by an auntie at Christmas. Most suspiciously, Honeybun would switch between these backgrounds by occasionally pressing a magic mushroom-shaped button, which even at the age of seven I felt was a little on the nose when it came to drug references.

I want to be clear on this. At the time this show felt to me like a totally normal thing to be screened on television. In fact, it was by a distance the most popular thing Television South West (TSW) produced.[1] I don't know if the birthday

---

[1] Full disclosure: Their other output was stuff like *Interpub*, a show in which various pub teams from across the TSW region would compete in arm wrestling, darts, a talent contest and a pub quiz. You can still watch the 1986 final online, which sees The Clifton face The Carpenters at The Rainbow House Hotel: '. . . neutral ground in the lovely seaside town of Torquay, great at any time of year,' says our host as the camera pans along a deserted street in the rain. It is an astonishing viewing experience, featuring music from local pub band The Scandals – who play

show genre stretched out to the rest of the country – I can't see why it would have – but it had taken Devon and Cornwall by storm. *Gus Honeybun's Magic Birthdays* was a West Country institution, like clotted cream or pasties but with none of the later-life heart implications.

It says a lot for the pull of Honeybun that each day viewers were tuning in in their droves to essentially find out about the birthday of a seven-year-old girl in Plympton who they had never met. And it wasn't just children's birthdays. It was rumoured that adults would also write in to get their names read out, just listing their birthdays as much younger than they were. Of course this was a more innocent time when grown adults pretending to be young children were greeted with less suspicion.

It must have been charisma that Honeybun had because he wasn't popular for being beautifully made and brilliantly operated. While Edd the Duck or Gordon the Gopher could express emotion and move easily to interact with their human friend, Gus looked like someone had stuck some grey fur on the pedal bin. He appeared to be a combination of cheap and heavy, like a puppet created to entertain children in an industrial corner of the Soviet Union. His movement comprised his head turning side to side like Linda Blair in *The Exorcist* or his ears flapping up and down

a medley of 'Sailing' by Rod Stewart and 'You'll Never Walk Alone' by Gerry and the Pacemakers – and stand-up comedy from Terry Scammell, who is wearing a leather tie.

like he had ticks. His trademark bunny hops were literally just the puppeteer moving him up and down while his much sought-after winks involved him moving his eyelid down and up with the elegance of a window blind that you hadn't quite got the knack of.

If I'm honest I hadn't thought about Gus Honeybun in years but then during the writing of this book a friend sent me a link to a huge piece of breaking news. It had come to light that beyond wishing people happy birthday and struggling to wink, Gus Honeybun had another role. One of his sidekicks, Ian Stirling (not that one), had been using Gus to send secret messages to the South West's LGBTQ+ community, announcing where parties were going to be through birthday cards containing code words such as 'Auntie Stella'. While I remembered Gus as just a charmingly crap puppet that I absent-mindedly sat through before *Home and Away*, it turned out he was a rabbit with hidden depths. Suddenly I found myself going down a Gus Honeybun rabbit hole (pun intended), watching old clips and reading on dedicated Honeybun fan sites about how he was a far bigger deal in the South West than I had ever realised.

It turned out that by the time I stumbled across Gus in the early '90s, he had already lived a life. He had arrived on TV in the South West in 1961, with the then holders of the ITV regional contract Westward TV claiming they had found him under a gorse bush, something which I assume was meant to sound sweet and quaint, but in reality made him sound like an old porn mag.

Despite this inauspicious origin story, Gus swiftly became more popular than Westward's human presenters and remained on screen for 20 years. By the time TSW took over local broadcasting in the '80s, Gus's stardom had reached new heights. He released his own single, had various merch and for some reason had his own branded bus covered in pictures of carrots that ran people around the Torbay area. His myth still lives on. I have just typed his name into eBay and found that a Gus Honeybun pencil sharpener from back in the day will set you back £75. I've clicked 'Watch Item' but I'm yet to make a firm bid.

In his pomp Honeybun had worked with a string of co-presenters, helping launch the careers of Fern Britton from *Ready Steady Cook* and Ruth Langsford, who went on to co-host *This Morning* with husband Eamonn Holmes. It may seem a dereliction of duty for me not to make a joke comparing Eamonn Holmes and Gus Honeybun at this point, however Ruth and Eamonn still regularly host the kinds of TV shows on which I would hope to promote this book and, while I wouldn't expect Eamonn to have read the whole thing, to take him down in the opening pages seems a gamble.

Such was the star quality of Gus that when TSW's contract came up for renewal in 1992, in what can only be described as a cocky move they got Gus to deliver their bid to the Independent Television Commission in person/ rabbit. Unbelievably they lost out when it was ruled that their bid was too high (I don't know how this can be a thing either). A company called Westcountry TV took over and shamefully one of the first things they did was to get rid of Gus. On TSW's last night of transmission, host Ruth Langsford was seen taking Gus Honeybun back to his moorland home, where he met his parents, brothers and sisters, and disappeared down a burrow for one last time.

Gus hasn't had much work since, although on my deep dive into some of the internet's more niche forums I did find reports that he went on to appear on the Atlantic FM Breakfast Show. I don't quite know how a silent puppet rabbit could work on the radio, but a gig's a gig I suppose. Poor old Gus; he deserved better.

The reason I am telling you this is, for me, Gus Honeybun represents a couple of things. Firstly, his existence is perhaps the ultimate example of just how strange growing up on Dartmoor in the '90s could be, even though it felt totally normal to me at the time. I grew up in a village where the bus came once a week. If you wanted to go from my village of Haytor Vale to the nearest town of Newton Abbot and you couldn't drive, you'd better want to go on a Tuesday morning. And you'd better make the 3pm bus back, otherwise you were getting a hotel for the next seven nights. Haytor Vale was a village so isolated and with such a lack of crime that throughout my childhood we didn't have a front door key. If we went out – or even on holiday – we would just shut the door and leave it unlocked, trusting that no one would walk into our house and steal our stuff. And they never did. The truth was it probably wasn't worth their while, we lived so far from anyone else that whatever they took it probably wouldn't have covered their petrol money. (Note to thieves: my parents have now moved and do lock their door, so don't try and use this knowledge to your advantage.)

The second reason I wanted to start by discussing Gus Honeybun is that I see him as the perfect illustration of how I spent my childhood. I was a boy so desperate to be sitting in front of the television that I would regularly make the decision to watch a rabbit wish people I didn't know a happy birthday rather than turn the TV off and do something else. When I tell people that I grew up on Dartmoor they often ask me what it was like to be raised around such unique scenic beauty, but the truth is I didn't really notice. I was far less interested in Britain's first granite railway than I was in watching *Gladiators*, *Neighbours* or *Pebble Mill at One* with Alan Titchmarsh. Youth may be wasted on the young but not nearly as much as woodland waterfalls and naturally occurring rock formations.

This is a book about growing up in the '90s told through the thing that mattered most to me, the television programmes I watched. For my generation, television was the one thing that united everyone. There were kids at my school who liked bands, kids who liked football and one weird kid who liked the French sport of pétanque, however we all loved *Gladiators*, *Neighbours* and *Pebble Mill at One* with Alan Titchmarsh (possibly not the third of these).

There are plenty of books and documentaries about the music, art or sport of the '90s, but none of these things were as central to our daily lives as the television. In the UK *Parklife* sold just over 1 million copies, *Definitely Maybe* sold just over 2 million copies, *How Do They Do That?* got 12 million viewers a week. For those who don't remember *How Do They Do That?*, it involved Des Lynam and Jenny Hull (me neither) explaining how people drew maps or how air traffic control worked. To repeat, 12 times as popular as *Parklife*.

These days we are constantly told that we are living in a golden age of television with Netflix and HBO creating shows that are more intricate, beautifully shot and intelligently written than anything that has gone before. But I want to ask you this. Which is the real golden age, the 2020s or the '90s? The answer, of course, is the 2020s – I'm not an idiot. I won't be trying to tell you that *Eldorado* was better than *The Crown* or that *Goodnight Sweetheart* was better than *This Country*. Because they really weren't – I've rewatched episodes of both and they've aged terribly. But the truth is that the shows I will talk about in this book meant far more to me growing up than a well-made Netflix drama means to me now. They are shows that helped me understand the world, work out who I was and how I wanted people to perceive me – often in ways that now make me cringe.

This book is my personal story and consequently I should warn people there are a couple of things that it isn't. It is not a comprehensive history of television in the '90s. There will be important shows that I don't talk about and there will be shows no one else remembers that I do, although by choosing to start by discussing *Gus Honeybun's Magic Birthdays* rather than *Twin Peaks* I have probably already made that clear.

Secondly, like anyone who had a relatively happy childhood, I may of course feel nostalgic for that time, but I am going to try not to tell you that the '90s was a perfect era in every way that we need to fight to go back to. This isn't my version of that book Jacob Rees-Mogg wrote about how the Victorians were so much better than us, but with Isambard Kingdom Brunel replaced by Jamie Theakston. It is an honest book about what it was like growing up in the '90s – the story of a strange kid in a strange place watching some quite strange TV shows – and if writing this book has taught me anything it is that I was a much stranger kid than I realised.

Gus Honeybun wouldn't exist now (for a start I imagine he was made of material that would be considered a fire hazard) and if he did exist it would be on a minor channel competing against hundreds of other channels and everything on the internet for our attention. In the '90s it was him or *Newsround*. And *Newsround* was for dweebs, even I knew that. Maybe the main reason that Gus was popular was simply because he was there, somehow given a slot on ITV at 5:10 in the afternoon, a much better channel and time than an industrial rabbit puppet and some birthday cards deserves. Most afternoons, I would be watching Gus in my sitting room with my family and my friends would be watching him in their sitting rooms with their families. Gus was a star in the West Country because his show was a shared experience. This is a book about a decade of those shared experiences.

'Get Your Own Back!'
The Broom Cupboard
CBBC, 3:50pm, 4 June 1991

We got our first big TV for the Italia 90 World Cup. There was no big build-up; my dad just turned up at home on the day of the first game with a huge TV in the boot of the car. He then proceeded to drop it in the driveway, causing a crack down the screen that was there until we upgraded again a few years later. Like living next to a noisy road it is amazing how quickly you get used to a crack in your TV screen. In fact we kind of missed it when it was gone – it was useful for judging marginal offside decisions.

This was the kind of exciting edge my dad brought to our lives – you never knew what was going to happen next. One morning you had a small TV and the next thing you knew you had a big one with a crack in the screen. At this time he would probably have been a builder – it is difficult to quite remember as he moved from job to job. His approach to business could best be summed up as trying to make lots of money for the minimum effort but in the process putting in a lot of effort and failing to make any money. He had a wide range of business interests over the years: one week he could be earning cash as a plumber, the next week he was writing a misjudged pitch for a TV show idea for Channel 4, and the week after he had decided he was going to sell a herbal cure for nits to other parents at the school gates.[2]

This isn't to say that my childhood was one of hand-to-mouth existence or running from the debtors after 1,000 bottles of nit cure hadn't shifted as hoped. My mum worked at a publishers editing those big hardback gardening books called things like *Herbaceous Borders through the Seasons* and my gran lived in the other half of the house on a naval widow's pension, so we were relatively comfortable. It's terrible to drop this in so early but I grew up with nothing much to complain about, which was lovely at the time but ruins any hope of this book winning the Costa Prize.

When I was three my parents had decided to move to Devon from Bristol with my gran moving down from London to live in the other side of the house (and, crucially, pay the deposit for the mortgage). My parents had chosen Devon to be nearer my dad's children from his first marriage in Cornwall and because my mum had always wanted to own horses, which in our terraced house in Bristol would have presented issues with both the RSPCA and keeping the carpets clean. Throughout my childhood, I was a huge fan of my half-siblings in Cornwall, but I never became a fan

---

[2] For the record, I swiftly shut down the herbal nit idea on the grounds that my whole childhood would have been ruined.

of horses, believing their heads to be unreasonably big and their feet to be unreasonably hard. Needlessly intimidating.

My parents swiftly adapted to Dartmoor village life by buying fleeces and developing strong views on how other people's barn conversions infringed on planning regulations, but really they remained who they were before we arrived – a couple of old hippies. It is easy to convince yourself that your parents are like everyone else's, but when one summer in your teenage years your dad uses his horticultural skills to grow dope in the greenhouse 'for something to do', you do have to wonder.[3] However, this summer of dabbling with being the next Howard Marks was an exception rather than the rule and mainly my parents' hippy past was just articulated by my dad still having a ponytail well into his forties. If you are wondering if it was one of those cool ponytails that men have, then the answer is no. There is no such thing as a man with a cool ponytail.

Despite the ponytail, having hippy parents didn't cause me any real issues and in fact meant that I lived a childhood with little pressure or rules. This may have led some children to go off the rails by sneaking out to the greenhouse with a

---

[3] While I have gone in hard on my dad's lack of business acumen and pony tail early doors, I should say this is mainly because it is much funnier to write about someone's faults. For balance, he also gave me the most useful piece of life advice I have ever received: "Be it losing your phone, scratching your car or buying something you don't need, you will waste £1000 a year to being an idiot. There's nothing you can do, so don't worry about it".

liquorice Rizla or handing in their RE homework a day late, but I didn't have that kind of rebellion in me. Instead I used this freedom to spend my childhood watching as much TV as I possibly could.

I have always assumed I grew up in a golden age of children's television but then everyone thinks that. Ask anyone of any age and they will tell you that the children's TV they watched from the ages of 7 to 11 was the only children's television that got it right, in the same way everyone believes that their family's Christmas traditions are the only correct way of doing things (Everyone must open one present at a time in turn, is that so hard?). However, I've now come to realise that far from the early '90s being seen as a golden age, it is one of the few eras of 20th-century children's TV that is never discussed in this way. People will talk about the pioneering first big children's shows of the '60s like *Bill and Ben* or *Andy Pandy*, the classics of the '70s such as *The Clangers*, *Bagpuss* and *Mr Benn*, or Roland Rat, He-Man and Timmy Mallett when the commercial shackles came off in the '80s. However, children's TV of the '90s seems to only be remembered by the people who were there.

In a way that's for the best, I'm quite happy for the children's TV of the early '90s to only be loved by my generation; isn't that how it should be? It would have been a hugely unsettling state of affairs to get home to find my mum already watching *ChuckleVision* on her own, calling me in by shouting: 'Come and look at this, Josh. Paul and Barry are having real problems carrying this antique grandfather clock up a spiral staircase – it's only going to go one way.' No, the best thing about kids' TV was that it was just for us.

These days CBBC and CITV are both TV channels in their own right, broadcasting throughout the day (and as a parent myself, can I just say, 'Thank God for that'). In the early '90s they were both just sections of the BBC1 and ITV schedules, handed the keys to the channel from around 3:30pm to 5:30pm, a period when children were free to watch TV but their parents still needed to get on with working on their herbal nit cure. I adored these two hours of the day, the time when I was in charge of the TV, switching back and forth between CBBC and CITV, trying to make the most of my freedom. (Strictly I also had the option of BBC2 and Channel 4, but it would take a very strange child to rush home from school to watch *Fifteen to One*.)

It was during this time that I first realised that watching TV was what I did best. While other kids would spend their free hours after school at football practise or riding around Dartmoor on their mountain bikes, I would come home, sit down on the sofa and not move a muscle for two hours. While on the surface the family moving to Devon gave me the opportunity for a childhood exploring nature and learning about wildlife, sadly my parents hadn't banked on just how good the output of CBBC and CITV would be. Riding a bike up and down a hill may be thrilling, but was it really as exciting as watching Neil Buchanan make a big picture of a washing machine out of piles of laundry on *Art Attack*? The answer was a resounding no.

I was mainly a CBBC man, in large part due to *The Broom Cupboard*. While CITV would just link the shows with a voice-over, the BBC's links were done by a presenter and a puppet pal[4] from *The Broom Cupboard* at BBC Television Centre, a cramped little studio with one unmoving camera shot. *The Broom Cupboard* had started in the '80s with Phillip Schofield and Gordon the Gopher, but by the time I was watching the anchors for the afternoon were Andi Peters and Edd the Duck, who had a green Mohican and an attitude to match (Duck, not Peters). Peters and Duck would spend the time between shows playing games, interviewing guests, reading out letters and generally talking too much about Take That for my liking. *The Broom Cupboard* was a reassuring constant every afternoon when I got home from school, except on that one terrible day of the year when without warning it was moved to BBC2 to make way for the Budget. As an eight-year-old, there was little to rival the awful panic that gripped you when you turned on CBBC to find that the BBC had finally snapped and replaced Edd the Duck with Norman Lamont, followed by the sweet relief of turning over to BBC2 to see the opening credits of *Maid Marian and her Merry Men*.

The programmes I loved the most on children's TV were the game shows, a genre that almost always meant one thing: gunge. I can only assume part of the deal for a kids' game show to be commissioned was that every episode had

---

[4] Please be aware that despite your current worries not all shows in this book will feature puppets.

to gunge someone for some spurious reason at some point. The gungiest show of all was *Get Your Own Back*, in which children would bring an adult on to the show to get their own back on them for something they had done (usually something quite mild like an uncle who had worn a bad shirt rather than a parent who had left the family broken by running off with a neighbour). The show was hosted by Dave Benson Phillips, who would wear huge colourful shirts and was one of the most hyperactive men who has ever existed. Had he been a child, his parents would have been having hushed discussions about how many E-numbers he was consuming. If the child beat the adult and got their own back (which they always did), Benson Phillips would gunge the adult and the child would get a Sega Master System.[5] I had spotted a loophole here and suggested to my dad that we should go on the show so that he could lose on purpose and I could win a Sega Master System. He told me he would rather just buy me a Sega Master System, which he never did.

CITV's main rival to *Get Your Own Back* was *Fun House*, which was hosted by 90's caricature Pat Sharp; a man in his thirties who had a feathered mullet, wore high-top trainers and would enter the studio on a BMX despite the fact he

---

[5] The Sega Master System was by far the best prize available on CBBC. The game show *50/50* saw children compete to win prizes for their school, something that surely no right-minded child wants. I can think of no better way to ensure a lifetime of bullying than your teacher pausing an assembly to announce you had won the class a set of new trundle wheels by appearing on a CBBC game show.

didn't work developing apps in Shoreditch. If that wasn't cool enough, alongside Pat were two cheerleading identical twins called Melanie and Martina, whose main job was to encourage the children through the games, in case spending a minute filling their trousers with gunge-covered balloons on TV totally broke their spirit and they burst into tears. I was desperate to go on *Fun House,* purely to take part in the 'Fun Kart Grand Prix', a round in which the contestants would race in the slowest go-karts you have ever seen in your life while wearing full protective clothing; sadly it was never to happen.

The main lie of these shows was that we were all meant to be at home cheering the children on, but for me this couldn't have been further from the truth. I was far too jealous of the fact that they were on the show and I was at home watching to shout encouragement at the screen as they won a ghetto blaster with cassette deck and FM radio. If I'm honest, if anything I actively wanted them to fail. It was like that myth that you are meant to support English football clubs in Europe even though you have no affinity for them. The children on these shows were Chelsea winning the Champions League, I couldn't be happy for them, I resented their success. I felt this anger most keenly towards the contestants on the greatest children's game show of all, *Knightmare.*[6]

---

[6] I thought it was a game show, although I have just read an interview with the creator Tim Child (who takes it very seriously) and he describes it as 'an interactive drama-based role-playing game'. To be fair there is every chance the creator of *Fun House* describes that as 'a combative gunge-led foam-house scenario'.

Knightmare was a show so good that it didn't even need to gunge people to keep you watching. Instead it involved four children taking part in a Dungeons & Dragons-style adventure, one of them putting on a large Viking hat called 'the Helmet of Justice' so they couldn't see where they were going, and the other three guiding them through a series of computer-generated rooms that had graphics which somehow managed to make the show feel both dated and ahead of its time all at once. The dungeoneer (child in helmet) would be guided through the rooms with instructions from their friends such as 'take one sidestep to your left' or 'take another sidestep to your left' and sometimes 'take two sidesteps to your left'. It was actually quite a slow experience all round. Along the way they would meet various characters straight from the fantasy playbook, who would say stuff like, 'Greetings, stranger. What be your name and purpose?', and then make them solve a riddle or choose between taking an extra life potion or poisoned apple. It never felt like a particularly tough decision.

I was desperate to go on *Knightmare* but for one worry: at the end of each episode the host Treguard – a man with a beard who often raised his voice to make it feel dramatic, like a less annoying Brian Blessed – would freeze the team on screen and say he would unfreeze them to carry on their adventure next week. I found this an absolutely terrifying prospect, believing it to be far worse than anything they did on *Get Your Own Back*. (I should add this does make me worry that as a child I was as thick as shit.)

However, once my friend Thomas had explained to me that this was purely a camera trick, it became my number-one dream to go on the show, so I was livid when a rumour went round that a group of children from a neighbouring school had been on *Knightmare* and managed to complete the adventure (a rare achievement). I didn't see the episode so have no idea if this was true, but the main detail I remember from this gossip was that one of the children was named Dicken Hairs (I can only assume he also went on *Get Your Own Back* to take this up with his parents). Perhaps this story was just a myth in my school or perhaps it was the case, either way it is a mark of how much these shows meant to me that, despite his name, I spent years of my early childhood desperately jealous of a boy called Dicken Hairs.

'No crowds, no chip shops, no Space Invaders'
Badger Girl
BBC2, 10am, 17 September 1991

While television at home was part of my day-to-day life, at school it was an exotic treat, a break from the norm like non-uniform day or a substitute teacher with a lack of self-confidence. The mere mention that the TV was coming out was as exciting as it got, as if there was a chance Mrs Kingsley would say we had learned everything we needed to for the year so we were just going to watch a few episodes of *The Crystal Maze*. In our hearts we knew it would just be another documentary on sedimentary rock, but learning from a screen rather than an old lady with a consistent aroma of Maxwell House was still a rare thrill.[7]

---

[7] I never saw it myself but there were always rumours at my secondary school of children with watches that doubled as TV remote controls, changing the channel when the teacher wasn't looking and everyone watching *Neighbours* without the teacher noticing. This felt a little far-fetched to me: *Neighbours* was on during lunch break.

Because you couldn't possibly have a television sitting in the corner of the classroom the whole time – how would anyone concentrate? – excitement would be built further as it was pushed into the room in a specially made wheely cabinet, welcomed by the awestruck crowd like the Queen going down the Mall. Ten minutes would then elapse as Mrs Kingsley – a woman of around 90 who I mainly remember for wearing open-toed sandals and having chronic bunions – struggled to find the right channel or, in desperate circumstances, failed to tune in the television at all.[8] By the time everything was sorted the atmosphere was at a level usually only seen in the moments before a Glastonbury headliner takes the stage, if that headliner was going to forgo playing 'Hey Jude' to instead tell us how the Aztecs stored their food.

My primary school had a TV but no video player, which meant that watching TV would involve us having to catch the programme live with the rest of the school day playing second fiddle to the BBC2 schedule. If we were especially lucky, the TV was turned on too early and we would get to see the end of the previous programme as we waited, lapping up the final round of *Going for Gold*, knowing this was as

---

[8] A technological issue of the time which involved someone twisting a tiny knob until it happened upon a channel and then having to work out which channel it was by cross-referencing what they could see with the listings in the *Radio Times*. It usually ended with you having three ITVs and no Channel 4 and having to start again.

good as life got. The two minutes when I should have been learning about the fact that Vikings had very long boats but was in fact watching a man from Switzerland answer trivia questions to win a fountain pen felt like pure freedom.

In the '90s there were two main programmes for primary school children: *Zig Zag* and *Look and Read*. *Zig Zag* had an opening title sequence reminiscent of the film *Tron*, which can only be described as being very misleading about what was to follow. Rather than a futuristic sci-fi tale about a man trapped in a computer game, we had signed up for 20 minutes of the presenter in a fleece standing on a freezing British hillside talking about the water cycle. While presenters on CBBC and CITV would inject energy (and hopefully gunge) into proceedings, presenters on *Zig Zag* took themselves far more seriously and information would be delivered not with excitement but with the pronounced and overly patient tone of someone trying to explain to an OAP how to construct an order in Nando's. It was the most boring television I watched as a child, but still far preferable to normal school.

Look and Read was the school show we all wanted to be watching. Each series would feature a different serial drama about the adventures of an intrepid young child into which they would slip some learning, almost unnoticeable to the average seven-year-old viewer. There you would be minding your own business watching an emotional scene about a boy befriending a stoat and then suddenly it would cut to a computerised character called Wordy – a kind of less annoying precursor to the Microsoft Paperclip – who would introduce songs about things like the sound 's' and 't' make when put together in a word. Seamless.

The most exciting of these songs was sung by a cartoon wizard called Magic E, who would sing about how he transformed words by adding an e on to the end: 'mad becomes made with me', etc. Magic E's ability to transform things with the simple addition of an 'e' made Gus Honeybun's magic mushroom button feel like a pretty subtle drugs reference after all. However, it is safe to say that this would have been lost on Mrs Kingsley who I am confident had never been to an all-night rave, mainly as all that dancing would have played havoc with her bunions.

The BBC had started the *Look and Read* series with a drama called *Bob and Carol Look for Treasure* in 1967, which was so long ago that it was a time when children were still called Bob and Carol. By the time I was at primary school they had left that kind of *Boy's Own* adventure behind for tales that ranged from kitchen sink drama to fantasy. There was *Geordie Racer*, the story of a child from Newcastle who liked running and pigeons, *Through the Dragon's Eye*, the tale of three children transported through a mural in Acton to a magical land of dragons called Pelamar,[9]

---

[9] After reading the first draft of this book, my editor said, 'I'm impressed you have done so much research,' to which I nodded sagely and accepted the compliment. I didn't tell him that the sad truth was that 90% of this information – for example, the plot to *Through the Dragon's Eye* – was still just retained in my mind from my wasted childhood.

and *Badger Girl* which, most excitingly for me, was set on Dartmoor.

The *Badger Girl* of the title is Debbie, a Londoner who comes to Dartmoor on a summer trip and ends up having to stop a pony rustling plot. She gets her nickname because of a badger-like streak in her hair and along the way befriends a badger she calls Stripy and a hermit called Badger Man, who lives on the moor and works to protect badgers. It was a very badger-heavy plot.[10]

The main reason we loved the show wasn't its high badger content but that Dartmoor was on television, something I can't remember happening at any other point in my childhood. In the opening scene as the bus winds across the moor, Debbie describes the area as 'No crowds, no chip shops, no *Space Invaders*, just grass and sheep', and I have to say, it's a fair cop. Maybe that's why they didn't make any other TV shows about it. I could write about how *Badger Girl* was an unfair London-centric representation of Dartmoor, a place that while remote was no different to the rest of the UK at the time but I would be lying to myself. If anything, *Badger Girl's* representation of being a child on Dartmoor didn't go far enough.

---

[10] *Badger Girl* was written by Andrew Davies, who would go on to be quite a big deal, adapting *House of Cards* and *Pride and Prejudice* for television and co-writing the iconic '90s sitcom *Game On*, but for the small amount of people of a certain age *Badger Girl* remains his defining work. I would have enjoyed *Pride and Prejudice* a lot more if Magic E had popped up halfway through to sing a song about the soft 'c' sound in Darcy.

My village, Haytor Vale, didn't have a chip shop. It had a pub that was always too hot due to the authentic Devonshire log fires and a post office that sold sweets by the quarter and those Mr Freeze ice poles that would cut the sides of your mouth with the sharp edge on their plastic tubing. The post office has since closed down.

Three miles down the road my school, Ilsington C of E Primary, stood opposite a thatched cottage and a village church. While Ilsington, with its school and church, was a step up from Haytor Vale, it was still a place of no crowds, no chip shops and no *Space Invaders*. Its pub, The Carpenters Arms, was run by a couple called Bill and Val, who had grown up in the village and took great pride in having only once in their lives travelled further than Newton Abbot, a market town around five miles away. They proudly told people they had been to Exeter, not liked it and so had never felt the need to leave the safety of the TQ13 postcode again.

At school I had four children in my year. To further add to the feeling that I was growing up in an Enid Blyton novel, the names of the other three were Thomas Bosence, Joanna Portus and Jennaveve Waghorn. To make up the numbers, children would be taught in classes that covered four school years, trying to find something the right level to challenge both 7- and 11-year-olds. Usually this would just be reading out the poem *Please Mrs Butler* by Allan Ahlberg, which to be fair was an absolute classic.

The school's staff consisted of two teachers and a secretary who had so little work that she would only come in two days a week. The main impact of her working part-time was that for three days a week there was no one to answer the phone and, with the teachers busy, this meant that had you called the school Wednesday to Friday the phone would have been picked up by a 10-year-old. While it may seem odd that children were excused learning to instead take down a message they really shouldn't have been privy to this felt totally normal to us. After all, it wasn't the only secretarial work that we were tasked with. Because the school was too small to have the means to cook school dinners on site each day we would answer the register by saying 'packed' or 'dinners', then one child would be tasked with counting up the number of children who said dinners and phoning the information through to a nearby school that did have a kitchen to get the food sent across. To this day I have no idea why such a crucial job was put in the control of a nine-year-old, but I suppose to be fair they did only ever have to count up to four.

Due to the school's links to the church opposite our assemblies would often be led by the local vicar. When I joined the school this was Reverend Glare – who once stormed out of a PTA meeting because a parent said something blasphemous – and for the second half of my time there it was Reverend Curd, who had a hand puppet dog called Patch, which lacked the charisma of Gus Honeybun but was far more likely to go to Heaven.[11] Patch never really convinced me that I should become a Christian, so much

---

[11] Once again, sorry about all the puppets; it will stop.

as convince me that puppetry wasn't the tough skill Jim Henson made it out to be. The church would host end-of-term services – a few hymns, a couple of readings (basically the boring bits of a wedding) – and the annual harvest festival, an event where once a year we would celebrate the harvest by bringing in tins of soup and beans and making a display. I always assumed harvest was mainly a field-based activity but it turns out it primarily took place in the dried goods aisle of the local Spar.

Watching television without a video player was very much the pinnacle of our multimedia experience at the school; the closest we came to the excitement of the TV being a period of time where for one lesson a week we just listened to the radio. Not while we worked, like builders, I mean we just sat and listened to a radio drama, all silently staring ahead like evacuees waiting for news from the front line.

This isn't all a way of saying 'weren't the '90s a better, a more innocent time?' because judging by reading this back, I didn't live in the '90s – I seem to have grown up in an overly romanticised depiction of the 1920s. In the play-ground, along with climbing bars and hopscotch, the main points of entertainment were a large tractor tyre – not hung on a rope like a swing but just lying on the ground like it had bounced over after a car crash – and a Bronze Age hut. I should add that by a Bronze Age hut, I mean the school had rebuilt one along Bronze Age methods rather than one being left untouched for centuries, although I understand why this wouldn't seem totally implausible to the reader.

While the Bronze Age hut was a nice way to combine learning about history with having something for children to run in and out of (that is essentially all we could really do with it) soon after I left the school it was removed after being condemned by health and safety. I can only assume the hut was done to such period detail that the bods from Devon County Council condemned it on the grounds it was 3,000 years old.

With all this history and natural beauty on our doorstep you would presume that at least our school trips would be exciting. In actual fact the main school trip I remember was in Year 5 when we spent the day at the Newton Abbot branch of B&Q. To confirm, yes, the hardware shop B & Q. I don't know if this was chosen for educational reasons or just because Mrs Kingsley needed to pick up a new spirit level; all I know is it was styled as a way of learning about how retail worked and the lowest moment of the day came when it was revealed we all had to eat our packed lunches in the car park so as not to disturb the shoppers. I assumed at the time that the trip was given the thumbs up at B&Q HQ, but that last fact makes me wonder if our teachers had just turned up and tried their luck.

Children around the country were watching *Badger Girl* and thinking, 'Bloody hell, that looks like a mad place to grow up' but at Ilsington C of E Primary School we didn't even realise that was meant to be part of the story. I assumed every school in the country operated like ours. Surely every child was listening to the radio and playing in a tyre while awaiting lunch to be delivered from a nearby school.

Badger Girl ends (spoiler alert) with Debbie appre-
hending the pony rustlers after Stripy the badger has taken
them down by biting their legs. As the rustlers are led away,
one turns to the policeman and offers one of the great TV
lines of the decade: 'I'll come quietly, officer. Just keep
that badger away from me.' Stripy the badger is returned
to the wild and Badger Girl decides she wants to return to
Dartmoor to visit him next year. I suppose the moral of
the story was *Badger Girl's* realisation that you don't need
Space Invaders or chip shops when you have badgers and
the majesty of nature. Which of course is utter bollocks – I
would have absolutely loved a chip shop.

'Kabaddi . . . kabaddi . . . kabaddi'
Kabaddi
Channel 4, 11:10am, 4 January 1992

I made my peace early in life with the fact that I wasn't going to be a professional sportsman. This isn't to say I didn't have some huge early sporting achievements on the heavily sloped playing field next to the vicarage, but the glory was fleeting. In my fourth year of primary school there was a national competition to judge the fastest children over 50 metres, with every child in the country submitting their times. When the results came in ours were some of the quickest in the UK, it seemed the children of Ilsington C of E Primary School were set to dominate British athletics for the next decade. Then my mum pointed out that our times may have been fast because we were running downhill. We weren't so much running as falling. Like that the dream was over.

It was around this age when it looked for a few months like I might become a footballer. Children's football matches would traditionally consist of every child chasing the ball around the pitch in a swarm. While I wasn't any more skilful than other boys my age, I realised I could just stand slightly outside the group, then when the ball popped out of the swarm I would be through on goal. For those few months I was a world-beater, then children realised they should stick to their positions and the jig was up. A career that looked so promising had peaked too early never to scale such heights again, like Michael Owen.

I didn't come from a sporting heritage. My dad's greatest sporting passion began at the start of the decade when he found an injured pigeon in our garden and nursed it back to health, like the old man from *The Shawshank Redemption*. The next thing we knew he had built a coop and if you have a coop, why not get a few more pigeons and if you have a few pigeons, why not go the full *Geordie Racer* and join a pigeon racing club? Before long my dad was spending his Saturday afternoons sitting in the garden waiting for his pigeons to return from places as far-flung as Andover or Wincanton. Unfortunately for him, the pigeons would fly all the way home at top speed before landing in a large tree in the garden and sitting there for hours, my dad unable to get to them to get the ring off their foot and stop the clock. Consequently my dad's Saturdays throughout the summer would be spent shaking a pot of seed with increasing frustration in an attempt to entice some pigeons down from a tree, muttering about how Mike Scott at the pigeon club would never believe his story.[12]

---

[12] The lowest moment of my Dad's career as a pigeon racer came when he decided to invest £150 in a top-level pigeon from which to breed a generation of winners. On its first trip outside the coop the pigeon flew away and never came back.

It is unlikely sport would have had much impact on my life if it hadn't been for the Italia 90 World Cup. Such was my love for Italia 90 that even now seeing a moment's footage of it or hearing Pavarotti's 'Nessun Dorma' can still send me into a shameful nostalgic reverie; talking with misty eyes about how football used to be so pure, how Italian stadiums have such a rare beauty and how Gary Lineker tans so well. It was here that I realised that sport didn't have to be about being slower or less able to swim than your friends, it could be about things I was good at, like collecting the 20-part Orbis World Cup sticker album with free ring binder – a product that contained not just the opportunity to stick down a picture of Neil Webb but also allowed me to learn facts as exciting as Andy Townsend's age and the address and phone number of the Yugoslavian Football Association. Italia 90 slotted me into my lifelong role as a spectator rather than a competitor and, really, isn't knowing lots about sport rather than taking part in it the real test of a man?[13]

Becoming a football fan in 1990 involved me making the decision that my favourite player was John Barnes (did the rap on 'World in Motion', was in the Lucozade adverts), subscribing to *Shoot* magazine and watching the English Football League on TV. This would be one game a week on Sunday afternoons and then some highlights of a midweek game if my mum remembered to tape *Sportsnight* on a Wednesday, which she never did. To me it didn't feel like

---

[13] No.

enough football, but little did I know it was about to get much worse.

In 1992 Sky bought the rights to the Premier League, prompting my parents to never get Sky TV at any cost for the rest of the decade. Their excuses ranged from the realistic 'it's too expensive' to the naively political 'we don't want to support Rupert Murdoch' to the unlikely 'you can't get planning permission for the satellite dish on a house in Dartmoor National Park'. As a child with little knowledge of the local planning restrictions it was checkmate.

Like any other football fan whose parents didn't like Rupert Murdoch/had planning permission issues (delete as appropriate), this meant I only had one option: to spend the decade filling the gap left by live football with, gulp, other sports.

Occasionally you hear people complain that the BBC doesn't have as much top-level sport as it used to, but that glory period must have been before I was watching it. I'm not sure a channel overflowing with top sport would begin every year by screening *World's Strongest Man*, a very literally named competition that mainly involved bright purple men who were weeks away from a heart attack lifting large stone balls on to Roman-style plinths in front of a crowd of 50 people on an overcast beach.[14] The main home of the

---

[14] If you think that is the bottom rung of BBC sport coverage you are mistaken. One year I remember spending a week watching the world championships of crown green bowls on BBC2, the crowd for which remains the oldest group of people I have ever seen in one place (and I once went to the filming of *Deal or No Deal*).

BBC's sports coverage was *Grandstand*, a weekly Saturday afternoon show featuring a variety of sports I didn't like and often didn't even know the rules to, but which I would watch religiously. *Grandstand* was styled as the place to be if you wanted to know everything happening in the world of sport but in reality consisted of a running order like this one I found for an episode online:

12.30 World Welterweight Boxing from Atlantic City

1.05 Swimming from Leeds

1.20 World Sports Car Championship from Brands Hatch

2.00 Horse Racing from Goodwood

2.05 Swimming from Leeds

2.30 Horse Racing from Goodwood

2.35 More Swimming from Leeds

3.10 More Horse Racing from Goodwood

3.15 Saloon Cars from Silverstone

3.35 Showjumping from Hickstead

4.30 Modern Pentathlon from Milton Keynes

I think we can all agree there is such a thing as too much swimming from Leeds.

Grandstand's only nod to my preferred sport of football was the Vidiprinter – an on-screen dot matrix printer that would print out the day's football results as they came in and even in the early '90s felt around 30 years out of date. A viewing experience that was so sterile that it was somehow tense, the Vidiprinter was most famous for spelling out the amount of goals in capitals if a team had suffered a real thrashing, just so you knew it wasn't a typo: Doncaster Rovers 1 Exeter City 7 (SEVEN), the capital letters really rubbing it in Doncaster's rubbish faces.

However, the place for the real sports junkies wasn't the BBC, but Channel 4, whose sport policy seemed to be 'get whatever the other channels don't want and shove it on a Saturday morning'. As a sport- and television-obsessed nine-year-old with four hours to fill until *Grandstand*, I offered them my complete support. There I could watch American football or catch up on the latest goings-on in sumo wrestling, the only sport I know in which the best player was nicknamed 'The Dumper Truck'. I have a vague memory that at one point Channel 4 even stooped as low as a show called *Pro-Celebrity Golf* in which professional golfers would tee off next to the likes of Terry Wogan and Bruce Forsyth. All things told, watching sport on Channel 4 was like eating vegan cheese – nowhere near as good as the real thing but just about better than no cheese at all.

Channel 4 even had their own version of *Grandstand*: *Trans World Sport*. Shown at around 6am on a Saturday (so as to leave time for a full hour of sumo wrestling after-wards), *Trans World Sport* was a magazine show that brought you (what it claimed to be) a round-up of all the important sports news and action from across the globe. While at the time I assumed their choice of sports was dictated by their rather quirky take on the most important stories of the week, it now seems clear to me that the shows were simply made up of whichever sports they could afford to buy the rights for.

The show would go from one sport to another, never connected, just swooshing between them like Sam from *Quantum Leap* not knowing which body he would jump into next. From Argentinian lacrosse to Norwegian handball to Dutch gymnastics to, somehow, more Norwegian handball. Each time, despite all experience, I would cross my fingers for British football before making my peace with the next five minutes being spent catching up on the Algerian long jump. As is always the case with being a sports fan, it's the hope that kills you.

The jewel in the crown for Channel 4's unhinged sports coverage was kabaddi, which for a few years they would cover for a whole hour every Saturday. If you aren't familiar with kabaddi it is essentially an Indian version of tag, involving two teams taking it in turns to try and touch a member of the other team without being grabbed by them. The added twist is that throughout this process the raider has to hold their breath, proving they aren't breathing in by repeating the word 'kabaddi' again and again. As an asthmatic, it was a tense spectacle.

Perhaps worried this wouldn't find a mass audience, throughout the coverage Channel 4 repeatedly hammered home that kabaddi was the biggest sport in India. I have no idea if this is true although there very rarely seemed to be many people at the matches and one of the top sides was called West Bengal Police, which didn't seem particularly professional. Kabaddi was the ultimate sports fan's deep cut. In the same way that some people say you aren't a Bob Dylan fan unless you have listened to *The Basement Tapes*, to me you weren't a sports fan in the '90s unless you had watched at least one episode of *Kabaddi*. Sadly, very little evidence remains of Channel 4's coverage, although I did find a petition on change.org to bring kabaddi back to the channel. 'There's a whole generation of youngsters missing out on the spectacle of half-naked Indians, starved of oxygen, trying to tag each other,' it states. It closed in 2013 with nine signatures.

One concrete impact of kabaddi, however, was to inspire my dad to turn on his Amstrad word processor and write to Channel 4 with his own idea for a TV show. While he was whiling away those hours in the garden waiting for a pigeon to come out of a tree, inspiration had struck. So once the pigeons were finally inside and he had lost another race, he wrote to Channel 4 pitching his golden idea, a TV show covering the latest goings-on in the world of pigeon racing. Over an hour we would meet the owners, watch profiles of the top pigeons and receive tips on how to get the most out of your bird. I don't know what I am illustrating here – how esoteric Channel 4's sport output was or how bad my dad was at judging a business opportunity? Probably both.

I wish I could say that Channel 4 were hugely excited and got my dad on the first train to London to discuss his idea; in fact, I wish I could say that Channel 4 replied. Sadly their response must have got stuck in the big tree in the garden. And so we were never to witness coverage of a middle-aged man sitting and waiting for some pigeons in his garden on Saturday morning TV. Although I have a terrible feeling I would have watched it.

'Contenders ready! Gladiators ready!'
Gladiators
ITV, 6:20pm, 10 October 1992

The lights circle around the Birmingham Indoor Arena, the cheerleaders G-Force wave huge red flags above their heads like they're part of a North Korean military parade and out come presenters Ulrika Jonsson and John Fashanu. 'Welcome to a very special night for British television: the 1992 Grand Final of *Gladiators*,' booms Jonsson. As hard as it is to believe when reading these words now, she wasn't being sarcastic.

Over the next hour we see why Ulrika was so excited as four members of the public take part in a series of bizarre physical challenges against musclebound, Lycra-clad Gladiators with names like Warrior and Saracen. They roll around in huge metal balls, fight using large cotton buds, run up a down escalator and, just in case this isn't enough entertainment, most of the games end with the Gladiators trying to dry-hump the contestants off a climbing wall or hanging rings. At the end of it all, senior staff nurse Vanda Fairchild and video editor Weininger Irwin are crowned the champions of *Gladiators* series one. When asked what he will do with the £5,000 prize, Irwin says he will 'invest the money in future endeavours in video editing', whatever that means. 'One day I will be the best video editor in London,' he adds. Once the cheers for this die down, Ulrika describes his approach as 'very confident indeed, but also very, very sensible'.

To comprehend why *Gladiators* felt like the most exciting thing in my life in 1992 you need to understand what Saturday night television was like before it arrived. Saturday evening was for television the whole family could enjoy together, young and old meeting like Allied and German soldiers playing football on Christmas Day in the no man's land between *ChuckleVision* and *The House of Eliott*. In Victorian times families spent their evenings bonding over charades by the fire; a century later charades had been replaced by *Noel's House Party*. The children could enjoy Mr Blobby winding up Radio 1 DJ Gary Davies while their parents could enjoy the slightly higher brow entertainment of Tony Blackburn being gunged. Or something like that.

Before *Gladiators* it felt as if Saturday night television was made for adults but with the idea that children would also be able to enjoy it. *Gladiators* was the first show that was aimed at children and adults had to get on board. It would have taken a very strange adult to sit on their own and enjoy an episode of *Gladiators*, although that is admittedly what I have just done before writing this.

It would be hugely overstating it to say that *Gladiators* needed to happen to Saturday night television in the same way punk needed to happen to music in the late '70s, but it is my book so I can say what I want. Suddenly I was spending my Saturday evening watching a man called Hawk rather than a man called Bruce Forsyth. I was cheering on Virgo rather than John Virgo. The Gladiators felt mysterious and exotic. We didn't know their real names or anything about them, they had their own theme songs and they wore tiny Lycra costumes[15] with pictures of things like swords or helmets on them. Squint your eyes and they could have been superheroes or WWF wrestlers, rather than bodybuilders from London satellite towns who had been renamed after birds of prey.

There was even a baddie, the most famous Gladiator of all: Wolf. Wolf threw his helmet down in anger when he lost. He trash-talked the contenders. He refused to accept he was going bald and continued to grow his rapidly thinning hair to shoulder length. I – like every child in the UK – loved him, only losing respect for him after an episode in which Warrior dislocated his kneecap and Wolf snapped out of character to help carry him off to first aid using his Atlas-phere (huge metal ball) like a stretcher.[16] The character of Wolf wouldn't have helped an injured man; he would have been too busy climbing on to the crash barrier to lightly taunt a ten-year-old in the crowd or disputing a decision

---

[15] Leotards for the women, pants and something that looked like a training bra for the men.

[16] I have no idea how they eventually got Warrior out of the Atlasphere, but I assume they didn't take him the whole way to hospital in it.

from referee John Anderson (a middle-aged Scottish man who was far more into enforcing the rules than you felt was needed on an ITV teatime show).

Everything about the show was exciting. While other shows were filmed in a TV studio, *Gladiators* took place in a building called the National Indoor Arena in Birmingham. This wasn't just any indoor arena, this was the National one, the Wembley of indoor arenas (if you exclude Wembley Indoor Arena). With its spinning spotlights, dry ice and cheering fans, the National Indoor Arena was the perfect amphitheatre for the modern-day Gladiators (also available as an occasional conferencing facility). *Gladiators* didn't have a studio audience, it had a crowd, full of excited people wearing huge foam hands and holding handwritten signs saying things like 'Lightning Strikes!' or 'Come On, Kym!' They chanted along with 'Another One Bites the Dust' when someone fell off a wall, they held their head in their hands when their friend tripped on the travelator and they shouted at Wolf when he quibbled over a minor rule infringement. This was the sport of the future. It felt like it was going to change everything – within a year Ian Rush and John Barnes would be forced by public demand to play in Lycra and change their names to Spitfire and Viking.

Even the presenters of *Gladiators* were exciting: Ulrika Jonsson – Swedish! – and John Fashanu – a real live still-playing footballer! Fashanu was an odd choice. While a footballer added an edge of glamour, he wasn't a particularly popular player, mainly being famous for playing for

Wimbledon, the most hated team in the Premier League. I have no idea why this quite average Premier League player was plucked out as the dead cert for TV presenting, any more than why Tony Cottee would have been asked to present *Blind Date*. Also, while I was fully aware that shows were pre-recorded, it always felt a bit much to me that Fashanu would be playing football on a Saturday afternoon for Wimbledon and then an hour later we would see him running out in the National Indoor Arena in a colourful waistcoat to host *Gladiators*. At least keep up some kind of pretence, guys.

Perhaps the biggest symbol of my unquestioning love for *Gladiators* was that I thought John Fashanu was an excellent host. People often dismiss TV presenting as easy, a job that simply involves smiling and reading out loud. I would implore those people to watch some clips of John Fashanu, a man who read the autocue with the look of a driver approaching a complicated roundabout in the wrong lane but trying not to let his passengers know he's panicking.

Fash conducted interviews with the manner of a man who had never had a face-to-face conversation but had read a pamphlet on how they worked and was willing to have a go. A random example on YouTube shows him speaking to a man called Tony who runs a gym in Caterham called Flex Appeal (a pun Fash doesn't seem to even notice).

Tony: 'I like going to the West End, see the theatre . . .'
Fash: 'What have you seen lately, anything interesting?'

Tony: '*Five Guys Named Moe.*'

Fash: 'Well tonight, Tony, you are going to meet five Gladiators named muscle.'

Interview ends

After events Fash would approach the contestants as they lay in a heap on a crash mat, having just been dry-humped until they lost strength in their arms, and ask the only question he had in his locker: 'How do you feel?' Once they had replied with something about giving it a good go, Fash would then dispense his catchphrase 'Awooga!', a word no one was sure of the meaning of but which really caught on in our playground. I had always assumed Awooga was Fash's one great piece of genius but, sadly, his ownership of it is disputed. In 2018, Craig Charles tweeted about a show he used to host called *Cyberzone* saying: 'I used awooga as the catchphrase which had been spoken by holly in red dwarf as the replacement sound of a Claxston we had fashanu on as a guest and he nicked it for gladiators. The mans a knobhead' [sic].

I didn't just watch *Gladiators*, I defined myself as a fan of the show in the same way children in the '70s were fans of the Bay City Rollers or children in the '80s were fans of that kid who died of a drugs overdose in *Grange Hill*. I bought the soundtrack album on cassette,[17] I got my hair cut into a flat-top like Warrior, and I even once sat through a whole

---

[17] 'The Boys are Back in Town' by Thin Lizzy, 'Another One Bites the Dust' by Queen, 'Since You've Been Gone' by Rainbow – basically the songs you would get on an album called *Top Gear Anthems*.

episode of *Tomorrow's World* because they had promised that at the end Wolf was going to try on a virtual-reality headset. I was that committed.

At school in the winter of 1992 *Gladiators* was our only topic of conversation[18] as we pondered on rumours that producers would speed up the travelator if a contestant was too far ahead in the 'Eliminator' and discussed breaking the cardinal rule of *Gladiators* and 'attempting to recreate the show at home'. All episodes ended with a warning about not committing this health and safety crime, which, of course, just put the idea firmly in your head. Before I knew it I was propping up a mattress on the stairs and attempting to climb it to replicate 'The Wall' or playing 'Duel' by standing on a milk crate and hitting a friend with a scarf. It turned out the main issue with recreating the events in your own home wasn't the health and safety implications but just that it was very difficult to recreate the excitement of *Gladiators* if you didn't own your own Atlasphere.

Gladiators ran for the whole of the '90s but my love for it – like all of my childhood obsessions outside of TV and football – couldn't have lasted more than a couple of years. In

---

[18] A lot of people of my age have stories of Gladiators visiting their school, but sadly the worlds of the Gladiators and Ilsington C of E Primary School never collided. My friend Ben grew up in Cardiff and had Cobra visit his school. He took a two-hour PE lesson, lifted up a teacher and at the end told them all to write down their names and addresses on a piece of paper. A week later a letter arrived and Ben had been signed up for a NatWest current account. Never meet your heroes.

later series they added more games and cast celebrities like swimmer Sharron Davies and previous *Gladiators* champion Eunice Huthart as Gladiators; the illusion was ruined – where was the mystery? We didn't want to know these Gladiators' names or backstory; the game was gone. Or maybe I was just now at secondary school and it suddenly all felt very childish to be basing my haircut on a man with 40-inch biceps and a picture of a knight's helmet on his training bra.

In later series, even John Fashanu was replaced as host by rugby player Jeremy Guscott; was nothing sacred? *Gladiators* turned out to be the high watermark of Fash's TV presenting career, although there is one astonishing footnote. In 2003 ITV planned to bring Fash back to Saturday teatime with a new vehicle called *Man vs Beast*, a show in which humans and animals would, finally, go head-to-head in physical challenges. The American show on which it was based included a sumo wrestler taking on an orangutan, a bear taking part in a hotdog-eating contest and, get ready to have your mind blown, 44 dwarves competing in a tug-of-war with an elephant. And if you don't think that sounds like elite-level sport, Shawn Crawford, who would go on to win gold in the 200 metres at the 2004 Athens Olympics, appeared on the show and comfortably beat a giraffe in the 100 metres only to lose to a zebra in his next race.[19]

---

[19] For more context, apparently the zebra false-started but won the rerun, raising the question, 'How is a zebra meant to know when a race has started?'

Sadly for Fash, ITV's version of the show was pulled on the week of broadcast after criticism from the RSPCA, Born Free Foundation and Dame Judi Dench. Fash had already taken the publicity shot, which remains online, of him trying to stare out a crocodile. Maybe *Gladiators* wasn't such an absurd idea for a TV show after all.

'You Can't Trust Anyone These Days'
Eldorado
BBC1, 7pm, 16 October 1992

I check my Twitter and Leslee Udwin has replied to my message.

'I hated it so much it would be a real trauma to think about it let alone talk about it. And my life now is so far removed from that. Would be happy to talk to you about almost anything else. No, actually, ANYTHING else but that. (By the way, Gin was one of my favourite people!!)'

Udwin is a film producer who, among other things, has brought the world *East is East* and *India's Daughter*, a 2015 documentary about the gang rape and murder of Jyoti Singh in Delhi that won international awards and praise, and led to Udwin being named the *New York Times*' second most impactful woman of 2015 (after Hillary Clinton). Off the back of this film she founded Think Equal, a global education initiative that aims to introduce social and emotional intelligence learning into early-year education – it counts Meryl Streep as a patron and has been supported by Ban Ki-moon. Such is the facile nature of my interests, I had found myself contacting her about her previous life playing Joy Slater in the BBC soap opera *Eldorado*.

I have never been a huge fan of soaps outside of *Neighbours* (which, as we will come to, wasn't a soap but a lifestyle). I have a friend who doesn't like football, he told me he was into it as a kid, but then at the end of the season it all just started again and he realised that it was endless – no one ever won. What was the point? That's how I feel about soaps. You are giving yourself over to something that is just going to go on and on, investing in a narrative in which you will never reach your intended goal, like joining the Liberal Democrats. As a result I have only once been excited for a British soap, the first episode of *Eldorado*, and that was only because my gran knew someone in it.

My gran was known to everyone as Gin (short for Virginia, unrelated to the drink, despite her fondness for it) and was a retired actor, a fact that will do a lot of the legwork if you are trying to imagine her. When we had moved to Devon with her we had split the house in two, and walking through the adjoining door you would be hit with a plume of cigarette smoke, Oscar Wilde quotes and theatrical anecdotes. Watching TV with Gin was as much a social activity as anything else, the programmes accompanied by a constant soundtrack of which people Gin knew and a small piece of trivia on them, rarely positive. The recurring comic actor Eric Dodson 'was nicknamed Doddy the Nose, darling' while John Savident, who played Fred Elliott in *Coronation Street*, 'used to carry a handbag'. It was tabloid dynamite.

Such were the circles Gin had moved in, on her mantelpiece in the kitchen was a photo of her talking to Ian McShane at a house party with her mouth open like she was shouting at him. A caption was stuck on the picture reading 'I've shouted at more film stars than you have had hot dinners, man!' When asked about the picture she would say she had no idea why she had it and that McShane had been 'dreadful. He turned up to the party with a kiss curl just so that people knew he was playing Disraeli, darling.' I had no idea what a kiss curl or Disraeli were, but I was impressed that she had met Lovejoy.

Gin's own acting career had begun in the '40s with the role of Mrs Dale's daughter Gwen in *Mrs Dale's Diary*, the first ever radio soap opera. She left the show after a few years and would tell the story that they had struggled to find someone with a similar accent to replace her, not realising that she had grown up in South Africa. Everything that happened to Gin was a far-fetched anecdote like this. She had gone to Summerhill School in the '30s, an unconventional institution where the children would vote on all the school rules and the teachers had to live by them. To me as a child that sounded like good sense, as a parent now it sounds completely insane. Possibly as a result of this childhood, Gin was one of the most gregarious and eccentric people you could meet. Hours of my youth were spent in her half of the house listening to her anecdotes while she smoked Silk Cut and drank Nescafé Gold Blend – offering me a drink in one of her collection of gift-shop mugs that she had got half-price due to the unpopularity of the names on them. Chats would always begin with the question: 'Would you like your tea in Neville, Sandra or Craig, darling?' before moving on to the real business of discussing what Gorden Kaye from 'Allo 'Allo! was actually like.

While Gin had retired before moving to Devon, in the middle of the '90s, like a cop in a movie, she got called back for one last job. A crew were filming some NatWest adverts starring Gary Olsen from 2point4 Children in Bovey Tracey and for some reason had come down to Devon without anyone to play 'old woman in the back of taxi'. They asked around the local area to see if anyone knew any old ladies who could act, found Gin and she took the gig. For a year we would occasionally see her on TV in the back of Gary Olsen's car as he delivered the advert's punchline 'I've got the old bag in the back' and she gave him a look she usually only reserved for Disraeli-era Ian McShane.

Hers was the ultimate life well lived. She had been on a ship going to South Africa during the war that had had to cut its engines as they suspected a German sub was below them ('everyone just went straight to the bar and got pissed, darling'), she had written romantic novels under the pseudonym Sarah Francis and she had been in a KitKat advert with Dot Cotton. I even vividly remember once having a discussion with her about how best to fit the word 'fuck' into conversation in the local post office if you had to get away with it. She was not what you would expect from a gran.

So it was within character when Gin revealed that one of her best friends had been given a lead role in the most expensive show ever launched by the BBC, *Eldorado*. 'Leslee Udwin is in it, darling; wonderful actress, it'll be marvellous.' As a child in a school where no one had ever known someone on TV (this was four years before the events of Gary Olsen and NatWest), I knew I was sitting on a hugely impressive trump card. On the morning of the first episode of *Eldorado* I went into school and told everyone the BBC were launching a great new show we were all going to love, and I should know as (slightly overplaying my hand) I knew the main character. We'll call this an early lesson in waiting to see how something goes before claiming credit because, as it turns out, *Eldorado* was the biggest TV disaster of the decade.

Eldorado was meant to save the BBC. Audience numbers were dropping and the licence fee was under threat (for once) so to turn things around they decided they needed a second prime-time soap opera, a wingman to *EastEnders*, a Robson to their Jerome. Tony Holland, who had created *EastEnders*, pitched them *Little England*, a soap about a community of Brits living on the Costa del Sol trapped together as outsiders in Spain. It isn't a bad idea on paper, but let's enjoy some of the hilarious decisions that were made after its commission:

- The production team were given just six months to get the show into production, a to-do list that included building a village from scratch halfway up a Spanish hillside in the middle of nowhere. They unsurprisingly failed to do this in time, meaning the village was still being built when they started filming, with the actors having to perform their scenes on a building site with diggers just out of shot.

- Characters from across the continent were added to the show to give it a more European feel so that the show could be sold abroad.[20] Bafflingly the scenes with just these characters in would be in Danish or Spanish with no subtitles, meaning the only people in the UK able to understand what was going on were language teachers and Peter Schmeichel.

- Once filming began they realised that the fact they had decided to build the whole town from stone meant that every word spoken echoed like the characters were down a well. At least if you didn't understand the Danish first time around it gave you a second bite of the cherry.

- In some roles they decided to cast actors who had never acted before in their lives but were just quite

---

[20] The only other show I can remember embracing the European project on TV at this time was daytime quiz show *Going for Gold* in which contestants from across Europe would take part in a general knowledge quiz hosted by the genial Irishman Henry Kelly. In a distinct advantage to the British contestants all questions were in English, meaning all they would have to do was buzz ahead of a contestant who was hearing the questions in their second language. Of all our sporting humiliations of the '90s, the fact our contestants didn't dominate *Going for Gold* comes pretty high.

good-looking. Dieter, the windsurfing instructor, was played by a German student whom a producer had found selling time shares on a beach. As they attempted to save the failing show he was cut from the cast, the actor being told, 'Dieter wouldn't teach windsurfing in the winter' (which is surely when the surf is windiest). The actor went on to move to England and go to drama school which, I am going to say, is surely THE WRONG WAY AROUND TO DO THINGS.

The launch of *Eldorado* is one of the decade's greatest demonstrations of hubris, the *Waterworld* of TV commissions, the Millennium Dome of soap opera.[21] The first episode was watched by 8 million viewers, but by the end of the month ratings had dropped to 2.8 million. The only real question is who in the name of God were those 2.8 million people who had decided to stick with it? Were there really that many Danish speakers in the UK?

Rewatching the first episode that had let me down so badly at the age of eight, I was a little underwhelmed. It has become such a poster boy for awful television that the fact it is just a bit shit was a slight let-down. It looks nice and sunny and the stone finish looks lovely as the show opens with a shot of some kids in the street playing football with a

---

[21] Sorry if that is a spoiler for anyone who doesn't know how the Millennium Dome went down and was waiting for the end of the book to find out.

cuddly toy. If it was a better show I'd think this image was a metaphor for something to come but the smart money is that they just hadn't managed to source a prop football on a remote Spanish hillside. We're then introduced to the main character I remember from the time, classic soap baddie Marcus Tandy (slicked-back hair, shades, linen suit – Ian Beale meets Sexy Beast) throwing the clothes of his girl-friend out of his window onto the square. Tandy is meant to be a high-flying businessman, however in the first episode we see his two businesses are a stables and a video shop, which is at best an unusual portfolio of interests. Especially as judging by the empty shelves the video shop only seems to stock about four titles.

After we meet Tandy things then go downhill as over the half-hour we are introduced to a string of unmemorable characters – from nightclub singer Trish to some Danish people I didn't understand – before ending with the awful reveal that the character of Bunny, a man in his forties, has married a 17-year-old girl called Fizz, whom he reveals to his friends from behind a huge cuddly toy. Looking at it now, perhaps the soft toy at the beginning was a portent of things to come after all and it was a much cleverer show than people gave it credit for.

* * *

Six weeks after I first got in touch, I received a message from Leslee Udwin out of the blue: 'OK, Josh, I've changed my mind!!! I'll talk to you about *Eldorado* if you want me to! X'. I talk to Leslee over Zoom as it is still lockdown at this point. She is a charming and charismatic woman with just the right edge of thespy delivery to her anecdotes. During our chat she drinks the biggest coffee I have ever seen, possibly needing to power her through another aspect of *Eldorado* that she hated.

She tells me that in an unlikely turn of events it was Alan Rickman's fault that she did the show: 'He said, "Of course you've got to do it; it's going to give you a platform." By that point I had made a film that released the Birmingham Six from prison, I'd been at the National, the RSC, I'd played Lady Macbeth at the Donmar Warehouse. I was, you know, a stuck-up ambitious actress. I knew Mark Shivas very well, who was Head of Drama at the BBC, and he said to me, "We've put more than half of our drama budget into this; there is no way this can or will be anything other than utterly brilliant."'

It is clear speaking to her that it had far more impact than I realised. What I had assumed was just a bit of a laugh about a German bloke who was learning to act was in actual fact for some people a horrific experience of feeling they had lost their career and reputation. I won't lie, it made me feel bad for laughing about the lack of videos on display in Marcus Tandy's shop.

'As soon as we did the first read-through I looked around and thought, "Fuck!" Because by then I'd seen the scripts. And as soon as the episodes started going out a friend in the UK sent me this wonderful advertisement for haemorrhoid cream she had come across saying "Makes even sitting through an episode of *Eldorado* bearable".'

I ask her if all the things I had heard about the set were true. 'They hadn't finished building it, so the first thing that would happen before a take is they would shout for the bulldozers to stop working,' she laughs.

'*Eldorado* changed me totally because I gave up acting. I thought nothing in life is worth that pain. I did one more thing after that – Arthur Miller's *A View from the Bridge* – and that was it. I didn't act after that; I became a producer.' I suppose the good news is that she became a hugely successful one. With that, Leslee moves the conversation on to our favourite stories of Gin and she seems a lot more comfortable.

I never watched *Eldorado* again after that first episode. Maybe I was too traumatised by the abuse it got me from school friends the day after broadcast or maybe, like the rest of the country, I just thought it was shit. It was almost certainly the second of these. In the end the show lasted for a year and three days, which feels like quite an achievement all things considered. There is a Twitter account that tweets updates on if it will ever be recommissioned – it has 114 followers. If they do bring it back they will need to find a new set as the village they built on the side of a hill is now a paintballing centre. Paintballing being the only thing to come out of the '90s that was actually less fun than *Eldorado*.

'We've created a séance, a massive séance'
Ghostwatch
BBC1, 9:25pm, 31 October 1992

In 1938 an Orson Welles dramatisation of *War of the Worlds* was broadcast on CBS Radio causing panic among an American populous who took it to be real and feared an alien invasion had begun. It would be easy for me to mock the Americans of the '30s and their rudimentary understanding of radio but that would be ignoring the Halloween in the early '90s when the BBC convinced me not that aliens were invading but that something far worse had happened: chat show host and national treasure Michael Parkinson had been possessed by a ghost called Pipes on live TV.

Halloween wasn't a big thing on Dartmoor in 1992. I'm not sure if this is because it hadn't yet taken off across the country or just that we were late to the party (it was almost certainly the second of these). The previous year a couple of friends and I had gone trick or treating, but with the demographic of our village consisting primarily of widows in their seventies and eighties, the evening was less about eating sweets and using whoopee cushions and more about repeatedly explaining the concept of trick or treating to confused OAPs. In fact the only highlight of the festivities was a woman giving us a pound and saying, 'Now fuck off.' To get a quid and hear a swear word at the same time was a huge thrill for an eight-year-old.

Halloween should have been massive on Dartmoor, the home of some of Britain's weakest paranormal myths and legends. I'm sure you don't need me to tell you that the moors are the home to the Nine Maidens, a circle of granite rocks that will put a curse on anyone who attempts to disturb them. In 1985 the crew for a film called *The Circle of Doom* added a tenth rock when shooting a scene, and days later the only tape of the film was – pause for dramatic music – lost in the post. It seems an oversight not to send something recorded delivery when you know you have messed with some cursed rocks hell bent on revenge, but what do I know?[22]

Most famous though are the events of August 1921 when an army officer was riding across Dartmoor on his motorcycle at night only for a pair of disembodied hairy hands to appear from nowhere and force him off the road. It was the third hairy hand-related accident on the road that year, with one victim describing the hands as 'invisible' (this was in the time before breathalysers). The *Daily Mail* sent reporters down to Devon to investigate, filing the front page

---

[22] I have just tried looking up the film on IMDb but it wasn't on there, proving their story. Spooky.

story 'Hairy Hands on Dartmoor'. I haven't read the article but I imagine it blamed Britain's lax immigration laws for letting the hands into the country in the first place.

Gin, of course, had an anecdote about being haunted, telling the story of a flat she lived in in Paddington in which items would be thrown around the room by a poltergeist. After she had moved out, the friend who had replaced her in the house approached her in the BBC canteen looking ashen and said, 'You bitch. Why didn't you tell me it was haunted?' While she took this as proof of the haunting, I was mainly excited to hear there was such a thing as the BBC canteen, a fantasy land in which you could queue for sticky toffee pudding between Nicholas Witchell and Greenclaws.

Despite all this firm paranormal evidence I wasn't any more afraid of ghosts than your average child who lives near a pair of disembodied hands with no respect for the Highway Code. In fact, I was excited rather than terrified when the BBC started screening trailers for a show called *Ghostwatch* with Sarah Greene from *Going Live!* telling us, 'On Saturday night we will be visiting the most haunted house in Britain. But will the ghosts be there?' (If this isn't scary to you on the page, do consider that while she said this she was genuinely holding a torch under her face). What I didn't know is that this was the trailer not for an actual live broadcast but for a 90-minute drama pretending to be a live broadcast in which Greene played herself being terrorised by the ghost of a dead paedophile. As you can imagine, it's quite a scary mistake to make at the age of nine.

Ghostwatch was not presented by people you expect to prank you. Sarah Greene was a woman too nice to laugh when someone phoned up *Going Live!* and asked Five Star why they 'were so fucking shit', while in the studio we had Michael Parkinson – a journalist, a Yorkshireman and a man so trustworthy that he now sells funerals on digital TV channels. If these two weren't enough to make me believe it was legit, alongside Parkinson in the studio was Mike Smith, Greene's real-life husband, in charge of the calls coming in from the 'public'. Once the hauntings began, Smith's powerless cries about the fate of his wife provided a personal drama you would never expect from a man primarily famous for hosting the early evening game show *That's Showbusiness*.[23]

The stand-out performance, however, is from Craig Charles, at the time primarily famous for playing Lister in *Red Dwarf* and as a live performance poet (more the first than the second, thankfully). Charles is given the role of the light-hearted foil on location, talking to locals on the street and interviewing an exorcist who, in a lovely detail, threw

---

[23] To add extra realism they asked viewers to call in on the traditional BBC phone number of the time, 081 811 8181: a number every child knew by heart due to its use on *Going Live!*. The '90s was a time when you knew phone numbers off by heart, as opposed to now when having a smartphone makes that skill completely unnecessary. This has led to the strange situation where I don't know my own wife's current phone number but I do still know the numbers of all my childhood friends.

up for a week after going into the house. What is most interesting about Charles's performance is that he seems to have made the decision to play the role of Craig Charles as an unbearably annoying bellend. He begins links by jumping out and shouting, 'Boo!' and makes jokes like, 'Call our witchboard, I mean switchboard.' Now, I'm not saying that is what Charles is like (I have never met him and I very much enjoy his funk and soul show on 6Music) but it is an intriguing decision for Craig Charles the man to make when deciding how to play Craig Charles the character. I imagine when it became clear to the nation that *Ghostwatch* was in fact fictional there was first a huge sigh of relief that ghosts didn't exist, and then an even bigger sigh of relief that Craig Charles wasn't the knob we had thought him to be.

Everything about *Ghostwatch* felt so real (sorry, Craig). The broadcast wasn't based in a traditional haunted house but a classic two-up two-down on a cul-de-sac in the London satellite town of Northolt, making it feel far closer to home than most ghost stories. As host Michael Parkinson says in the introduction, 'No creaking gate, no Gothic towers, no shuttered windows, yet this house has been the focus for an astonishing barrage of supernatural activity.' It's like Brookside Close but with a ghost instead of a man called Sinbad.

The show is centred on the Early family – mother Pamela and her daughters Suzanne and Kim – who for the past year have been terrorised by a poltergeist. The ghost, known to them as Pipes because Pamela originally told her daughters the sounds they were hearing were just the house's pipes, has been throwing stuff around the house, creating loud noises and left cat-like scratches on Suzanne's face.

Watching the show again, what strikes you is that it is perfectly paced with, and I mean this as a compliment, the first 45 minutes making you feel like you are watching a very boring live show about a ghost that isn't going to turn up. The presenters themselves seem totally unconvinced, Smith mocking his wife for telling a story about how she was once haunted by a ghost who played the harpsichord and Charles larking about in a werewolf mask like a twat. In horror it is the moments of anticipation that scare you the most and *Ghostwatch* is heavy on the anticipation – it turns out watching Sarah Greene make a coffee for the cameraman to fill time can be absolutely terrifying.

As the show slowly develops, strange things begin to happen and we find out more about Pipes. The youngest daughter Kim shows us a picture she has drawn of him that can only be described as absolutely fucking grotesque, Greene making the strange decision to put the picture on the fridge like Kim has drawn a lovely cat rather than a ghost with an empty eye socket. Kim then tells us that Pipes resides in the basement of the house, a room referred to throughout as the glory hole, a term that I can only assume hadn't gone mainstream by the early '90s.

The second half of the show builds like classic horror until scratching and thumping is coming from the walls and Greene is running round the house chasing down Pipes like it's a terrifying episode of *Challenge Anneka*. As the older daughter Suzanne develops scratches on her face, in a brilliant touch Parkinson says events are so remarkable that they will be staying with the coverage rather than going to the next programme. Eventually things start to be flung from walls, we hear the sound of cats coming from the glory hole (come on now, you're better than that) and the show loses the video link to the house. Then someone calls in and says he was the social worker for a man who lived in the house. He was a paedophile who killed himself under the stairs and he had a dozen cats that were trapped down there with him, which scratched up the face of his corpse. To give you an idea how scary it is when rewatching it I had to pause it at this point to gather my thoughts and calm myself down. In fact, if I'm honest with you, I am yet to unpause and I'm mainly writing this current sentence because I am frightened and want an excuse to delay pressing play.

OK, I've done it now and can report that by the end, Pipes has taken the opportunity to not just terrorise a house but the nation. As a wind whips through the TV studio we realise that he has taken control of the broadcast and the studio ghost expert Dr Parker shouts at Parky, 'We've created a séance, a massive séance.' The show ends with Parkinson alone in a deserted studio, possessed by the voice of Pipes the ghost. Holy shit.

Watching the show again as a 37-year-old with the full knowledge that it isn't real, the whole thing is completely terrifying. And then I remember I originally watched it as a nine-year-old under the impression that the events were genuinely happening. My friend Thomas had been staying over for Halloween and we watched *Ghostwatch* the next day on tape, my parents deeming us too young to stay up but fine to traumatise ourselves at 10am. Despite watching it the next day we had no idea it wasn't real, although looking back if Parky had been possessed by a ghost on live TV you presume my parents would have heard about it on the news at some point and told us. Instead we watched it petrified throughout, sure that this changed everything we knew about the world, ghosts existed, we had seen one and it was coming to get us through the television. And then Gin pointed out there was a cast list in the *Radio Times*. I would love to say that made everything OK but my only memory of the rest of the day is that Thomas was going swimming with his family and I decided to go along because I was too scared to be on my own. When you consider I couldn't swim due to a childhood allergy to chlorine but still wanted to go, you realise just how scared I must have been. I was happy to spend my afternoon sitting at the side of a swimming pool eating Iced Gems and watching my friend swim lengths if it meant I didn't have to sit at home trying to process the hour of my life when I thought Sarah Greene was being chased by a dead paedo.

Thomas and I assumed we were the only losers stupid enough to think it was real, but as the week went on it turned out we were not alone. On the night of the broadcast the BBC received 20,000 calls from worried viewers during the show. I'm not going to say they hadn't expected this reaction but they had put five operators on the switchboard. Three women went into labour during the show, a vicar phoned in to say that even though he knew it wasn't real they had raised demonic forces, while another caller claimed the BBC were going to have to pay for a new pair of trousers as her husband had shat himself. The following week Sarah Greene had to go on *Blue Peter* to reassure children that she was OK, while in a documentary released to commemorate the ten-year anniversary of *Ghostwatch*, Parkinson says that even his own mum thought it was real, phoning him up afterwards and asking what had happened to Pipes – strangely more concerned about the fate of an evil ghost than her own son. All in all, going to a swimming pool, even though I couldn't swim, was quite a mild reaction.

In their defence the BBC were clear they never meant to trick people, pointing to the fact they had put credits at the end, there was a cast list in the *Radio Times* and the continuity announcer had mentioned it was a drama, although you can still watch that intro and it is quite a vague nod to it.[24] People complained the intro would be of little help

---

[24] That intro in full for those interested: 'Now on BBC1 Screen One presents an unusual and sometimes disturbing film marking Halloween. Over the centuries there have been numerous reports of ghosts and ghouls but the line between fact and fiction has always been unclear. Using the modern idiom of the outside broadcast, Michael Parkinson, Sarah Greene, Mike Smith and Craig Charles star in *Ghostwatch*.' I doubt that would have helped me since, as a nine-year-old, I wasn't totally across the phrase 'the modern idiom'. In fact I'm still not totally confident I know what it means now.

if you had just turned on to the show after five minutes, although arguably it would have slightly ruined the experience had they had to stop every five minutes to remind viewers it was still just a drama.

Most tragic was the news that a teenager with learning difficulties had taken his own life five days after the broadcast, leaving a suicide note about his fear of ghosts. The coroner didn't mention *Ghostwatch* in his verdict but it was another sign of the impact people believe the show had.

One of the reasons so many people felt so angry about the show was that it came from such a trusted source. In the 1990s, television was how we got our news and information; the BBC felt like our most revered institution, even after *Eldorado*. Imagine if they staged a terrorist attack on *The One Show* or *The Great British Sewing Bee* announced that Russia had launched a nuclear missile, that is what this felt like. (In reality both of these things would be amazing and I would heartily endorse them going ahead.)

There is footage online of a show called *Bite Back* – a programme seemingly based on viewers sitting in a studio with BBC producers and telling them they are shit at their job – from two weeks after *Ghostwatch* had aired. People are livid. One man says, 'You betrayed the trust people put in the BBC,' like a lover has cheated on him, while another complains he was one of the few people who got through on the phone lines but all he got was a message that the lines were engaged, totally misunderstanding what getting through on a phone line means. Host, Sue Lawley, sums up the controversy by saying, 'Intelligent people felt duped' – presumably she couldn't have given a shit if they had tricked some thickos.

I could pretend I felt angry about *Ghostwatch* but after the initial fear that ghosts had taken over the television and that my life would never recover had subsided, I found it thrilling to think the BBC had tricked me like that, even unintentionally. It is difficult to think of a more audacious moment in the history of the Corporation. After all, what is the licence fee for if it isn't to prank the nation's nine-year-olds into thinking Parky has become possessed?

Ghostwatch was perfect for a moment in time. It couldn't have the same impact were it to be made today – social media would be full of people discussing that it was just a drama from the moment it started. In other ways it was years ahead of its time, made a decade before the found footage horror films like *The Blair Witch Project* or *Paranormal Activity* made us familiar with the techniques it used. No one had any reason to think the BBC were reinventing the mediums of television and horror, let alone doing so on a show featuring Mike Smith. I just did a straw poll of friends my age and almost all can remember watching it, believing it was actually happening and still feeling scared thinking about it today. In a way it was the defining live television event of our youth. The children of the '60s had the Moon landing, the children of the '80s had Live Aid and we had Sarah Greene running away from a poltergeist.

In recent years *Ghostwatch* has had a critical renaissance, the generation of children that were traumatised by it when it was first broadcast have now embraced it, with the release of anniversary DVDs, articles about it in broadsheets and even a special 25th anniversary screening of *Ghostwatch* at the BFI. My friend attended the night and after the film had finished they were treated to a Q & A with the writer Stephen Volk, a perfect sign of just how seriously the film was now being taken. The lights came up, the floor was opened to discuss one of the most brilliant and controversial pieces of television in the history of the BBC and then someone's hand went up to ask the first question: 'Had you not heard what a glory hole was?'

'Just a friendly wave each morning'
Neighbours
BBC1, 5:35pm, 5 February 1993

I recently read an article by the music journalist David Hepworth discussing how the early period of The Beatles is often overlooked by critics, discarded as disposable pop music. 'We must accept the fact the greatest pop group of all time didn't consider it beneath them to make their records for 14-year-old girls,' he writes. I don't know if he would offer a similar defence for Australian teatime soap operas, but if he's not going to then I will, because if there is anything in '90s television that didn't get the respect it deserved it was *Neighbours*.

Neighbours was the first show that I didn't just watch but I feared missing, knowing that it was all anyone would be talking about at school the next day (apart from the one poor kid whose parents didn't have a TV as they felt it was a bad influence, an unimaginable decision which should surely have led to a call to Childline). Such was the rapt attention with which I watched *Neighbours*, I accidentally developed the world's most useless superpower and to this day I can name the actor for every character in the show between 1992 and 1994. Not because I want or need this information but because it is lodged in my mind, absorbed through osmosis from watching the credits day after day. Susan Kennedy – Jackie Woodburne, Hannah Martin – Rebecca Ritters, Lou Carpenter – Tom Oliver. To put this in perspective, I don't know the name of the current Australian prime minister (unless it is Lou Carpenter).

Such was my love for *Neighbours*, in the school holidays I would watch it twice a day, the initial 1:45pm showing and the repeat at 5:35pm. I'm not sure what I hoped this would achieve, maybe I imagined I would pick up on subtleties the second time around like a film buff rewatching *Citizen Kane*, or another important film I haven't seen because I was too busy watching *Neighbours* twice a day. It is crucial to underline for people that weren't aware of this that, yes, when Neighbours arrived on our shores, the BBC made the decision that it was a show of such quality that it needed to be screened twice a day. On BBC1, the country's main channel. It was a show treated with the reverence only usually reserved for the news or the Queen's Speech. And this, of course, felt totally fair.[25]

---

[25] Even *EastEnders* fans had to wait for Sunday afternoon for their repeat when the week's three episodes would be screened in one long omnibus edition. I am aware that watching *Neighbours* twice a day shows a strange level of over-commitment, but surely nothing compared to those losers who would spend their Sunday afternoons watching an *EastEnders* episode that had the running time of a feature-length Hollywood movie.

Neighbours had arrived on the BBC in January 1986 and instantly became one of the biggest shows on TV. By 1988 the Scott and Charlene wedding episode was the third most-watched TV show of the year, with an audience of 19.6 million.[26] The cast instantly became megastars, taking advantage of the love bestowed on them by the British public by moving from acting into pop stardom. Not just Kylie Minogue and Jason Donovan but also the actors no one gave a shit about. Craig McLachlan had a Number 2 hit with a cover of Bo Diddley's 'Mona' (not that we knew it was a cover – we assumed Craig had penned it himself because in the video he was holding an acoustic guitar) and even Stefan Dennis, who played the evil businessman Paul Robinson, had a Top 20 single with 'Don't It Make You Feel Good', a dreadful elec-tropop song that was far more sexually charged than you expect from the owner of Lassiters cafe and bar complex. Imagine the man who plays Ian Beale releasing a single and it actually charting – that was the power of *Neighbours*.

---

[26] A small note about TV ratings. Back in the '90s when there were only four channels, top shows like *EastEnders* would get around 15 million viewers. These days, due to the rise of the internet, streaming and people spending their evenings reading this book, shows get nowhere near that – *EastEnders* gets around 4 million. The only things that get 15 million viewers now are huge sporting events or Royal weddings. In other words, the chance of a Scott and Charlene-size audience happening again depends almost solely on England winning the World Cup or Prince George growing up and marrying Kylie, the second of these being more likely.

Neighbours even achieved the ultimate badge of honour by causing a moral panic. As the show took hold of the nation's youth, the tabloids reported on parents' worries that British teenagers were now talking with an Australian inflection in their accent, with every sentence going up at the end like a question. As I write this I can't leave my house because of the global Covid-19 pandemic; in some ways it is impossible not to argue that the '90s really was an easier time.

This intonation panic was part of the wider narrative – as soon as *Neighbours* became popular people started to worry it was bad for the nation's youth. How could a rubbish imported soap opera with rickety sets and even more rickety acting have such a hold on our children? What kind of witchcraft is this? The answer was simply that *Neighbours* showed us teenagers in a way we had never seen before.

Like all children over the age of eight I was already excited about my future life as a teenager and impatient for it to begin, confident in the knowledge it was simply going to be a better version of my current life. Every school holiday my older brothers and sisters would come and visit from Cornwall and their teenage lives sounded other-worldly. My brother Henry wore shell suits and a Nike Air Jordan T-shirt and had a cassette tape featuring a recording of 'Rhythm is a Dancer' by Snap!. My brother Jake had an acoustic guitar on which he could play a workable version of 'Everybody Hurts' by R.E.M. My sisters Fran and Kate would pepper their visits with stories of their nights out at the Harbour Lights, a sticky-floored local nightclub where they would not be ID'd on entering. How could I not aspire to live the life of someone who had three shell suits or attended a local nightclub that was once visited by Wimbledon striker Dean Holdsworth?[27]

Outside of *Neighbours* it felt like I rarely saw teenagers on TV at all. Today, CBBC is staffed by cool young presenters who look like they could make it to the boot-camp stage of *The X Factor* (but probably no further) – in the '90s on children's TV we had Treguard in his Knightmare Castle and Pat Sharp riding a BMX in his mid-thirties. We couldn't live vicariously through their love lives, to be honest it felt like that was an area best left well alone. Even Radio 1, the home of young music for young people, was staffed by people like Mike Reid, a middle-aged square who would complain about the drug implications of the new single by The Shamen before heading off to hobnob with Douglas Hurd at the Tory Party Conference.

On the rare occasions we did see teenagers on British TV, it wasn't in the fun and carefree way we hoped. Characters on *Grange Hill* would go through teenage pregnancies or drug addictions, which felt a little heavy for a show broadcast at the same time as *Fun House*. You didn't get this kind of drama with *Neighbours*. Even on the occasion that they did a story about teen pregnancy it included an appearance by the ghost of the unborn baby's dead father to tell the

---

[27] A night that ended with him involved in a tabloid kiss and tell (not involving one of my sisters, I should add).

mother she was about to have a girl, so it wasn't strong on kitchen-sink realism.

Neighbours was a show that confirmed to me what I had heard from my brothers and sisters – being a teenager was going to be great (and even if something did go wrong at least I would be visited by a helpful ghost). It didn't crush our dreams too early. The characters had relationships that went wrong, but they didn't ruin their lives and by the next day they were smiling and having a milkshake in The Hungry Bite again. You learned nothing about life from an episode of *Neighbours* except that you could become a lot more attractive to the opposite sex by taking off your glasses.

British soaps felt dark and depressing in comparison. The only time in the history of *EastEnders* when they tried to inject some humour was when Frank Butcher turned up on Pat's doorstep wearing nothing but a spinning bow tie. Imagine watching a soap for ten years waiting for something funny to happen and then it's that. In 1994 *EastEnders* cast *Carry On* actress Barbara Windsor as Peggy Mitchell and everyone assumed that would bring some fun to Albert Square. Within months Peggy had started a hate campaign against Mark Fowler after she found out he was HIV positive and then contracted breast cancer. It wasn't a hoot.

Like all the best things for young people, the greatest thing about *Neighbours* was that our parents didn't understand why we liked it. A lot of adults at the time put its popularity down to us being attracted to the sunny Australian lifestyle. This missed the point. If we were only watching to see the sunny weather then Judith Chalmers would have been a lot bigger cultural figure at my primary school. The truth was if we had wanted to be outside in the sun we wouldn't have been inside watching *Neighbours*.

The most exciting aspect of *Neighbours* coming all the way from Australia wasn't the sunshine but the rumour and speculation it created. The story that got us most excited in my school was that *Neighbours* was filmed on an actual real street that actual real people lived on in an actual real place called Melbourne. Obviously now I realise that just referred to the external scenes but at the time I would ponder on the issues this would present the families who had *Neighbours* filming in their houses while they got on with their day, feeling sorry for the child who would be trying to watch *Round the Twist* in their living room while in the kitchen Jim Robinson was loudly dying of a heart attack.

Another exciting consequence of *Neighbours* coming from abroad was that we were watching the past, because the episodes shown on the BBC were actually 18 months behind those being shown in Australia. Children in school would claim to have heard outlandish future storylines from Australian relatives, trying to convince us they had it on good authority that Lou Carpenter had been murdered, Brad Willis had died in a surfing accident or, worst of all, Paul Robinson was working on a new single.

The proof of the 18-month lag came in 1992 when Kristian Schmid, who played Todd Landers, came to the UK to present *Going Live!* alongside Phillip Schofield and

Sarah Greene (although he only did the job for a few weeks due to issues with his work visa). Schmid was sporting a long ponytail but in *Neighbours* Todd Landers still had short hair. Finally, a glimpse into a *Neighbours* future we could be sure of. We hear a lot about how boring watching paint dry is, but I for one can't tell you how exciting it was to watch Kristian Schmid's hair grow slowly over a year and a half, knowing what awaited. A year or so later the UK audience saw Todd Landers' life tragically cut short, unlike his hair which by this stage was very long.

To me everything about *Neighbours* was exciting. Sometimes it was preposterous, sometimes it lacked a handle on reality, but that was part of the reason why I loved it. I was willing to overlook – and in fact embrace – the unlikeliness of storylines like Julie Martin deciding to go back to school to finally pass her HSC despite being in her thirties, ending up in the same class as her daughter and then being expelled for cheating in a test. This may have been an unlikely scenario but it was an entertaining one, in the same way Julie's eventual death was given a quirky edge when her body was found at a murder mystery weekend.

Watching *Neighbours* was not about looking for plot holes. We weren't worried that Marlene Kratz went on a three-month cruise around the world and then was just never mentioned again. We couldn't have cared less; in fact, I have just Googled this to check I'm not imagining it happened and according to a *Neighbours* fan site: 'It was later revealed in *The Official Neighbours Book* that

Marlene didn't return because she married the captain of the cruise ship.' Of course she did – the most absurd reason was always the one *Neighbours* would choose. *Neighbours*, after all, was a show that had a storyline about a piece of cursed rock bringing bad luck to whichever character had it in their possession. A show that took time out to depict a dog's dream about marrying another dog.

Neighbours fans didn't even question the greatest liberty of all, when actors were suddenly replaced and someone else would play their character. When Caroline Gillmer (didn't need to Google it) who played Cheryl Stark was taken ill, rather than write the character temporarily out of the show they just brought in another actor for the role for a couple of months. An actor that didn't even have the same colour hair. Without comment, Lou's red-headed wife Cheryl turned up with blonde hair and, more importantly, a different face. No one batted an eyelid. Two months later she changed back, and no one mentioned a thing.

Despite all this I want to be clear on something, *Neighbours* was good television. Bad television is something that bores you, contains characters you don't care about and makes you wonder if you should be turning over to watch *Home and Away*. *Neighbours* did none of these things. I was more emotionally involved in the storylines and felt a stronger affinity to the characters than with any other show I watched growing up. I wanted to live these characters' lives, even though by this point I had no idea what it was like to kiss a girl or go on a never-ending cruise.

Disappearing down a *Neighbours* wormhole on YouTube while researching this book, I found myself watching Ramsay Street matriarch Helen Daniels' death scene. Helen, a character who had been in the show from its launch until she left in the late '90s, dies at home surrounded by family watching the home video of her grandson Scott and Charlene's wedding. In a classic piece of *Neighbours* amateurism, they obviously only have the footage filmed for the show of Scott and Charlene's wedding, so when they cut to the supposed home video it is made up of emotional close-ups, wide crowd shots and the implication that Scott and Charlene hired an expensive crew of at least six cameras to film their special day.

But despite this liberty I was surprised by how much better the scene was than I remembered. It is genuinely well acted and full of semi-meaningful dialogue in which the characters tell us about Helen's place on the street over the years. Then as the video ends, Helen, who has just returned from hospital to be with her family, closes her eyes and dies. And why not? Isn't that how we'd all like to go, surrounded by our family and watching *Neighbours*? Either that or at a murder mystery weekend.

As Dr Karl Kennedy turns up and confirms that Helen has died, we see her granddaughters crying and then the scene fades to the credits, not the normal credits with all the actors names I remembered and the iconic upbeat *Neighbours* theme tune, but a sad piano version of the song accompanied by images of Helen throughout the years on the street.

Sitting alone watching this on my laptop I couldn't believe it but I genuinely felt myself welling up. I'm not sure if it was because I was upset that Helen had died or simply that watching a show that used to be so central to my life as a child made me feel overcome by nostalgia. Either way, I can't emphasise enough how sad this piano version of the theme tune was. Maybe *Neighbours* could do serious after all.

My love of *Neighbours* continued until I became a teenager when I began to lose interest – perhaps I resented it for making me unrealistic promises about what my life would entail. Or maybe by that point I had just moved on to watching shows about adults and imagining how exciting their lives must be. *Neighbours* managed to carry on without me and continues to this day on Channel 5, like a band playing village halls 20 years after they had their last hit single. I haven't watched it in years, but that doesn't mean I won't always have a place for it in my heart. We will always have that long, crazy summer when Cheryl Stark had a different face.

'Swing Your Pants!'
Live & Kicking
BBC1, 9am, 2 October 1993

I hate to brag but I was quite a big deal at primary school. Sadly, I now suspect this wasn't a consequence of my unrivalled charisma and social skills at the age of ten but just an illustration of quite how small the school was. By the time I was in year 6 I was one of the only two boys in the top year, so really Thomas and I were top dogs by default.

It didn't take much to be cool at Ilsington Primary, after all, 1993 was the year that the whole school got into marbles. A new tourist attraction, the House of Marbles, had opened three miles away in Bovey Tracey and while many may presume that Devon is full of thrilling tourist spots and attractions, the amount of time my friends and I spent in the cafe, glass-blowing exhibition and marble-dominated gift shop over the next 12 months would call that into question.[28]

---

[28] I have just been on the House of Marbles website and the frequently asked questions is a superb read. From 'What is your most expensive marble?' (Answer: £650) to, strangely, 'What is a lavatory?' (Answer: A traditional term

Even at the time I suspected marbles was an odd thing for us to be into. When my brothers and sisters came to visit from the metropolitan environs of Cornwall, they would discuss their love of Neneh Cherry or bodyboarding, before looking at my marble collection with confusion, like I was not their brother but a Victorian child who had time-travelled into their era in a made-for-TV Disney movie. Stung by this and desperate to be more like my older siblings with their seemingly unattainable Cornish lifestyle, I developed a new passion: pop music and the Top 40. While at school I would still spend time discussing how they got that swirl pattern into the middle of the marbles, I knew I wasn't a complete square because at home I was learning the lyrics to 'The Key, The Secret' by Urban Cookie Collective and memorising the results of the *Smash Hits* Poll Winners Party (Mark Owen, Best Haircut, every year . . .).

Every Sunday between 4pm and 7pm I would listen to the Top 40 on Radio 1, recording the songs I liked on cassette. An early version of Napster-led piracy that would go on to destroy the record industry, the main issue with this kind of bootlegging was that the beginning and end of each song would be ruined by the voice of Bruno Brookes, a Radio 1 DJ whose actual name was Trevor. It was a thrilling

for what many people refer to as a toilet, a WC, a loo, so follow the sign to the lavatories because there are no toilets). I have no idea why the word toilet is banned at the House of Marbles, presumably due to a long-running beef between the marble and porcelain industry.

if unsatisfying way to start a record collection, the fact you couldn't afford to buy the songs on cassette reinforced every time a track ended and you heard Bruno say, 'Up three at two it's Shaggy with Oh Ca . . .' followed by a hard cut into the beginning of 'Young at Heart' by The Bluebells.

Most of my pop knowledge, unsurprisingly, would be gleaned from the television. Like all children born in the UK before the internet ruined everyone's fun, every Thursday evening I would turn on *Top of the Pops* to watch artists mime through their latest singles in front of teenagers too self-conscious to dance. However, unlike in the '70s and '80s when *Top of the Pops* was the beginning and end of pop music television, by 1993 it was just one of the shows you needed to watch if you wanted to know the exact songs you should be listening to as a ten-year-old.

On Saturday lunchtime the *ITV Chart Show* offered a similar experience to *Top of the Pops* but on a much smaller budget. The show had no presenter or live performances but made up for this by linking together music videos with cutting-edge (for around 1985) computer animations of cool modern gadgets like space rockets and pinball machines. It was MTV made on a ZX Spectrum by a dad.

The whole show was styled like you were watching it on a VHS player. Videos would be shown for a few seconds only for it to suddenly say 'Fast forward' before skipping through the rest of the song. Before each break you would see three seconds of the next song coming up before it said 'Pause' and went to an advert for Clearasil. On rare occasions you would even get the treat of it saying 'Play' and you would be able to settle back for a full three minutes of 'Tease Me' by Chaka Demus & Pliers. There were few experiences as disappointing for a ten-year-old in 1993 as seeing the *ITV Chart Show* fast-forward through Snow's 'Informer' only to play the whole of UB40's cover of '(I Can't Help) Falling In Love With You'.

As you would expect I saw being a music fan as not just about enjoying the songs but as a challenge to learn every related fact about the artists I could. A lot of these facts would be provided for me by the Sunday morning pop music magazine show *The O-Zone*. By far the coolest thing on CBBC, *The O-Zone* was hosted by trendy young presenters like Zoe Ball, Philippa Forrester and Toby Anstis – two-thirds of whom I was completely in love with – and combined music news (M People win top award!) and behind-the-scenes interviews with your favourite acts (Whigfield tells all about that dance!). It was through this show that I learned previously off-limits trivia such as Ray from 2 Unlimited's favourite keyboard and that the singer in 4 Non Blondes was actually a woman.[29]

---

[29] If you think I had no use for this pop trivia you clearly weren't in my Year 5 music lessons the week we all had to give a talk on a musical topic of our choice. While others chose to talk about musical instruments or hymns from assembly, I simply played Culture Beat's 'Mr Vain' and then revealed to the impressed class that lead singer Tina liked cats. Instant street cred.

However, if you wanted to know all you needed to know about music and pop culture for the prepubescent, there was only one show that really mattered: BBC1's three-hour, Saturday morning, live entertainment behemoth *Live & Kicking*. Presented by Zoe Ball and Jamie Theakston – a duo who felt like cool grown-ups that just happened to be on kids' TV – *Live & Kicking* featured pop star guests, comedy sketches, American cartoons and, predictably, gunge. Like all the best live entertainment shows of the decade, it was a brilliantly just-under-control mess – *TFI Friday* for those yet to discover the joys of alcohol.

Live & Kicking was a one-stop lifestyle show for children of primary-school age. Here you could see pop stars not just performing their single but holding a prop phone so that viewers could call in to nervously ask them where they got their ideas from. Meanwhile, the rise of video gaming was catered for by Vac-Man, which would see a child trying to win a tempting but inevitably disappointing goodie bag by playing a Pac-Man rip off down the phone. This mainly involved the child attempting to control a man hoovering up rubbish by shouting, 'Left vac, right vac,' in a hugely confusing spectacle that I was very disappointed never to take part in.

Comedy on *Live & Kicking* was provided by the greatest children's entertainers of all, Trevor and Simon, a surreal double act who would get the pop star guests to act in sketches or sing along with their hippy characters before shouting their catchphrase, 'Swing your pants!' More excitingly, at the end of the show they would dress as gnomes and do a *Juke Box Jury*-style review of the new releases, with guests asked to water a flower in front of them depending on how much they liked the new tune from Let Loose. Trevor and Simon were far closer in tone to Vic and Bob than kids' TV had any right to be and I loved them for it.

But there was also a serious side to *Live & Kicking*. We learned to live a moral life through *The Raccoons*, a cartoon about a group of raccoons attempting to defeat the arch-capitalist Cyril Sneer that would underline the message of each episode with a voiceover at the end (just in case we had missed the point that recycling was good). Elsewhere, a cool American called Aric Sigman would offer advice about the problems of growing up as *Live & Kicking*'s agony uncle, a job that for some reason always seemed to involve him giving us the advice that if we were worried about our first kiss, we should just practise on our own hand. This seemed to me to be a completely useless tip; if you didn't know how to kiss, how would your hand help? Your hand can't offer helpful feedback or give you confidence-boosting compliments – it is a part of you. Pointless.

On Saturday afternoons after *Live & Kicking*, my parents would take me to Newton Abbot so I could look at the single I had just seen East 17 promoting before deciding that I would just tape it off the radio. Newton Abbot is a small market town on the edge of the moor that had seemingly been briefed about all the most popular shops in other towns but instead had decided to do its own versions.

Instead of a John Lewis there was Austins, which prided itself on being a department store so big it was actually spread over two (quite small) shops on opposite sides of the road. Instead of McDonald's it had a Wimpy.[30] Instead of Pizza Hut there was Pizza House. It was like one of those computer games that can't afford the rights to the names of real footballers so gives you a front two of Ryan Greggs and Ruud van Mistelroum.

Perhaps Newton Abbot's strangest shop was on the outskirts of town. Standing at the side of the A38 dual carriageway, Trago Mills was a huge discount store, for some reason housed in a purpose-built black-and-white mock Tudor castle with grounds roamed by peacocks. There's a sentence that kept getting weirder as it went along. Inside Trago, the stock seemed to be exclusively chosen because it had failed to sell elsewhere: a book department full of hardback copies of Vicki Michelle's autobiography, a sport department with 200 fishing rods but no footballs and a computer games department that seemed to only deal in games for discontinued Atari systems. With its faux historical setting and idiosyncratic stock ordering, Trago remains the only place I have ever been that allowed you to both imagine your life as a 16th-century monarch and purchase a compilation of *American Gladiators* on VHS in the same morning.

---

[30] Instead of a Big Mac or Whopper, Wimpy's speciality was a rolled-up sausage called a Bender in a Bun. Tasty.

To add to Trago's surreal air, around the grounds of the property were billboards calling for Britain's exit from the European Union with slogans like 'Europe is selling Britain by the kilo' while inside the store they had refused to stop using imperial measurements. Owner Mike Robertson's obsession with getting his right-wing agenda across at all costs extended to the company's adverts in the local papers, one side of which would draw attention to half-price garden furniture while the other would feature a stream of consciousness essay about the state of the world, signed under Robertson's pseudonym Tripehound. I am confident he is the only department store owner whose adverts have led to him being sued for libel by Ted Heath.

Despite my parents' political differences with the owner, we were regular visitors and it was there that I made a purchase that would send my credibility sky-rocketing even further: a set of disco lights. While this may sound quite a sad purchase for a child who spent 80% of his life alone watching television, my friend Thomas and I had a plan. We would combine these lights with my encyclopaedic knowledge of the charts (October '92–December '93) to start our own after-school club (and rave). Marble Mania was born.

Marble Mania wasn't particularly marble-themed but had been named to piggyback on the latest craze, in the same way Wayne Lineker exploited the word Lineker to get people into his nightclubs. Taking place after school on Friday, it was a simple format: everyone came to my house, there was a shop in which we would sell things from our bedrooms we didn't want any more, then we would all watch *Neighbours* and have a disco. This involved me turning off the sitting-room lights, popping on the disco lights and playing a mix tape my brother had made for me that contained 'Rhythm is a Dancer' by Snap!, 'On a Ragga Tip' by SL2 and other fresh cuts from across the Cornish border (I didn't want to use my own tapes for fear Bruno Brookes chipping in on each song would break the spell).

The genius of Marble Mania was that we would charge £1 each for entry – every parent would pay it for their child because they didn't want to miss out and we would get to keep the money. Parents were essentially paying Thomas and me for my parents to look after their kids. With no over-heads we were seeing upwards of £8 a week each. I don't want to overstate things but it is the kind of thing you read about in a biography of Alan Sugar.

Such was the success of Marble Mania and my conse-quent rise in popularity that this was where my first kiss occurred. Sophie was one of the three girls in the year below me but I didn't let the age difference get in the way of things and had been in love with her since I was nine (and she was eight). Sophie was a lovely girl and marginally more attainable than Philippa Forrester from *The O-Zone*, although my abiding memory of her was that she used to get five separate chocolate bars in her lunch box every day. It was astonishing to see – a Penguin, a Breakaway, a 54321, a Trio and a Club, all in the same box. I should say at this point that I liked Sophie for who she was and not because she was a ready source of surplus Penguins throughout the school week, although this certainly didn't hinder her attractiveness.

I didn't think I had a chance with Sophie any more than the other four boys at my school within a year of her age, but then one Marble Mania everything changed. Maybe it was the reputation I had as a nightclub owner, the romantic nature of 'On a Ragga Tip' or perhaps it was that someone else just decided we were now boyfriend and girlfriend (it was that one) but suddenly we were a couple. The two hours that we were together and the one kiss we shared were a giddy high unmatched so far in my life. I had it all: a girlfriend, a night-club and enough money to finally buy 'Deep' by East 17.

Sadly it wasn't to last. Later in the same Marble Mania, Sophie was standing on a duvet and, in what I can only assume was a power play or misjudgement of how physics worked, challenged me to take it from under her feet like a magician with a tablecloth. Emboldened by the success of my club/kissing, I assumed I could, Sophie went over and I was dumped. Maybe that was how relationships worked or maybe hers was an overreaction based on the fact she was on a sugar low, having not had any chocolate in the last hour – it remains a mystery.

All I do know is the next day I watched *Live & Kicking* knowing now for certain that Aric Sigman was of no use. Maybe your hand could prepare you for the technical side of kissing but it couldn't prepare you for the heartbreak.

'Pot as many balls as you can'
Big Break
BBC1, 7:30pm, 20 November 1993

Can you separate the art from the artist? Are you allowed to enjoy *Annie Hall* despite the fact it was directed by Woody Allen? Is it acceptable to watch the films of Charlton Heston despite his support for the NRA? Was it OK to enjoy *Big Break* despite the fact it was presented by Jim Davidson?

When we moved to Devon in the late '80s, my dad bought a quarter-sized snooker table 'as a present to himself'. I never really got to the bottom of what this phrase 'present to himself' meant and how it differed from just buying something, but it is a technique I have taken on, and as such I would like to use this platform to thank myself for being so generous in recently buying myself a SodaStream.

The quarter-sized snooker table was placed in our dining room instead of a dining table, my dad rightly assuming that we were far more likely to want to play pool than eat dinner in a room without a television. Despite being quarter-sized, the table was still too big for the dining room and if the white was left in one corner of the table, the proximity to the wall meant it was almost impossible to play your shot. To this day I am one of the few snooker players who has mastered playing a shot with the cue angled vertically down. My dad later invested in a small cue just for playing from that corner but it didn't prove to be a workable solution; it just meant we found ourselves attempting to sink a long red with what was essentially a chopstick, a skill I have found little use for in later life.

It may be difficult to believe now but at the time snooker was one of the most popular sports on television, still riding the tailwind of its '80s heyday when it became one of the nation's favourite sports through a combination of people getting colour TVs and Steve Davis doing a Bisto advert. Such was snooker's popularity in the '80s, when the 1985 World Championship final between Dennis Taylor and Steve Davis went down to the final black it was, if I remember correctly, watched by more viewers than there are humans in the world (must remember to check this . . .).

The snooker players of the '80s were all huge stars with their own distinct characters: Dennis Taylor wore his glasses upside down, Steve Davis earned the nickname 'interesting' because he was dull and Alex Higgins was popular for being an emotionally volatile alcoholic. There really was some-thing for everyone. Things peaked in 1986 when Chas & Dave and the Matchroom Mob (half a dozen famous players managed by cockney impresario Barry Hearn) released the single 'Snooker Loopy', reaching the dizzying heights of number 6 in the charts. Steve Davis, who featured on the single, has since described it as 'the end of music and snooker as a credible force'; I would question if that was a thing in the first place.[31]

It will not surprise readers at this point in the book that I watched any snooker that was available on TV. In fact, snooker was one of the few sports I wouldn't just watch but would also play, although admittedly this was mainly because if I kept the door open I could see the TV from the dining room, so could carry on watching *Saved by the Bell* as I pretended to be Jimmy White.[32] Consequently, I was delighted when BBC1 launched the snooker-based game show *Big Break*, which saw members of the public answering questions and famous snooker players potting balls to win them prizes (dishwasher, telephone with answer machine, mystery holiday, etc. – the kinds of things my dad bought himself as a present if he was feeling particularly generous).

Big Break had everything. Trick shots, tension and one of the great TV theme tunes, 'The Snooker Song' by Captain Sensible. I have since found out that 'The Snooker Song' is from the Mike Batt musical of *The Hunting of the Snark*.

---

[31] Davis now genuinely splits his time between being a snooker pundit and DJing at festivals playing avant-garde techno music, so he would know.

[32] I later met Jimmy White on a radio show and made quite a tame joke about the fact he lost in a record six World finals. He looked crestfallen. It still makes me shudder with shame to think about it.

What a moment it must have been for people who didn't know this and went for a night out at the theatre only to halfway through think, 'Are they playing the theme tune to *Big Break*?' I can only hope to one day be in the West End watching *The Phantom of the Opera* only to be surprised as they burst into the first verse of the theme to *Beadle's About*. This is a joke, of course, as I have no interest in ever going to watch *The Phantom of the Opera*.

Big Break was hosted by the unlikely double act of snooker player John Virgo and terrible man Jim Davidson. Virgo had presumably got the job because he was the funniest snooker player in the business, which you are right to think isn't a huge claim. Before *Big Break* he was primarily famous for his party trick of coming on and doing impressions of other snooker players to fill the time if tournament matches finished early, something for which he was almost always available as he usually went out in the first round. Rewatching the first episode of *Big Break*, what is astonishing is how little he changed his act for prime-time BBC1 – in the first episode alone he makes three separate jokes about Terry Griffiths being a slow player. While this may sound like a lot of jokes on a niche subject, to be fair to Virgo, Terry Griffiths was an amusingly slow player.

Despite his Griffiths-heavy set, to me John Virgo was hilarious. Each week he would wear a funny waistcoat and deliver a series of deadpan catchphrases like 'pot as many balls as you can' and 'Goodnight, JV'. And boy was Virgo deadpan.

It is impossible to work out if he was brilliant at playing a dour man or if he just was one. Like all great performers, the question was where does the TV John Virgo begin and the real John Virgo end? Usually doing a joke about Terry Griffiths taking ages to chalk his cue, it turned out.

Sadly, possibly blinded by my love of Virgo, *Big Break* was responsible for one of the great TV regrets of my childhood: the years I considered myself a fan of Jim Davidson. As far as I could tell, Jim Davidson was just a chirpy man who hosted *Big Break* and *The Generation Game*. What wasn't to like about this man who put Stephen Hendry off a long red by doing an impression of Private Frazer from *Dad's Army*? As it turned out the main thing not to like was that outside of *Big Break* his output consisted mainly of sexist and racist jokes. But surely it was the BBC's job to check these kinds of things, not mine.

Davidson had come to prominence in the late seventies when he came second in the TV talent show *New Faces*, a Stavros Flatley for the Three-Day Week generation. To give you a taste of his schtick, his stand-up featured stories of a black character called Chalky White (sample line: 'daylight come and I gotta sign on') and in 1980 he released a cover of 'White Christmas' that was performed by Jim – with depressing predictability – in a Jamaican accent. It stalled at number 52 in the charts, which is some consolation I suppose. If you want to sum up Davidson's world view, years later I saw him on an episode of *Today with Des and Mel* and when Des O'Connor asked him what he would do were he to be prime minister for the day (quite a dangerous question to Jim) he replied: 'Well, first I'd give a bit more money to the pensioners,' which of course got a huge round of applause from the ageing studio audience, before he added: 'And then I'd pull up the drawbridge.' The audience applauded again.

It would be easy to take Davidson's comedy apart to show what kind of act he was – the controversies section of his Wikipedia page does a pretty good job of that – but I think it'd all be too bleak. To tell you all you need to know about him let's look at one of his stranger pursuits, his adult pantos. If you aren't aware of Jim Davidson's adult pantomimes, they took traditional pantos and applied his sense of humour to them. Jim had done the impossible – made panto worse. In 1995 he toured his first adult panto *Sinderella*, which according to the cover of the VHS was '"Sexist, naughty and totally outrageous", the *Sun*'. Yes, the pull quote they had used contained the word 'sexist' – that was a selling point. If you were worried that Jim wouldn't deliver on that claim, the image on the front of the VHS is Jim dressed as Buttons while in front of him a woman is leaning over and pulling up her skirt to reveal her stockings, suspenders and bare arse. This was the year he became the host of *The Generation Game*.

A seven-minute clip of the show exists online and I can only say it is a relief it is only seven minutes. It seems it is mainly a mix of jokes about the performers being pissed and blue puns, but not nearly as good as that makes it sound. In 1999 Davidson toured his second adult panto

Boobs in the Wood, he did *Sinderella Comes Again* in 2004 and in 2015 he performed *Sinderella 2: Another Scottish Romp*, which was sadly cancelled halfway through the run due to Davidson's 'unacceptable behaviour' (going to the pub mid-performance still in his costume). I say 'sadly cancelled', but it was probably a good thing. According to a review I read, one character in the show was called Bonnie Prince Long Cock and the plot was that Cinderella was unable to go to the ball as she was on her period. Holy Moly.

It's hard to believe that in the mid-'90s I considered myself a fan of this man. Maybe it was simply that, away from his live comedy, Jim was a great light entertainment host, in the same way that Enoch Powell was a great orator. In that first episode of *Big Break* he is certainly a genial presence – it really is a very passable impression of Private Frazer – but you can see hints of the real comic seeping through. He makes a running joke of flirting with a contestant called Jill until she says she can't cook, and he replies, 'That's her elbowed then.' When Jill eventually wins, Jim tells her: 'You're going to be a wealthy woman, and you're not even divorced yet.' Say what you will about him, but he has a consistent world view.

It feels astonishing that Jim Davidson was such a big name on BBC television when I was a child, weirder still that this felt totally normal. Maybe due to his output, when I think of him now he is a comic from the '70s but the truth really is that his main era of success was the '90s. It was *Big Break* arriving in 1991 that made him a BBC household name and four years later the Corporation doubled down by making him just the third ever host of the flagship Saturday night show *The Generation Game*. It is nice to imagine that decades are neat sets of ten years, each with their own personalities and themes – the '80s was about Thatcherism and yuppies, the '90s was about Britpop and Girl Power – but this is never true. *Big Break* is a show that took a sport that was popular in the '80s and a host that should have been left in the '70s and ran for 200 episodes across the '90s, far longer than almost every show we associate with the decade.

When I started to write this book I thought it would be easy to sum up the '90s as a consistent narrative with all the TV shows telling a different part of the same story, but that is not how it works. Sometimes putting these shows together is like trying to make sense of a *Now* album that contains both 'Wonderwall' and the 'Macarena'; just because things happened at the same time it doesn't mean they all fit together. The sad truth is, if you watched TV in the '90s, you would have almost certainly seen Jim Davidson.

'Have you no shame?'
Neighbours (again)
BBC1, 5:35pm, 25 April 1994

A few weeks ago I got home from the pub and switched on the TV to find that Channel 5 were showing a two-and-a-half-hour-long clips show called *The Most Shocking Moments of the '90s*. While normally I wouldn't choose to watch a Channel 5 clips show with a longer running time than *Goodfellas*, part of me felt it was my duty to this book to open a bottle of wine and spend the small hours of my evening watching a show that had managed to bag interviews with both Darren Day and Bez.

While the show contained all the usual clips you would expect of '90s TV lows – drunk chat show guests, the OJ Simpson trial, a clip of Simon Cowell as a contestant on a quiz show that really stretched the definition of the word 'shocking' – what struck me most was what was missing, the single most shocking piece of '90s television, something I maybe only remember because it happened on the show I loved the most, *Neighbours*.

Having previously convinced you beyond doubt that we should show *Neighbours* a bit more respect, I feel I now have to put forward the other side of the argument. For two weeks in 1994 (1993 Australian time), *Neighbours* was the worst show on television, broadcasting a storyline so breathtakingly misjudged and so jaw-droppingly offensive that to this day I cannot understand how it isn't seared on to our collective memories. Seeing George Best being slightly embarrassing on an episode of *Wogan* is nothing compared to the deep shame of the fortnight that the Lim family moved to Erinsborough.

Up until the arrival of the Lims, the demographic of Ramsay Street had been as achingly white as the audience of a Jim Davidson tour show. So you would assume it would be quite a progressive step for the monocultural cul-de-sac to welcome its first Chinese family. Sadly this wasn't to be the case as the writers decided to squander this opportunity and base the Lims' short stay on the street almost entirely around a storyline in which – and I can't believe I'm writing this – Julie Martin accused them of barbecuing her dog.

I'll just leave that there for a minute for you to take in. Julie Martin – she of the light-hearted storyline about going back to school in her mid-thirties – accused Ramsay Street's first Asian family of barbecuing her dog. In 1994. On the BBC. Not once but twice a day. Even at the age of ten I couldn't help but think, *'This cannot be fucking happening.'*

Part of me has always assumed the Lims to be a phantom memory. Surely if this had actually happened it would still be talked about constantly, like World War II or Kinga with the wine bottle. At the bare minimum you would think it would have made it into the 150 minutes Channel 5 had put aside for shocking '90s moments (I can't emphasise how underwhelming this Cowell clip was). However, after some research, I am relieved to report I didn't imagine a thing, and the Lim family's time on Ramsay Street was genuine.[33]

There isn't much evidence of the Lims online, but the *Neighbours* fan site perfectblend.net lists the saga in the show's '20 embarrassing moments' (huge understatement), alongside Toadie taking part in robot wars and middle-aged teacher Susan Kennedy getting amnesia and suddenly thinking it was the mid '70s and she was 16. Maybe it was the content of the Lims' storyline that made Susan think it was still the '70s.

Best (or worst) of all, if you want to view it for yourself the highlights of the storyline are available with just 40,000 views on YouTube. Bearing in mind the content, it has done well not to be taken down from the platform. Watching it for the first time in 25 years is a strange experience, the blood

---

[33] I should be clear I am relieved it happened, not because I feel it is a good piece of TV but purely because I don't know what it would say about me had I imagined the whole thing and clung on to it for 25 years. To be honest, I probably wouldn't have put it in the book.

draining from my legs as I realise it is actually somehow worse than I remembered. It begins when the Martins' family dog Holly has gone missing and Julie asks around the street to see if anyone has seen her. Seeing his chance, Lou Carpenter decides this is the perfect opportunity to wind Julie up with a classic prank: hinting that the Lims barbecued her dog. Sadly, Julie (being completely bananas) believes him and confronts the mother of the Lim family, Jenny. What follows is a dreadful cross-purposes conversation that no one would have in any situation ever:

Julie: I know our dog was in your yard last night.
Jenny: Yes, she paid us a visit.
Julie: So you admit it?
Jenny: Admit what? She wandered in and played with Tommy until it was time for dinner.
Julie: Have you no shame?

I'm sure we can all agree that as a realistic misunderstanding it doesn't work at all, but I am not sure that should be our main issue here. Let's focus on the core problem of the racist dog barbecuing accusation, something of which Julie says: 'That sort of thing may be OK in your country, Mrs Lim, but in Australia we consider it barbaric.' Oh God no.

I should be totally clear at this point: the Lims didn't barbecue Holly, as Julie soon finds out when the dog turns up. Cue two of the most absurd lines of dialogue in the history of television. Firstly we hear Julie's husband Philip utter the immortal words, 'I hope having a racially prejudiced wife won't affect my business relationship with Raymond Lim.' Then, when Julie is told to apologise to Jenny, she says, 'So she's allowed to be as rude as she likes to me but I make one remark about her eating my dog and I'm the bad guy?'[34]

Perhaps most stunningly, perfectblend.net gives some context to the genesis of the storyline: 'When accusations of racism were levelled at *Neighbours* in the early '90s (presumably due to the entirely white cast), they decided that they would tackle the issue in a way that only *Neighbours* could. In 1993, the Lim family made Ramsay Street their temporary home.' So this was actually meant to be the solution to Ramsay Street's whiteness problem – a Chinese family moving in and being accused of barbecuing a dog. I'll say it again, oh God no.

You could argue there is little to be gained by looking back at the past and judging it by the morals of today, but I would say that were you to look at this *Neighbours* episode and judge it by the morals of the 1920s you would struggle.

---

[34] Also, side point: why is Lou Carpenter getting away with this scot-free? He's the one that suggested it in the first place, so actually I would say the fact he voiced the idea, even as a joke, says a lot about him as a man. Although maybe I should cut him some slack: he'd had a tough time since his wife Cheryl completely changed her face and hair for six weeks earlier in the year.

Perhaps because Julie was not a character we were meant to like, in some dreadfully backhanded way the writers were trying to make a point by showing her up to be an idiot. But that moral seems to be 'don't presume Chinese people have cooked your dog', something I would argue goes without saying.

Usually being reacquainted with vague memories from your youth brings a nostalgic joy, a feeling that these were more innocent times; however on some occasions the opposite is true. While it is easy for me to write off *Big Break* as a silly game show I don't really care about, the fact I loved *Neighbours* more than life itself makes this far harder to take. After all, it is difficult to call yourself a fan of any show that is willing to end a storyline with a character saying the words: 'I'm sorry I said you ate our dog. It was very rude and ignorant of me and it'll never happen again.'

'Something called the internet'
Tomorrow's World
BBC1, 7:30pm, 29 April 1994

It is half seven on a Wednesday evening and Kate Bellingham is introducing *Tomorrow's World* viewers to another technological advance that, like everything else featured on the show, will soon probably be forgotten.

'The one person I know is connected is Bill Clinton,' says Bellingham, before revealing that she had written to him that day and excitingly had already received a reply. 'Thank you for writing to President Clinton via electronic mail,' she reads from the screen, as it becomes clear that she has in fact received one of the first ever examples of an out-of-office email. Despite this, Bellingham is delighted with the response, but then the tone changes as she adds with a slight bitterness that she can't email British Prime Minister John Major because 'he doesn't have a modem'.

Despite John Major's lack of support, Bellingham is very excited about the possibilities of this new technology, telling viewers we will soon be able to use 'something called the internet' to transform our computers into 'a mammoth interactive entertainment centre', making it sound less like the future of human communication and more like something you would take your three-year-old to when you have run out of ideas on a Saturday afternoon.

To up the excitement levels, Bellingham avoids the word internet at all costs, instead throwing around a much more box-office term: Information Superhighway. A phrase she uses an astonishing seven times in four and a half minutes. At one point even referring to 'the building of information superhighways' like they were a physical thing.[35] The opportunities of information superhighways seem endless. Bellingham tells us that in the future we will be able to look at every painting ever painted in our own home and that we could be watching *Tomorrow's World*, wonder where the presenter got their clothes from and then just buy them online there and then. A future that would seem more appealing if she hadn't opted for the appalling '90s fashion choice of a waistcoat over a T-shirt.

But while Bellingham is excited by a future where you can dress like your favourite *Tomorrow's World* presenter while looking at a picture of Monet's 'Water Lilies', from this evidence it would have been impossible to tell if the

---

[35] Full disclosure: I am so bad with technology that I am only 60% confident that information superhighways aren't a physical thing. In fact, if I'm honest, I'm not even sure what a superhighway is. I'm presuming that big wide expanse of tarmac with no markings you get after you have just paid on a toll road.

information superhighway would take over the world as *Tomorrow's World* anticipated or would it go the same way as their previous predictions like robot snooker players and paper pants. You can judge for yourself because Kate Bellingham's four-and-a-half-minute love letter to the information superhighway is available on YouTube and has 221,000 views. YouTube, for those who are unaware, is on something called the internet, which has really taken off.

*   *   *

My primary school had one computer. Not for the adults to run the school – that was done with pen, paper and typewriter – but for the children to join the technological revolution. The purchase of the BBC Basic was a kind of tentative halfway house approach to the new age of technology, that we should show willing with this stuff but not go overboard. Much in the same way that I currently own £50 of cryptocurrency.

The BBC Basic computer – a name that was brutally honest with itself about what the machine could achieve – was designed for the BBC's computer literacy campaign and was as exciting as that makes it sound. It had launched in the '80s as a rival to the ZX Spectrum, meaning my school was somehow already lagging behind in the technological revolution before it had even really started. It wasn't even the best of these two '80s rivals. While children with a ZX Spectrum could play classic video games like 'Jet Set Willy', 'Manic Miner' and 'Daley Thompson's Decathlon', those with BBC computers could play 'Every Second Counts', a game based on the Paul Daniels-fronted early evening game show. Consequently for my six years at primary school, the BBC Basic sat in the corner of the hall deservedly ignored while children discussed how the teachers should have just bought a SNES.

Ilsington Primary had been stung before with cutting-edge technology. Arriving one Monday morning, we were told by Mrs Mantell that they had purchased a fax machine and pupils could now send and receive faxes. On the one hand this was very exciting, on the other it didn't feel particularly relevant to us seeing as none of us were moon-lighting as high-powered New York real estate agents. We need not have worried though as it was explained to us that the nearby school at Widecombe-in-the-Moor (no relation) had also bought a fax machine and we could now message our friends over there.[36] We didn't know it but we were witnesses to the first technological steps towards globali-sation and the interconnectedness of the world, in this case across six miles of desolate moorland to another bunch of underwhelmed ten-year-olds. For a week the teachers excitedly got us to send faxes back and forth to Wide-combe about what we were up to (faxing mainly) until the

---

[36] These were not our friends but in fact huge rivals, as proved every year in the inter-school Area Sports Day. An event in which we would invariably finish bottom, partly due to the fact that my year didn't have the numbers to field a full team for tug of war.

excitement of the new fad ran out. The following week the fax machine was disconnected and put in the cupboard, like that Breville sandwich toaster you OD'd on for three days before never using again.

It was a perfect summation of how the technological revolution impacted on my life in the '90s. Something would come along, provide a bit of a distraction, turn out to be rubbish and then we would go back to watching TV. It happened to the best of them: Global Hypercolour T-shirts, Tab Clear transparent cola, the information superhighway. If I had written this book in the year 2000 I probably wouldn't even have felt the need to mention the internet, such was its lack of impact on our lives. But now – in a world where the internet's hold on my life is such that I have had to put my phone on the other side of the room as I write this to reduce the temptation to check a Plymouth Argyle message board – it feels I need to be clear for those that weren't there just how little impact the internet had on our lives before the turn of the century. Getting the internet was like signing up to an early medical trial. The drug would one day change lives but at that moment it did very little and had the terrible side effect of preventing you from making phone calls on the landline (which at the time was your only phone).

Despite our natural distaste for new technology, attempts were made to make the internet seem exciting to us. Mainly this involved it being presented to us as the height of cool, with the word 'surfing' thrown around like it was going out of fashion (and let's be honest, it was). That's right; you didn't just go on the internet, you surfed it. It wasn't for nerds with computers, it was for cool dudes with shark's tooth necklaces and knee-length, quick-drying shorts. In the library at my secondary school there was a book that taught young people how to use the internet. The illustration on the cover has to go down in history as the most pathetic picture I have ever seen: a teenager with a sideways baseball cap and large unbranded trainers surfing on a computer keyboard.

I have no idea why the secondary school had this book. Even though they had gone a step further than my primary school and had an IT suite of 20 old computers, they had absolutely no ability to go online. It was in here, however, that I had my first experience of cybercrime – arriving for our weekly hour of IT, we found that someone had stolen all the mouse balls, making every mouse unusable. The teacher thought for a second, came to the conclusion that she had absolutely no idea how to get around this insurmountable problem and IT was cancelled.

In 1996 – two years after *Tomorrow's World* had alerted the nation to the information superhighway – my parents decided to go where my school wasn't going to and the Widdicombes got the internet. The Packard Bell Pentium 75 – which like most computers of the time existed in a huge white plastic box called a tower that would sit on your desk and provide enough heat to toast a marshmallow – came with the ability to get online and a free CD-ROM of the encyclopaedia Encarta. It is perhaps a good illustration of how underwhelming the internet was that when it first arrived in our house I genuinely believed Encarta was far more likely to be central to our future.

If I typed the word football into Encarta I got information on football. If I wanted to read about football on the internet I needed exact website addresses, cumbersome strings of words that were impossible to scribble down when read out on TV or radio. There is a YouTube clip of Pete Tong reading out his website address on his Radio 1 show for the first time, and it remains one of the greatest moments of the decade: 'We'll post that out of the BBC home pages of the internet,' says Tong. 'It's very complicated but here it comes: http, colon, forward slash, forward slash, www, dot, bbcnc, dot, org, dot, uk, forward slash, bbctv, forward slash, radio1, forward slash, p, slash, tong, forward slash, index, full stop, html.' This simply could not be the future.

Even if you were to get the address right it was never worth it. After I had desperately managed to scribble down the address for the *Live & Kicking* website, I found it just consisted of a few pictures of Zoe Ball and Jamie Theakston with literally no option to buy the clothes they had worn on the show or view their favourite famous paintings. In fact, all you could really do was look at these pictures as it was impossible to know how long it would take to download them. 'Download time 5mins 34secs' would suddenly change to 'Download time 16 days' then back down to 'Download time 2mins 12secs' then back up . . . To repeat, this simply could not be the future.

According to Wikipedia (a kind of modern version of Encarta), the Dotcom Bubble lasted from 1994 to 2000. I'm sure it did for investors and nerds on the west coast of America but not for schoolchildren on the west coast of England. In my house in the 1990s the internet was, at best, a flawed vision of a rubbish future and, at worst, the reason you missed a phone call from your mate because your mum was trying to download a photo of Monty Don. I could see no way in which this was anything more than an embarrassing fad that would soon be forgotten.

In 2018, 24 years after *Tomorrow's World* bemoaned John Major not having a modem, files were released that showed it wasn't just BBC presenters who were disappointed in him. Some of Major's advisors at the time were concerned that if he didn't get an email address he wouldn't be able to keep up with hip young Labour leader Tony Blair. 'Internet users will be a growing group of opinion-formers, and I can just imagine Tony Blair showing how he belongs to a new generation by signing up,' wrote Damian Green of the government's policy unit. Sadly for internet-savvy Tories, Major didn't sign up, with many of his advisors believing email was a passing fad. So it wasn't just me that knew it wasn't going to take off – I was in tune with the leader of the nation.

Major's internet-pushing advisor, Green, went on to become an MP and served as First Secretary of State under

Theresa May. However such was his commitment to the exciting world of surfing the information superhighway, he was forced to resign in 2017 after he was shown to have lied to colleagues about pornography on his work computer.

'Finish him'
GamesMaster
Channel 4, 6:30pm, 20 September 1994

It was the most excited I had ever been about a trailer. The computerised voice – as with any computerised voice, both futuristic and naff at the same time – asked a simple question: 'So, games fans, are you ready to challenge the GamesMaster?' Unsurprisingly I wasn't ready to challenge the GamesMaster, but I was more than ready to watch some other sun-starved nerds have a go.

As with any technological trend that threatens television's monopoly on people's time – be it YouTube, Twitter or kabaddi – commissioners had responded to the rise of computer games in the only way they knew how – by making a TV programme about it. Each week the GamesMaster – a disembodied floating head played by eccentric TV astronomer Patrick Moore, naturally – would be setting children and a strange array of celebrities cutting-edge computer game challenges.[37] How could you not be excited by a TV

---

[37] In researching this I found out that due to the competitive nature of the computer gaming, *GamesMaster*, hilariously, fell under the

show that featured Frank Bruno playing 'Sonic Blast Man' and 2 Unlimited playing 'Fatal Fury 2'?

The '90s was the golden age of computer games. And no, I won't be taking any questions on that. In the '80s video games had been a curiosity, a fun diversion that may or may not have been left there with the BMX and Bananarama, but the launch of the Sega Mega Drive in 1990 and the Super Nintendo Entertainment System (SNES) in 1992 changed everything. By the time they had been superseded by faster but less fun machines in the late '90s, they had sold 80 million consoles between them worldwide.

The stars of this golden age were the face of Nintendo, Mario Mario[38] – an Italian plumber – and the poster boy of the more grown-up Sega Mega Drive, a blue hedgehog called Sonic (more grown-up being a relative concept). Super Mario World, in which you guided Mario through a land of tortoises, mushrooms and pipes to try to save Princess Toadstool, sold 40 million copies, spawned a film starring Bob Hoskins and a number 8 single featuring the game's theme tune under some bad rapping. On the other hand, Sonic the Hedgehog wasn't a plumber, so they both had their positives.

jurisdiction of the Channel 4 sports department. Of course it did: kabaddi, sumo wrestling, 'Earthworm Jim' – it makes sense. Do you have any motor sport on Channel 4? Yes, we do – 'Super Mario Kart'.

[38] That isn't a typo – Mario's surname was Mario, hence the Mario brothers. The only other person I know of to befall this fate is Gary and Phil Neville's dad, Neville Neville.

The best game of the time, however, was available on both the SNES and the Mega Drive. 'Street Fighter II' was a beat 'em up (fighting game) in which you could play as characters like Blanka, who had been raised by electric eels and so could course electricity through his body, and Dhalsim, whose mastery of yoga meant he could stretch his limbs to metres long. Like everyone else living in east London, I have been to a few yoga classes and this has never been brought up as a potential benefit, although I must admit I have never got beyond intermediate. Even if it was unrealistic about the benefits of breathing and stretching, 'Street Fighter II' summed up just how exciting computer games now were. The SNES and the Mega Drive had changed people's understanding of video games and now dominated the industry; arguably no two objects had a greater cultural impact on the '90s. I had a Commodore 64.

The Commodore 64 was first released in 1982. Arguably a good rule of thumb for playing computer games in the '90s is that your computer shouldn't be able to remember the Falklands War, but there you go. While the games on SNES and Mega Drive came on cool modern cartridges, the games on the Commodore 64 came on cassette tape. Before playing any game you would need to put the cassette into the deck, press play and wait for at least 15 minutes while it loaded. This allowed you time to focus on other things, like thinking about how good it must be to have a Mega Drive.

I hadn't shunned the Sega/Nintendo stranglehold intentionally, I just didn't know it was happening until it was too late. One Saturday in the early '90s my dad and I had wandered into the Newton Abbot branch of Dixons and seen a computer demonstrating a game called 'International Soccer'. My mind was blown, as until this point I had no idea football could be a computer game. I assumed it was brand new technology, secured an agreement with my dad on getting the Commodore 64 for Christmas and left feeling very smug indeed. I have just checked and 'International Soccer' was released in 1983, the year I was born. Still, I was delighted, doubly so when I unwrapped my Commodore 64 on Christmas Day to find that it didn't just come with 'International Soccer' but also a game called 'Fiendish Freddy's Big Top O'Fun', in which you were given the white-knuckle thrill of performing all the skills necessary to run a successful circus – from tightrope to trapeze to badly mistreating endangered species.[39]

Despite the rise of Sega and Nintendo in my peripheral vision at this time, I adored my Commodore 64. You have to remember there was a brief period when I was into marbles, so in many ways a Commodore 64 felt positively modern. Also, it had some great games. The 'Dizzy' series followed a talking egg with a face and boxing gloves called Dizzy who solved puzzles on treasure islands, 'Rocketball' saw you compete in a futuristic sport where people played netball on roller skates while 'Daley Thompson's Decathlon' allowed you to enjoy the thrill of the Olympic Games by whacking

---

[39] Joke, before anyone complains.

your joystick from side to side as fast as humanly possible to make your little Daley Thompson run. For a decade this was how all athletics games operated and led to the premature death of a generation of joysticks.[40]

A couple of years later I finally decided to join the '90s and upgraded from the Commodore 64. Not to the SNES but, in a bizarre doubling down, to the next Commodore up, the Amiga. The Amiga was like a slightly more highbrow version of the SNES or Mega Drive. While they were games consoles, the Amiga was a computer that played games. It had a keyboard and mouse, so that if I had wanted I could word process or build a spreadsheet. I never did this, of course, but it was nice to know the option was there.

The games were different on the Amiga as well. You didn't have Sonic or Mario. Instead, you had 'Lemmings', a puzzle game in which you had to prevent suicidal Lemmings from dying, 'Cannon Fodder', a war game in which every soldier you lost would be commemorated with a small grave and poignant music, and 'Civilisation', in which you had 4,000 years to build a society from a small tribe into world conquerors (not played in actual time). I once stayed up so late playing 'Civilisation' with my brother Henry that we overslept and missed a lunchtime gig by the band Dodgy.

---

[40] For those too young to remember joysticks they were the precursor to today's controllers and were basically a large lever that could go in one of eight directions. They were not the innuendo that is currently running through your head.

This is perhaps the most '90s anecdote in this book. Or indeed any book.

While the Amiga had its fair share of shooting and jumping games like the SNES and Mega Drive, in reality you were far more likely to spend your time building a profitable and well-run theme park. If I'm honest with myself, it was the more middle-class end of the games market – your parents sat on the sofa and read the *Guardian* while you sat in the corner of the room deciding if your society should operate a feudal or democratic system of rule.

If the Amiga was uncool, it did have one edge over the Big Two – due to the fact that the games existed on copyable discs, it was ripe for piracy. If you had a friend who had the game and you had a blank disk, within seconds you could have the game for free, as long as you didn't mind breaking the law. Enough time has passed now for me to admit that, to my shame, I was too much of a square to do this. While other Amiga owners were copying and sharing their games, I was the one paying full price for 'Nick Faldo's Championship Golf' (£26.99!) when I didn't even like golf. 'Sensible Soccer', perhaps the greatest football game of all time, sold one original copy for every 19 pirated copies in circulation on the Amiga, and I of course had one of those full-price copies. Like someone who listened to repetitive dance music but didn't take drugs, I was someone who had an Amiga but didn't go in for piracy – the worst of both worlds.

Despite this I can't think of an item I loved more growing up than my Amiga. Such was my passion for it that when we had to each do a presentation about something meaningful to us in an RE lesson, I brought in my copy of 'Cannon Fodder'. I assumed the class would whoop in agreement as I discussed the unrivalled originality and playability. Then the guy before me got out a photo of his dead dog.[41] I had misjudged the room.

While my teacher didn't approve of my choice, what did she know? Like *Neighbours,* computer games weren't for grown-ups. This was the best thing about them – they were something my parents' generation couldn't be a part of on any level. Even if they didn't like the TV we watched they understood it; it had a reference point in other TV they did like. Worse than that, they often liked the music we liked, telling us they 'dug' Oasis because they sounded like The Beatles, instantly destroying any element of cool teenage rebellion we thought we were operating on. But computer games were from a world they didn't inhabit. Playing with Matchbox cars in the '60s didn't help them to control a motorcycle and punch someone on 'Road Rash' in the '90s. You would ask your parents if they wanted to play and they would pick up the joystick and hold it the wrong way round. The deep shame. Trying to get someone born before 1965 to use a joystick properly was like trying to get an Amazonian tribesman to pop a series link on your Sky box.

---

[41] For clarity, this was a photo of a dog that had since died, not a photo of a dead dog. That would have been awful.

Computer games were a subculture for the young, and the people that made *GamesMaster* understood this. Consequently it had the same DIY spirit as the best Channel 4 shows of the time – television that felt all the better for being cheap and on the verge of falling apart at any moment. I would have watched any old shit about computer games and loved it (in fact, in writing this book I have begun to realise I would have watched any old shit about anything and loved it), but *GamesMaster* was a much better show than it needed to be.

The show was hosted by a sarcastic Scotsman called Dominik Diamond who wore big, stylised suits and had been in a sketch group at university with David Walliams and Simon Pegg called David Icke and the Orphans of Jesus. Diamond didn't seem to give a shit about anything. He starts series four by describing the contestants playing by saying: 'Each week we will select people, some of them physically attractive, some of them laughably ugly.' He later introduces celebrity guest Frank Skinner as 'star of every single TV show in Britain this year' and when interviewing a kid who is about to play 'Mortal Kombat'[42] just asks him

---

[42] 'Mortal Kombat' was an astonishing computer game to put on TV at 6:30pm. A beat 'em up like 'Street Fighter II', it took things to the next level by having 'finishing moves' in which you could rip the head off your opponent or pull out their spine and see their innards go everywhere. And people complained about the *Brookside* lesbian kiss.

what his favourite flavour of crisp was (Cheesy Wotsits). I loved Dominik Diamond.[43]

Each series of *GamesMaster* would have a different setting like it was a different level of a computer game. From a series on an oil rig to one in Atlantis to a series in Hell. The Hell set meant series four featured fiery pits with audience members trapped in cages while players were brought on by dwarves dressed as death. When Frank Skinner comes on, he describes the set as 'a gothic *Tiswas*', which perfectly sums up not just the set but the show as a whole. Rewatching it, the show holds up brilliantly from the mad set to the caustic host; in fact, the only underwhelming element of the viewing experience is the computer games. It turns out that watching two 12-year-olds from Burnley playing 'Cool Spot' isn't the televisual gold I remember it to be. In fact, the only real fun of the games is that Diamond gets to commentate, taking the piss out of the graphics or just really sticking the boot in when a child messes up.

---

[43] Diamond didn't host series three due to it being sponsored by McDonald's and was replaced by Dexter Fletcher, a man with one of the most baffling CVs in showbiz. As a child star he appeared in *Bugsy Malone*, *The Long Good Friday* and *Press Gang*, before he transitioned to working actor and followed that up with becoming a huge film director, making the Elton John biopic *Rocketman*. All this and he also hosted series three of *GamesMaster*. Diamond returned for series four, which was still sponsored by McDonald's, but he must have got over it.

For each game Diamond was joined by a computer games expert at his side, a Mark Lawrenson to his John Motson. These men (and from memory they were all men) were the first real hint to me that perhaps computer gaming wasn't the cool subculture I thought it to be. Judging by these experts, computer games weren't played by fashionable and sociable lads but a group of interchangeable geeky blokes in Jesus and Mary Chain T-shirts and NHS specs – plus one complete bellend called Dave 'Games Animal' Perry (a self-given nickname). Perry wore a bandana, described himself as the greatest games player in Britain and got in a mood on the *GamesMaster Christmas Special* when he lost on a snowy level of Mario 64. It may have been this kind of role model that meant I have never really trusted any adult that plays computer games.

These days grown-ups play computer games and we are meant to be fine with that, and not just grown-ups with nicknames and bandanas, proper grown-ups. Maybe I'm just a product of the decade I grew up in (there is little doubt about that) but I can't get on board with this. If I'm honest with myself, when someone tells me they are a 'gamer', a bit of my respect for them dies, never to grow back. I love Dara Ó Briain – I think he is one of our greatest comics – but when I remember he plays computer games to relax it reminds me that we all have our faults. It is something I can never really get past, like finding out an adult likes WWE wrestling or collects trainers.

Worst of all, computer games have changed to reflect this market. A few days ago I was talking to a friend about a PlayStation game he was playing called 'The Last of Us', in which you control a smuggler tasked with transporting a teenage girl across a post-Apocalyptic America. He described the game as a series of tough moral decisions that at points had made him cry. What's wrong with being a talking egg? Is that not fun any more? If I want to make a tough moral decision, I will consider if I can claim a laptop I would have bought anyway as a business expense. If I want to cry, I'll just type 'Helen Daniels death scene' into YouTube, thank you very much.

People tell me these computer games are now great art, an opportunity to contemplate the human experience rather than just jump on a mushroom, but I liked jumping on a mushroom. I feel about modern computer games like I feel about prog rock: just because it is complicated doesn't make it better. I used to play a game growing up called 'Championship Manager' in which you would buy and sell football players, pick the team and then watch each game unfold. It was simple, brilliant and addictive. According to the promotional material, in its modern-day equivalent – 'Football Manager 2020' – you now have to man-manage the egos of the team, personalise your training for each player to reflect your tactics and take full control of your youth development centre. What a boring game.

I promised myself that this book wouldn't hark back to the '90s like it was a better time where everything was superior, but I have made the tough moral decision to break that promise to myself. The '90s was the golden age of computer games. They were simple, stupid and something unique to our generation that our parents couldn't understand. I don't mind missing out on the emotional journey of 'The Last of Us'. I was there when computer games first took over the world, although in hindsight I should have probably got a Mega Drive.

'Do you wanna bet on it? You bet!'
You Bet!
ITV, 7:05pm 25 February 1995

I told a friend about this book recently and she just looked at me and said, 'So is that just going to be you describing all the mad TV shows that we used to watch?' It felt a slight slam on my literary pretensions, but what are you going to do? The truth was I knew what she was asking me. It would have been much easier if she had just cut to the chase and said it: 'Will you be writing about *You Bet!*?'

You Bet! is either the best or the worst idea for a programme in the history of television; I still can't quite decide. The show would feature members of the public attempting challenges while a celebrity panel bet on their chances of success; on the surface quite a simple and run-of-the-mill format. The key to the madness was the challenges that were undertaken. Quite simply, challenges that shouldn't exist, no one should spend time learning to do and, most importantly, had no right to be televised. Let alone on Saturday night on ITV.

One week, a man would have three minutes to break the tops off six boiled eggs using a Caterpillar 320B excavator (big digger) while blindfolded, and the next week a man in a soundproof booth would have to identify Queen songs purely by the way a flame moved in front of a speaker (losing one of your senses was often part of the task). It is the kind of show that you think you must have misremembered but then you watch a few[44] clips on YouTube and it is all there, it happened. Prime-time TV featuring a three-minute segment in which someone has to recognise cast members of *The Bill* by their ears.

The show was hosted by Matthew Kelly, a nice smiley man with a fuzzy beard who felt like the human embodiment of the Honey Monster. His main job was to interview contestants – who had the social skills you would expect from people who could recognise every Eurovision entry ever from the first five seconds of the song[45] – and talk to a celebrity panel seemingly booked with the instruction, 'Imagine the most unlikely group of people to ever be found in a room together.' Please welcome the celebrity guests for series 3 episode 6 . . .

Letitia Dean, Barry McGuigan and Bobby Davro.

---

[44] 16

[45] A challenge which Kelly introduces with the astonishing joke: 'What involves a panel of international judges and almost every country in Europe? No, not the Nuremberg Trials, the Eurovision Song Contest. Which is like the Nuremberg Trials but less fun.' Holy shit.

Is that a good or bad week? Who knows. Better or worse than series 7 episode 15?

Tony Jarrett, Michael Fish, Mike Gatting and Mo Moreland of the Roly Polys dance troupe.

Each week felt like the worst ever answer to that question about your dream dinner party. 'I think my dream dinner party would be celebrity reporter Ross King, swimmer Nick Gillingham, Bernard Cribbins and Mr Motivator (series 8 episode 6). Either that or Bob Holness, Suzi Quatro and John McCririck (series 2 episode 8).' If you don't know who all these people are, don't worry; I didn't know a lot of them at the time and that was when they were famous.

It wasn't an easy gig for the celebrities, whose job was to come up with spurious reasons why they thought each contestant would pass or fail the task based on absolutely nothing. When discussing whether the contestant will recognise cast members of *The Bill*, John Virgo says he believes she can do it because he spoke to her earlier and she was able to name every member of the Sri Lankan cricket team. Then Bob Carolgees bets that she won't be able to do it because when she spoke to Virgo she thought he was Matthew Kelly.

The beauty of *You Bet!* was that it managed to run a strange gauntlet of being both totally unhinged and completely mundane at the same time. Somehow they took random celebrities, oddball members of the public and challenges based around cracking eggs with a digger and turned it into a show that ran for ten series on Saturday night TV. I find the fact it existed heart-warming, a sense of the triumph of the nerds. These are contestants who almost certainly weren't the coolest kids at school – in fact, they were almost certainly the uncoolest – but now due to their ability to recognise Premier League players only by their knees, they were on Saturday night TV being lauded for their strange superpowers. Perhaps my knowledge of every actor in *Neighbours* wasn't quite as shameful as I first thought.

You Bet! was a show where the weirdness just kept on giving. I would love to say that the most joy I have had in writing this book has been rediscovering a great dramatic performance or inspiring documentary, but in actual fact it is probably just reading *You Bet!*'s Wikipedia entry. A source which tells me that *You Bet!* was based on a European game show, called *Wetten, dass . . ?*, which was the biggest German language TV show in the world and featured guests such as Britney Spears, Tom Cruise, Cameron Diaz, Naomi Campbell, Michael Jackson, Arnold Schwarzenegger, Bill Gates and Mikhail Gorbachev. Presumably Bernard Cribbins wasn't available.

Astonishingly, the paragraph on the *You Bet*! Wikipedia page implying there was a TV show in which Mikhail Gorbachev bet on whether a man could throw 50 Aerobies to a Jack Russell in a minute wasn't the one I found most difficult to get my head round. For further down was the news that the first couple of series of *You Bet!* were hosted by Bruce Forsyth[46] and each week would close 'with Forsyth doing a rap'. Was this the greatest piece of Wikipedia graffiti ever or have I somehow forgotten television's most unlikely hip-hop and light entertainment crossover?

To back up their claim Wikipedia goes on to transcribe the rap (along with the audience shouting back every 'You Bet!' line): 'Do you wanna bet on it? You bet! Well you'd betta get on it? You bet! So don't fret, get set, are you ready? You Bet! Goodnight, God bless, I'll see you next week, bye!' (Wikipedia offers up a hyperlink to the word rap, just in case that was the bit of the sentence you were questioning.)

My first question: Is this the only rap that has ever ended with the line 'Goodnight, God bless, I'll see you next week, bye'? My second: Since when was Bruce Forsyth a rapper? And not just any rapper, one at the absolute vanguard of the movement, rapping on TV in the UK in 1988, the same year Public Enemy released 'It Takes a Nation of Millions to Hold Us Back' and N.W.A. released 'Straight Outta Compton'. On the West Coast it was N.W.A., on the East Coast it was

---

[46] I'm not sure how happy Bruce was about losing the gig. I just double-checked his autobiography to see if he mentioned *You Bet!* and found the following slam: '. . . it was announced that Matthew Kelly would be taking over as the host for the next series. This was good news for Matthew, veteran of *Game For a Laugh*. According to newspapers, he had recently had to sell his family home to pay a big tax demand. Doubtless it would have been even better news if he'd heard about his change in fortune before he moved!' Ouch!

Public Enemy and in Elstree Studios it was Bruce Forsyth, the host of *Play Your Cards Right*.

It will come as little surprise that I could find no other mention of Bruce Forsyth's career in rap online, but what I did find was a full-length episode from *You Bet!* hosted by Brucie, and I can honestly say I have never skipped to the end of something so quickly. So, to answer the question, 'Did Bruce Forsyth used to rap on Saturday night television?' I am disappointed to say, 'Not really.' As it turns out Wikipedia have used the word rap as a very broad term (perhaps they should click on their own hyperlink) and sadly the 'rap' is just another of Brucie's famous audience participation catchphrases. A more cumbersome version of 'Nice to see you, to see you nice' but just with a bit more rhythm. I suppose 'Goodnight, God bless' was a bit of a giveaway.

But while I was disappointed with what I found surely the fact I had believed that Bruce Forsyth would end *You Bet!* with a rap was the perfect illustration of just how unlikely the whole show was in the first place.

'Blobby, Blobby, Blobby'
Noel's House Party
BBC1, 7pm, 25 March 1995

Until I was ten, the South West's premier theme park was Flambards (just off the A394, ample parking available). Part historical museum and part regional amusement park, Flambards allowed you to enjoy both the Britain in the Blitz exhibition (opened by Dame Vera Lynn) and one of those roller coasters that doesn't go fast enough for you to need to be properly strapped in. More importantly, to my knowledge it was the only theme park in the UK to feature a Gus Honeybun-themed ride. Presumably not because they had exclusive rights, just that no other theme park would ever consider doing such a thing.

Then in February 1994 everything changed: Flambards had competition. The King of Saturday night TV Noel Edmonds announced that he would be launching his own theme park in Cricket St Thomas, Somerset. It was the perfect location – close enough to Dartmoor to make it a big local news story but far enough away from the rest of the country to make the idea of building a theme park there a hugely misjudged act of faith.

Little evidence remains of the giddy build-up to 'Britain's first TV theme park', but you can still watch an advert in which Noel implores the nation to come to 'Cricket St Thomas, near Chard', the addition of the phrase 'near Chard' not being quite as helpful to the country's thrill-seekers as he imagines. Despite the location it is clear that Noel is confident. In an interview to promote the park, he tells the watching press that he believes the theme park will outlive his show *Noel's House Party*, before adding rather bleakly: 'It'll probably outlive Noel Edmonds.' Presuming that was a vote of confidence for the park rather than an announcement he was at death's door, Noel was right to be cocky. After all, the park would feature – and indeed have a whole world named after – the biggest star in the UK in 1994. Welcome to Blobbyland.

Like someone who claims to have been a fan of a stadium-filling band since they saw them play to 20 people in the Camden Barfly, I had been a fan of Mr Blobby right from the start. Not because I was some kind of talent-spotting Svengali but simply because I watched *Noel's House Party* religiously.[47] *Noel's House Party* was an hour of games, sketches and pranks broadcast from a studio made to look like Noel Edmonds' country house in the fictional village

---

[47] Sadly, despite the title, *Noel's House Party* had little in common with house parties as I would come to experience them as a student. At no point did we see Edmonds drinking Malibu and Lilt from a mug or throwing up in a sink after having a whitey.

of Crinkley Bottom. And if the fact the village was called Crinkley Bottom didn't get you laughing, then the rival village of Dangly End would surely seal the deal. And in the unlikely event that Dangly End didn't get you, Noel would begin the show by reading out funny stories from the local newspaper, the *Crinkley Bottom Observer*. What I am saying is it was brilliant.

By the time I became aware of Noel Edmonds he had been one of the biggest stars in Britain for a couple of decades and had become the kind of TV personality who was such a big deal he was described as 'TV presenter and businessman', a role which mainly seemed to involve him being seen flying his helicopter if ever there was a need, and often if there wasn't.[48] He was an astonishingly charismatic and slick live TV presenter and a man who, whatever the era, always seemed to have misjudged the shape and colour of his jeans.

Thanks to Edmonds, *Noel's House Party* had an amazing frantic energy like no other show of the time. One minute you would be watching NTV, in which Noel would surprise a viewer by cutting to a secret camera in their living room. The next minute there would be a knock at the door from a

---

[48] For the record this isn't Noel's only choice of vehicle. He also drives a black taxi and keeps a mannequin in the back so that he doesn't have to pick people up. The mannequin is called Candice Cannes and in 2013 she released a techno track called 'Are You Ready?' in which a woman's voice uttered suggestive phrases that could have been said on *Deal or No Deal*. This fact is unrelated, but it is still good for people to know to help build up a picture of Noel.

neighbourhood character played by Vicki Michelle or that bloke who plays Boycie in *Only Fools and Horses*. After this you would watch 'Grab a Grand', in which celebrities as bookable as Kriss Akabusi or Graham Gooch would jump up and down, catching banknotes being blown about by a wind machine. Finally and most importantly, as with any show that knew how to entertain, the whole thing would end with someone famous getting gunged, ideally that bloke who plays Boycie in *Only Fools and Horses*.

Like anyone who wasn't insane, my favourite part of the show was the Gotcha Oscars (changed simply to the Gotchas from series 2 after legal issues with the Academy Awards, no really) in which Noel would prank a celebrity from his contacts book and inevitably reveal them to be a little short-fused but a good sport once they realised they were on camera and being watched by the nation. This was where Mr Blobby came in.

For the second series, Noel decided a good way to prank celebrities would be by tricking them into thinking they were appearing on a new children's TV show and then making the shoot a living hell. Then, just as everything was kicking off, the character leading the fictional show, Mr Blobby, would take off his head to reveal Noel inside with his trade-mark beard and swept-back hair.[49] The joke was that Mr

---

[49] My friend Elis once did warm-up for *Deal or No Deal* and described Noel's look as like a lion who had gone to a fancy-dress party dressed as a human.

Blobby – a huge pink pear-shaped rubber figure with yellow spots, goggly eyes and a giant yellow bow tie – was such a terribly thought-out and one-dimensional character that we couldn't believe the celebrities actually bought it. What no one could have expected is that Blobby instantly became the most popular thing on *Noel's House Party*, and then the most popular thing in the UK.

By the next series Mr Blobby had transcended the Gotchas and had become part of the main show, perhaps doing a sketch with the cast of *Casualty* in which he would fuck everything up or maybe just barrelling in through the door of the house and saying 'Blobby, blobby, blobby' before knocking over a vase, a table and, perhaps, Neil Morrissey. The reality was that by now Mr Blobby had outgrown *Noel's House Party*. He wasn't just on TV, he was on every conceivable piece of merchandise, from duvet covers to pink lemonade. Such was his celebrity, no one even needed the word Mr any more, now he was just Blobby, like he had the infinite fame of a Madonna, Diana or Rylan.

By Christmas 1993, just over a year after his first appearance on screen, Blobby had become so famous that the worst single of all time, 'Mr Blobby' by Mr Blobby, was in a two-way chart battle with Take That's 'Babe' for Christmas Number 1. If I had to articulate how bad 'Mr Blobby' by Mr Blobby was, in one simple fact I would say that it contained fart sound effects for comedy value. If I had space for a second fact I would say that Jeremy Clarkson was in the video. Listening now it feels less like a single and more like a test to see if the nation would buy literally anything with Mr Blobby written on it. Perhaps the only positive that can be taken from its success is the image of Gary Barlow a few days before Christmas listening to the fart sounds coming from Radio 1, knowing that was the song the nation deemed superior to his heartfelt ballad about getting back together with a babe.

With a number one in the bag the next logical step could only be the Mr Blobby theme park; after all, Mickey Mouse had his own theme park and he hadn't even had a Top 10 hit. And so it was that Blobbyland at Crinkley Bottom allowed the people of Britain to finally visit Mr Blobby's house, Dunblobbin, spend their money at The Gunge Shop and dine at the Mr Blobby Haute Cuisine Emporium (once again, no really). As Noel had predicted, the park was initially a huge success and by the end of the second season, Blobbyland at Crinkley Bottom had clocked up over a million fans coming through the gates and, most astonishingly, one couple had used it as a wedding venue (surely, surely, something they regret).

I, however, had no interest in visiting. My initial fondness for Blobby had faded as his fame had grown. While I was more than happy to sit at home and watch him take the piss out of Garth Crooks or Valerie Singleton on *Noel's House Party* at the age of ten, by the age of 11 I considered myself too grown-up to enjoy his rubbish single or drink lemonade that wasn't its 100% natural transparent colour.

While I was simply a bit sniffy about Blobby, his success made others absolutely furious. People hated him like they hated Thatcher in the '80s or Honey G in the 2010s. And not just people you would expect, but people who really shouldn't have cared. I was searching for evidence of this and found an article not from the *Sun* or the *Mirror* but instead from the *New York Times*. Attempting to make sense of what had happened in the UK, the author cannot comprehend Blobby's 'appeal to this nation of Shakespeare, Milton and Philip Larkin', explaining to their confused readers how 'some commentators have called him a metaphor for a nation gone soft in the head. Others have seen him as proof of Britain's deep-seated attraction to trash.' Which I think we can all agree is pretty rich coming from an American.

But here's the problem. Isn't slagging off Mr Blobby for being vapid, annoying and, basically, crap totally missing the point of why he existed in the first place? Rewatching the Will Carling Gotcha when the character of Mr Blobby still felt fresh and new to the studio audience reminded me of why people had, for a short period, loved him. The audience cannot believe how funny it is watching this absurd pink figure utterly torment the captain of the England rugby team. Blobby crashes into the rugby posts and knocks them over, the floor crew get annoyed with him for messing up each set piece and eventually we see Carling get so frustrated that he gives Blobby a sly kick up the arse. It is essentially a man who doesn't realise he is being pranked causing physical pain to another member of the crew on a children's TV show, and it is hilarious.

The problem with Mr Blobby was context. When he started, his role was to annoy celebrities. The problem was that once he was taken out of that context, all we were left with was the most annoying celebrity of all and sadly that is what most people remember. Is it possible that Mr Blobby was the most misunderstood TV star of the '90s? In fact he wasn't an annoying marketing exercise but actually one of the funniest and most anarchic characters of the time, an agent of chaos in the vein of Johnny Rotten, Johnny Vegas or Liam Gallagher. In truth is Blobby actually one of the most rock 'n' roll figures in '90s culture? In him are we seeing the classic trickster figure in mythology like the Norse god Loki or who the Native Americans call Coyote? Can we all agree I have pushed this defence too far?

These days Blobby is often put forward as a symbol of the worst of the '90s, his existence somehow seen to represent a facile and meaningless decade. But this is wrong on two counts. Firstly, he was very funny pissing off Will Carling. Secondly, he has no real relationship to a wider '90s culture. He existed completely in his own world; there was no fashion for Blobby clones or other 7ft rubber characters built to annoy celebrities for our entertainment. In short, there was no one like Blobby. If anything, the main cultural comparison I would draw to Blobby is from a more modern era. With his rapid surprise ascent to fame, realisation that he actually had little to offer outside of his original setting and then swift descent through public shaming, his career feels less like something from the '90s and far more like that of so many reality TV stars of the 2000s.

Perhaps if the popularity of Blobby represents anything it is about Britain itself, whatever the era. The British people's willingness to embrace Blobby and put him at Number 1 ahead of Take That or visit his theme park ahead of Alton Towers wasn't about embracing quality and meritocracy; it was simply about our love of sticking two fingers up to the establishment, a joy that is hard-wired into every single one of us. Even Noel Edmonds. Mr Blobby is LadBaby, Boaty McBoatface, Wolf from *Gladiators* and (whisper it quietly) Boris Johnson.

Whatever the reason for his success, by 1996 the unthinkable had happened: Mr Blobby's unique brand of two-dimensional charm was struggling to stand the test of time. He had been sidelined from *House Party*, failed to follow up on his chart success and, most heartbreakingly, people were no longer willing to travel to Somerset to go to the Mr Blobby Haute Cuisine Emporium. Blobby was quietly dropped from Crinkley Bottom and it was renamed the Cricket St Thomas Wildlife Park, wildlife being something that feels less like a once-in-a-generation fad.

That was the last that I thought about Blobbyland until a few years ago, when photographs surfaced in the newspapers of the park in the present day. Never demolished, Dunblobbin sat derelict in a now wild woodland, moss growing on its roof and weeds sprouting through the white picket fence. In the bedroom Blobby's yellow-spotted bed was strewn with detritus from the park, like Tracey Emin has adapted her most famous work for the viewers of *Fun House*. Further into the woods the pink and yellow toilet sat alone, surrounded by stinging nettles and covered with what was hopefully mud. The whole thing looked like those photos you'd see in the *NME* of Pete Doherty and Carl Barât's flat at the height of the Libertines, just with slightly more pink and yellow and slightly less heroin.

The images have a creepy air, like stills from a horror film about a Saturday night TV-obsessed murderer who lures people back to his woodland lair. It had apparently become a place routinely visited on strange semi-pilgrimages, with stories that it had become a venue for illegal raves, the perfect collision of two very different '90s phenomena. Those who had been there had left graffiti on the walls, outside Blobby's front door someone has spray-painted 'Erol', while in huge letters on a wall inside Dunblobbin it simply says 'Noel Edmonds, stop pretending *Deal or No Deal* is more than it is'.

A couple of years after Crinkley Bottom had closed and Blobby had disappeared from our screens, *Noel's House Party* came to an end. Edmonds put on a brave face, saying: 'I am delighted this decision has been made. I feel as though a huge weight has been lifted off my shoulders,' before adding less magnanimously, 'We have suffered very badly because the Ronan Keating show on before us has turned out to be a disaster. That's dragged down our figures.' Never one to miss out on a bit of self-promotion, Edmonds went on to claim that 'history will prove that *House Party* was one of the most successful entertainment shows of all time'. While that is the kind of quote that you would love to laugh at in hindsight, he was 100% correct.

On 20 March 1999 the final episode of *Noel's House Party* was broadcast, with Blobby brought back for one final sketch. As the episode came to an end, Noel gave one final heartfelt speech, telling viewers: 'It's an overworked expression when people say "it's the end of an era", but for BBC Television, the entertainment department, for me, and possibly you, it really is the end of an era. I hope your memory will be very kind to us. After 169 [episodes], bye.' He then went upstairs to the exit at the top of the set and was squirted in the face with a fire extinguisher by Freddie Starr.

In the years that followed, Noel would go on to host over 3,000 episodes of the daytime game-show-cum-positive-thinking seminar, *Deal or No Deal*. However, this was just the tip of the iceberg. He also started a phone line to give life advice to your pets, appeared on *This Morning* to say that electromagnetic pulses and positive thinking can cure cancer and set up an online radio station to aid his battle with Lloyds Bank over the collapse of his company Unique. Named Positively Noel, the station's aim was for Lloyds staff to blow the whistle on the company in between tracks themed on his case such as Kate Bush and Peter

Gabriel's 'Don't Give Up' and LunchMoney Lewis's 'Bills'. For other celebrities this would feel like the strangest chapter of their career, but really it was nothing compared to the time Noel created the biggest character in the UK by accident, topped the charts and then launched his own short-lived theme park.

'I'm here in the scorpion house at London Zoo'

999
BBC1, 9:30pm, 7 April 1995

At the age of 11 I said my goodbyes to the other three quarters of my school year and moved to South Dartmoor Community College, a perfectly nice comprehensive school in the nearby town of Ashburton. Like a lot of schools at the time it seemed to always be halfway through a rebuild – it had a brand new science block but I was taught RE in a Portakabin, and it had a sports hall with a multi-gym but a school bus in which the heaters didn't turn off.

While this was a much bigger school than Ilsington Primary, it was still clear I was in Devon rather than *Grange Hill*. The location of the school six miles across the moors from my house meant that I would get at least a week off every winter when snow meant the bus couldn't get up the hills, and every year on the week of the Devon County Show all children of farmers would be granted the week off to attend, no questions asked, like it was a religious holiday. I was briefly friends with a farmer's son but never asked him about this loophole. Sadly our friendship didn't last beyond the one time I went to his house and rather than watch TV or play on the computer he insisted that we go hunting with ferrets. Not my scene.

While I didn't feel that only having four children in my year at primary school was strange at the time, it completely failed to prepare me for secondary school; year size: 200. My best friend Thomas Bosence had passed the 11+ and gone to the boys' grammar school in Torquay, meaning I was left alone to try and form an identity within the throng. Suddenly the cache I had earned through being across every storyline in *Neighbours*, possessing 'Rhythm is a Dancer' on cassette and hosting a marble-themed after-school club seemed worthless. In fact, were the last of these facts to get out, it could have been actively damaging.

When a footballer goes into a new dressing room they will often speak of trying to establish themselves by standing up to the big personalities, showing they are not weak from day one. I opted for the exact opposite strategy and decided the best course of action was to completely disappear. This meant attempting to fit in and be unre-markable in every way. I adopted the correct haircut (undercut Years 7–9, French crop Years 10 and 11), wore the correct shoes (Dr Martens Years 7 and 8, Kickers Years 9–11) and was academic enough to be in the higher groups but never good enough to be identified as a boffin. I sat halfway down the school bus (not near enough to the front to be a square but not close enough to the back to get caught up with the main personalities of the bus, the Chapman brothers),[50] I never took part in musical or dramatic productions, never stood for head of house or student council and in my time I only got one detention and that was when the whole class was given detention so I was doing it to fit in.

Such was the success of my disappearing strategy that a couple of years after leaving school I was sitting on the train with a friend, talking about the people we had gone to school with, and the girl in front of us turned round and asked if we had gone to the same school as her as she knew a lot of the people we had mentioned. Recognising her, I said yes, explaining that we were called Ian and Josh and that I knew her name was Holly as we had been in some of the same classes as her. She looked at me blankly, completely unable to place my face. Holly had sat on the same table as me in maths and science for the final three years of school.

I should be clear that this doesn't mean I was without friends: not having any friends would have drawn attention to myself. Instead I would position myself quietly on the periphery of friendship groups, certainly part of them but not the person you remember, like Howard in Take That.

[50] This was not the controversial visual artist brothers Dinos and Jake Chapman. The Chapman brothers on bus ASB5 were called Philip and Nicky and mainly used to do impressions of Jim Carrey rather than create artworks depicting scenes of hellish torture in small plastic figurines.

A lot of comedians talk of discovering their comic ability when making a class laugh so as to avoid being bullied, but this is not something I can identify with. I found a much better way to avoid being bullied was for the bullies to not realise I existed, a skill that isn't much use for a career in comedy but one I have implemented on a number of underwhelming panel show appearances.

It is with a heavy heart that I should warn people that this decision to go socially off-grid for most of my teenage years means that if you are hoping for this book to accelerate in an orgy of debauchery, illicit relationships and rebellion then you are going to be left hugely disappointed.[51] However, if you are hoping the lack of party invites would lead to me doubling down on spending my time watching television rather than snogging girls then you are in luck. After the relatively fast romantic start of a kiss at Marble Mania at the age of ten, the five years of my secondary school was a romantic wasteland as barren as the moors my bus would get stuck on during the snow.

I would compromise on anything to go under the radar and fit in at secondary school. Perhaps the strangest of these attempts to stay unnoticed was that I was a secret vegetarian. I had been raised as a vegetarian by my hippy parents but this was a rarity in Devon in the '90s, a place in which – to recap – farming was treated as a religion

---

[51] For those people I can promise a disastrous attempt at taking soft drugs towards the end of the book, so it won't be a complete washout.

and children hunted with ferrets for pleasure. Such was the lack of demand for vegetarian food that our local pub The Carpenters Arms had one veggie option on the menu: a dish called bean pie, which was, quite simply, baked beans covered with Smash.

While at primary school the fact I was vegetarian didn't really feel like a worry, once I got to secondary school and was looking to cover up any difference or weakness it became a huge issue (entirely in my own head and of my own making). This didn't mean I made the decision to start eating meat – I wasn't rebellious enough for that – but simply that I decided to keep the fact I was veggie from my friends. When visiting friends' houses, I would have to make excuses that for some reason I wasn't hungry or would like the chicken and rice without the chicken. If going to Wimpy I would claim I had ordered the spicy bean burger simply because I wasn't in the mood for meat. When on a week-long school trip to York, I claimed a clerical error had led to me being listed as veggie and now I suppose I would have to put up with the food. You would think by this point it would have been easier to fess up but I was in too deep and continued this for five years. By the end of school, to my knowledge no one suspected, almost certainly because you would never think that someone was trying to cover up being a vegetarian – it is not something that anyone has ever done.

If this was a TV drama my total willingness to bow to the peer pressure and fit in would have led to me trying heroin or being caught stealing an All Saints CD from Woolworths, but thankfully neither of these things were an option due to my lack of access to hard drugs or a Woolworths. It did however lead me to do something far worse: change my TV tastes to impress my peers. In particular this meant watching a show I actively hated but for some reason, still unknown to me, was the most popular show at school: 999.

The basic premise of 999 was that serious BBC newsreader Michael Buerk would narrate a series of reconstructions of horrible real-life accidents that would have resulted in death had the emergency services not saved the day. It operated in a place somewhere between those 1970s public information films in which children die playing on rail tracks and an episode of *Casualty*, with overlong reconstructions of people thinking they were about to die, usually played by an actor but astonishingly sometimes played by the victim themselves.[52] All in all, why wouldn't it be the most popular show with 11-year-olds, it had everything they love: stunts, peril and Michael Buerk.

I hated 999. It was terrifying, unpleasant and presented in a way that left you in no doubt that, to quote the big lottery hand, it could be you. On *Crimewatch UK*, the other show of the time that showed terrifying reconstructions, host Nick Ross would sign off by telling you that statistically you were unlikely to be the victim of a crime, ending

---

[52] On the one hand this would add an air of authenticity, but on the other the complete lack of acting experience could really take you out of a scene.

with his catchphrase 'don't have nightmares'. On 999 it felt like Michael Buerk was implying it would almost inevitably happen to you, saying things like, 'It was just an ordinary trip to the shops, like we all take every day.' I couldn't stand it and yet, because I had no interest in forging an independent personality, I would force myself to watch it every Friday night.

Buerk didn't just provide the voiceover for the show but would appear on camera to link the near-tragedies together from a location related to the incident, allowing the viewer to have fun guessing what awful life-shaping hell you were about to witness. One week he would be standing next to a fire engine holding a huge metal cutter, the next he would be standing sweating in a shirt and tie at the side of a municipal swimming pool. I just clicked on a random episode online which began with him announcing, 'I'm here in the scorpion house at London Zoo.' Fuck. That.[53]

Wherever he was it was going to be a grim watch. The escape at the side of the swimming pool involved a girl who got trapped under the water in a whirlpool after her hair got sucked in one of the water valves. The reconstruction mainly

---

[53] Astonishingly, in an interview to promote the show Buerk admitted he had originally wanted some of the rescue attempts to fail, saying: 'In my simplistic way, I felt a lot hinged on suspense – would the person get out of this ghastly predicament? – and that was lost if every item ended with survival.' If you didn't enjoy 999, just remember, if Buerk had got his way it could have been far worse.

involves people panicking and a camera shooting from underwater just in case we weren't sure how awful it would be to be trapped drowning in a whirlpool.[54] I mean this: 999 was a horrible show. A low-budget *Final Destination*.

Perhaps the best way I can sum up the kind of things that went on in 999 is simply to present a post from an internet forum I found with the header 'Do You Remember 999?'. It creates the perfect picture of the fun times to be had watching the show:

'I remember footy team struck by lightning, javelin, lost in snowy mountains, man impaled on pool cue, nut allergy, wasp sting shock, baby choking on apple core, man with hole in throat falls in river, and loads more.'

It comes to something when wasp sting shock is a bit of light relief.

While, thankfully, a lot of those clips don't stick in my memory, this is one that stands out in particular. Javelin was 999's biggest hit, Michael Buerk's 'Wonderwall'. Ask anyone if they remember 999 and it'll be the first thing they mention. If you put '999 BBC' into Google, 'javelin' is the first predicted word. And yes, it is more or less what you presumed and hoped it would be, the story of the

---

[54] The video for '999 Whirlpool rescue' on YouTube cuts out after five seconds and goes to a small section of the *New Adventures of Superman* and back again, showing it has just been ripped from an old VHS. I cannot be clear enough on this: taping over the *New Adventures of Superman* with an episode of 999 should be a criminal offence.

schoolchild who tripped and got a javelin through the neck. A real-life version of those apocryphal stories teachers would tell you to get you to behave, like when my music teacher Mr Wickenden said he had seen a child flick a glockenspiel beater straight into another child's eye and it had got stuck there (simply couldn't happen).

Somehow though javelin is the one clip I have looked for researching this book that I cannot find anywhere. I should be clear though, the fact I can't find it doesn't mean I'm doubting its existence; I know javelin happened. Partly because I have asked my friends about 999 and they all mention it, partly because I have just read a tweet saying 'There isn't a week that goes by when I don't reference that episode of 999 with Michael Buerk when the kid gets a javelin through the neck' and partly because whenever I close my eyes I have been able to see it since the first time I forced myself to watch that episode in the mid-'90s. I wish I had just got into shoplifting instead.

'Pass it to him'
Fantasy Football League
BBC2, 11:10pm, 14 April 1995

If I could have lived anywhere at the age of 12 it would have been in David Baddiel and Frank Skinner's flat. I don't mean this as a throwaway comment to make a point; it was genuinely something I would think about most days, piecing together what life would be like if Baddiel and Skinner allowed me to move in and be their flatmate. What obsessed me about Baddiel and Skinner wasn't that they were comics – I had no interest in that, at least consciously – but that here were two people whose identity seemed to be based almost solely on watching football on TV. In Baddiel and Skinner I had found heroes to whom I could aspire.

I had been introduced to Baddiel and Skinner through *Fantasy Football League,* a weekly late-night football show hosted from a replica of their real-life flat (a less opulent but more appealing home than Noel's house in Crinkley Bottom). From here they would make jokes about minor details in clips of the week's football, welcome celebrity guests like Peter Cook or Damon Albarn through the front door and generally convince me that being a football fan was a pure and moral code to live your life by. While a lot of shows for football fans keep references broad so as to not exclude people, *Fantasy Football League* took the opposite approach. To understand the jokes you would need an almost encyclopaedic knowledge of the game. Sketches would be based on England assistant manager Phil Neal's tendency to repeat everything Graham Taylor said or *Football Focus* presenter Ray Stubbs' strange way of pronouncing the name Peter Ndlovu. It was a show that made John Virgo's Terry Griffiths jokes seem positively mainstream.

When I interviewed Frank Skinner a few years ago he described their more oblique references as their 'no surrender' jokes, lines that producers or the channel felt were too niche but they stood by as they knew it made the show what it was. And he was right, this is exactly why the show appealed to me; it felt like here was a place where the nerdiest part of my personality was finally being rewarded. *Fantasy Football League* made me feel like I was part of a special gang, perhaps in that way hooligan firms gave a different type of football fan a sense of connection. While they got their feeling of belonging from meeting in underpasses to shank someone for supporting a different football club, I got mine from staying up late watching BBC2 and recognising a good lookalike for Francis Benali.[55]

Fantasy Football League had come along at the perfect time, a unique moment in British football, a no man's land between the unprofessional and rudimentary set-up of the '70s and '80s and the moneyed and corporate game of the 21st century. When Sky bought the rights to the Premier League in 1992, suddenly the game was rich. Before this deal ITV were paying £44 million for four years of coverage; by the end of the '90s Sky's four-year package was costing them £670 million. It created an environment where riches and new ideas were streaming into the game but the players were still going on the lash after training and – in the case of Manchester United's Lee Sharpe – getting their mum to run their own fan clubs (with annual BBQ and free monthly cassette tape of Lee talking about what he's been up to with his life).

Throughout the '90s, footballers weren't elite sportsmen, they were blokes. They had names like Trevor and Clive

---

[55] It should be said that while *Fantasy Football League* started out as an alternative show for nerds like me, Baddiel and Skinner would of course go on to write the official England song of Euro 96, 'Three Lions', with Ian Broudie. A song that went to number one, was sung by the nation and remains the greatest football song of all time (jog on 'World in Motion' fans, it doesn't even mention football till John Barnes turns up with his rap). However, like any true fan, I preferred life when Baddiel and Skinner were just an exclusive late-night thing.

and – despite being in their twenties and running around for a living – they somehow all looked like they were in their mid-forties and losing sleep worrying about their children's escalating university fees. Looking at my sticker albums of the time it is hard to convince myself that these were young men in their physical prime. There was Scotland goalkeeper Jim Leighton, who would play without his false teeth, Bulgaria's World Cup 94 hero Yordan Letchkov, who had the bald head and tired face of an Oxford University don, and Alan Shearer, who was 26 when he was top scorer at Euro 96 but somehow already looked like a middle-aged regional sales rep who spent his life on the road in a Ford Focus.

Shearer started his career at Southampton, my nearest Premier League club at a distance of just 127 miles from Haytor Vale. Even with football, an industry which based its popularity on having teams in every town and city across the country, Devon was not the place to be. If Southampton achieved anything in the '90s it was to perfectly illustrate the contradiction of the football era, remaining in the Premier League throughout the decade despite operating at a hilarious level of amateurism.

Southampton played at The Dell – a ground so cramped that one stand got shorter and shorter as it went right to left to fit in the building behind it – and their main reason for remaining in the Premier League was Matthew Le Tissier, a player who would win every Goal of the Month on *Match of the Day*, but also a man who would have two Egg McMuffins from the McDonald's drive-thru on the way to training. Le Tissier should have played 100 games for England; he ended up playing eight. However, such was Southampton's reliance on him that when Alan Ball took his first training session as the club's manager in 1994 he put the team on the pitch, pointed at Le Tissier and said, 'Our tactic is pass it to him.' This is not the game plan of a team in the best league in the world, it's what an under-11s team does when they have a player who has hit puberty early.

Perhaps the greatest illustration of the level of profession-alism at Southampton came in 1996 when manager Graeme Souness received a phone call from World Footballer of the Year George Weah, recommending they sign his cousin, Ali Dia. Souness wasn't going to turn down a tip from the best player in the world and didn't just sign Dia but put him straight on to the bench for the game against Leeds that Saturday. The problem was that it hadn't in fact been George Weah on the phone but a prank caller and Dia wasn't a professional footballer but just some bloke chancing his arm. So I think we can agree it is hilarious that after 32 minutes Le Tissier picked up an injury and Souness brought on Dia in his place. Dia went on to score the winning . . . Of course he didn't. He was so shit that he himself was substituted later in the game, he swiftly left the ground and was never seen by the rest of the Southampton team again.

This was the problem. As much as the Premier League tried to promote itself as the futuristic face of football, it was actually a place where you could still get a game by prank-calling a manager. It wasn't just Southampton who were a shambles. When hugely successful, stock market-floated megabrand Manchester United played at The Dell in 1996, they left the pitch 3-0 down only to return for the second half in a completely different kit. It turned out that their heavily marketed new grey away kit had prevented the players from seeing each other against the background of the crowd. Le Tissier played in the game for Southampton and later admitted he hadn't noticed United had changed kits until someone in the car park asked him about it after the match; he was that kind of player.

I was delighted by this victory for Southampton, not because I had any strong feelings for them but because growing up, I hated Manchester United with an unhealthy passion. I hated their bitter and angry manager Alex Ferguson; their arrogant French striker Eric Cantona; the fact I imagined Lee Sharpe didn't have veggie options at his Fan Club BBQ. My main issue, however, was that their unique combination of trophies and glamour meant that everyone at my school 258 miles from Old Trafford supported them. On non-uniform day, hundreds of children would turn up in one of the three (three!) current Manchester United shirts available, claiming a lifelong loyalty to the club based on the fact their uncle used to be a season-ticket holder or that their gran had once stopped so Bobby Charlton could use a zebra crossing.

While I was willing to feign an interest in 999 to fit in with my peers, feigning an affection for Manchester United was a step too far. A true fan of *Fantasy Football League* wouldn't choose to support Manchester United, they would choose to support their local team like the show's super-cool guests Nick Hancock (Stoke City), Danny Baker (Millwall) or TV astrologer Russell Grant (Brentford). And so it was that I became a fan of Plymouth Argyle.[56]

Being an Argyle fan had huge benefits. While all the Manchester United fans at my school could only follow their games on *Match of the Day*, I got to go to Plymouth's matches. While in my head this made my life like that of Baddiel and Skinner, in reality it often meant being driven to the games by my mum, a woman who, as an act of motherly love, had got herself into football only to find that she completely lacked the mentality to enjoy it. Each game would be soundtracked by her constantly muttering to herself, 'Oh, no!', 'Don't do that,' or 'Why are they so rubbish?' She found no happiness from the matches until the rare moment the final whistle went and we had won, which actually put her in sync with most of Plymouth's fans.

While Manchester United played at 60,000 capacity all-seater super stadium Old Trafford, Plymouth's ground, Home Park, could be best illustrated by a stand named the Barn Park End, which housed the away fans on a bare

---

[56] Full disclosure: Exeter City and Torquay United were actually nearer to our house but Plymouth were that little bit better so I chose them. What a startling lack of ambition to be a glory supporter but to still only choose Plymouth Argyle.

concrete slope with no roof. In the '80s the Barn Park End had apparently backed on to a zoo and the story goes that during one game a wayward shot looped out of the ground and was followed seconds later by the trumpeting of an elephant that had been struck by the ball. However, by the time I was watching the zoo had gone and the Barn Park was simply a slope so exposed to the elements that if the rain was heavy enough away fans would have to be beckoned out of the stand by stewards and moved into the grandstand for their own safety, like children being called in from the rain by their parents.

Obviously as home fans we didn't have to put up with this kind of degradation, we sat in the Lyndhurst Stand which had plastic seats and a roof and was consequently deemed quite luxurious. This was until the late '90s when it was shut down after failing a health and safety inspection and we were moved to a different part of the ground for a couple of matches. Once the relevant but imperceptible upgrades were made, we were moved back into our seats and a few games later the ball was cleared onto the roof above us and a rusty piece of metal fell down into the stand below. It turns out the lack of roof on the Barn Park End was actually a clever health and safety measure.

When I began supporting Plymouth in 1991 they were in the division below the Premier League. Swiftly after this, to the astonishment of everyone in the West Country, they appointed England's Italia 90 goalkeeper and record caps holder Peter Shilton as player-manager. Shilton was one of the most famous footballers in England and seeing him turn up to play for Plymouth felt like a strange clash of two previously separate worlds, like Cobra turning up to take your PE lessons (and allegedly sign you up to a NatWest current account).

Shilton's time in charge of Argyle was incredibly exciting, by which I mean he proceeded to get us relegated, struggled with a gambling habit and got sacked. But why would we stop there? A few years later we signed the legendary Liverpool goalkeeper Bruce Grobbelaar, perhaps the most famous goalie in the country apart from Shilton, partly due to his unrivalled success and partly because he was facing a court case into alleged match fixing. A king of multitasking, Grobbelaar carried on playing for Argyle during the trial, spending the week in court and turning up for games at the weekend without training (which it has to be said did show). In good news, Grobbelaar was cleared, but in bad news, a year later we were relegated again.

As football moved forward into the brave new world of the 21st century, somehow I had chosen a team that was going backwards. By the end of the decade Plymouth sat two divisions below where we had started, the ground was falling apart and, somehow, we were now worse than Exeter. Meanwhile, in perhaps the most dramatic two minutes in the history of English football, Manchester United scored twice in injury time against Bayern Munich to win the Champions League and complete an unprecedented treble, winning the league, FA Cup and European Cup in one season. They were the greatest team in the history of English football.

But still, I had a sense of moral authority that Manchester United fans at my school could only dream of and Frank and David would have been proud of me. Or at least that is what I told myself.

'What a wonderful guy'
Beadle's About
ITV, 7:15pm, 13 May 1995

Gin watched TV in the way I now use Twitter, not to further her cultural horizons or increase her knowledge but just to keep track of the people she hated the most in the world. We would spend evenings sitting in her living room with its antiques drinks cabinet and bookcases of leather-bound biographies of Laurence Olivier while she gleefully held forth about Noel Edmonds ('terrible little man') or Des Lynam ('less "Dishy Des" and more "Dismal Desmond", darling'). Gin could manufacture an issue with anyone if the show was boring enough not to hold her complete concentration. *Blind Date* host Cilla Black ('awful voice'). World tennis number one Monica Seles ('doesn't need to grunt so loudly'). American magician David Copperfield ('look how many shirt buttons he has undone, conceited').

She was not alone, the '90s was a decade in which you would quite happily watch people you hated on television.

These days if you turn on the TV and see someone you cannot stand (Romesh Ranganathan, Rob Beckett, etc.), you will just turn over to one of the hundreds of other channels or, perhaps, turn off the TV altogether and read a book (look at your phone). In the '90s there were three other channels, and the odds were that the people on those channels could be just as annoying, you just had to watch the person that annoyed you the least.

Top of this love-to-hate list for the nation was Jeremy Beadle. 'He's so awful, darling. Did you see what he did last week?' Gin would say, before describing the previous week's episode of *Beadle's About* in minute detail even though she had seemingly watched it against her will. On this she was in tune with the country: Jeremy Beadle held a strange position in popular culture. On the one hand his show regularly got 15 million viewers, on the other hand he was once voted the second most-hated man in Britain after Saddam Hussein.

Beadle's About saw Beadle, Britain's self-appointed prankster-in-chief, play hidden camera stunts on members of the public. These stunts could be anything from digging up their garden to smashing a replica of their car to, well, it was usually one of those two. Once the victim was closing in on a nervous breakdown – but still just about providing good content – the prank would climax with one of the people who was ruining their life removing a fake beard and revealing they were in fact Jeremy Beadle. It turned out the best disguise for a man with a beard was just a slightly bigger beard.[57] Presumably people would be talking to the disguised Beadle thinking, 'Well, it does seem unlikely that my car would be lifted up by a crane and dumped into the sea but this man can't be Jeremy Beadle – he has a slightly bigger beard than I would expect.'

Beadle was an unlikely TV star. A middle-aged man in big suits and colourful ties, he looked like the children's cartoon character King Rollo and presented shows with the overly friendly manner of a stepdad trying a little too hard with his new wife's kids. He felt less like a Saturday night TV presenter and more like a middle manager you wouldn't want to get stuck with at the office Christmas party. But for a period it felt like he was always on TV. On top of *Beadle's About* he was the first host of *You've Been Framed*, a show in which members of the public submitted home videos of themselves falling off garden swing chairs and taking insane gambles with rope swings above rivers. It seemed Beadle was happy to host any show as long as it involved the humiliation of the public on some level.

Such was Beadle's fame at this time, in 1993 a man was arrested for trying to pull a policeman's beard off,

---

[57] For those unfamiliar with Beadle's trademark facial hair, he had that rare style that combined shaved cheeks with thin little lines of beard running down the jawline to connect the sideburn to the goatee. The only other man I have ever seen with this beard is Craig David, although sadly I have no proof that Beadle was his inspiration.

Left: Always good to match the food on your face with your hair colour.

Right: Gus Honeybun, nightmarish creature and Westcountry legend.

© Mike Alsford/Shutterstock

Left: My Elton John phase.

Left: Me and my dad, Tom. When you can wear a leather jacket that cool, vegetarianism has to take a back seat.

Right: The bustling streets of Haytor Vale (post office since closed down). © *Ilsington Parish Council*

Left: My mum, Sarah, and my legally required '90s curtains haircut.

Left: Ramsay Street's most annoying family: Julie, Phillip, Debbie and Hannah 'Button' Martin.

Right: Just minutes later, Parky would be possessed by a ghost, awful really.

In the cold light of day, *Gladiators* was absolutely absurd.

Josh Widdicombe, 8, of Haytor, shows off his prizewinning vegetable insect.

Above: My far cooler Cornish siblings, Kate, Jake, Henry and Fran, showing huge *Stranger Things* vibes (me, leaning over and facing the wrong way).

Below left: Gin, the most entertaining person I have ever met. Pictured with me in an appalling shell suit and in her acting heyday.

Below right: Winning a prize at the local flower show for a vegetable animal made by my dad. Deep shame. *Courtesy of Mid-Devon Advertiser*

Left: Name a more iconic duo… I'll wait. © *BBC Picture Library*

Right: The '90s most annoying and preposterous character, pictured with… Well, you can do your own joke here.

© *BBC Picture Library*

Left: *Live and Kicking.* Turns out it is impossible to over-decorate a children's TV studio. © *BBC Picture Library*

Above: Liam and Noel stay humble as they receive a Brit Award.

© Trinity Mirror/Mirrorpix/Alamy Stock Photo

Right: The future of British guitar music.

Left and below: Two of the decade's most iconic adverts. Nicole and Papa, and the Milky Bar Kid (Dartmoor version).

© The Advertising Archives

Left: Don't worry, Gareth, this'll be the last time you suffer penalty shoot-out pain at the Euros.

© BBC Allstar Picture Library Ltd/ Alamy Stock Photo

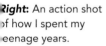

Right: An action shot of how I spent my teenage years.

Left: The world's greatest pop star in the world's greatest bar. © Jeff Spicer/Alpha Press

Above: Lads, lads, lads! '90s time capsule, *Men Behaving Badly*.

© Fremantle Media/Shutterstock

Right: Nasty Nick owns up to the terrible crime of stealing a pencil.

© WENN

Left: Final day at school, pictured with my far cooler and more alternative friend, Robin.

presuming him to be Beadle. By this point we were living in a world in which Jeremy Beadle was so ubiquitous that a member of the public presumed they are more likely to be Beadled than arrested. To be fair we don't know the context of the incident. If the police were investigating the man's car mistakenly being crushed into a small cube, then I can understand his error.

It seems strange that there was a time when these kinds of pranks meant Beadle stood out as the worst person on television (to my knowledge Saddam Hussein wasn't primarily seen as a TV personality). We live in an age when Simon Cowell is employed on two separate TV shows to revel in telling people that their dreams are nothing in front of the nation; Beadle would at worst spend 20 minutes making you think you didn't have a car any more. Contestants on reality shows in the 21st century are offered psychological aftercare to help them deal with what has happened to them, in the days of Beadle, ITV would just have to re-lay your patio and everything was back to normal.

Even Beadle's most extreme stunts felt good-natured, perhaps his greatest being when he convinced Janet Elford, a 59-year-old farmer's wife from Dorset, that an alien had landed in her garden. Elford arrives home to find a crashed meteor surrounded by police before a (clearly plastic) alien appears from the rock in front of her. Amazingly she falls for it completely and is talked into trying to communicate with the alien by the police. 'What do you want from us?' she says in the kind of slow, calm tone that you only really reserve for talking to creatures from another planet. Getting no response (obviously) she then follows it up by asking the greatest question anyone could ask an alien life form: 'Do you want a cup of tea?'

For all the temporary humiliation it would always be made clear by the end that the victims loved being Beadled; when he ripped off his beard they were always delighted to see him. Delighted in the way you are delighted to wake up from a nightmare, but delighted all the same. Then once the prank was over, Beadle would interview them in the studio and they would say what great fun the whole experience had been, the excitement of being on TV outweighing the fact that their 15 minutes of fame almost exclusively involved them telling a fake traffic warden to fuck off.[58]

Perhaps the only time the show became genuinely uncomfortable was when Beadle tricked a man called Vincent Spiteri into thinking that his Essex driveway had been converted into a stop-off for European lorry drivers. To be blunt, it is a ten-minute clip of a man having a break-down surrounded by actors playing comedy Europeans; judge for yourself if that sounds like your kind of thing. The prank is not even a minute in before Vincent has smashed

---

[58] As a child watching *Beadle's About*, the swearing was perhaps the best bit of the show, the first time we had ever heard swear words replaced with a bleep. This of course was far more exciting than actual swearing as you can use your imagination to guess which one syllable word they might be calling Jeremy Beadle.

all the sauces from a burger van onto the floor, so by the time a man pretending to be an Italian lorry driver is pissing in his hedge he has lost it. By the end Vincent is swearing and throwing punches all over the shop, at one point hitting five actors with one swing. And then Beadle turns up as a Frenchman: striped T-shirt, beret and, of course, big beard.

Back in the studio, Vincent is sitting there for the traditional post-prank interview with Beadle, attempting to smile. Jeremy leans in, 'Did you enjoy it?' 'Yeah,' says Vincent, his arms crossed. And so concludes the interview. 'What a wonderful guy,' says Jeremy, the only evidence of this being a ten-minute video of him smashing stuff up and swearing. It's safe to say Vincent didn't vote for Saddam.

'Shitelife!'
The Brit Awards
ITV, 8:30pm, 20 February 1996

For Christmas in my first year in secondary school I requested my first proper album by a proper band, Blur's *Parklife*. For the next four months I listened to this album exclusively on repeat until for my birthday in April I received *Definitely Maybe* by Oasis (I then switched it up and listened to them both on repeat). I would love to say that I had been won over by the excitement of British guitar music being reborn through a Kinks and Beatles-influenced celebration of the unique intricacies of the English psyche, but the reality is I was 12 so I probably just quite liked the tunes to 'Girls and Boys' and 'Live Forever'. Either way it was these two albums that would fundamentally shape my music tastes for the rest of my teens; there would be no more Urban Cookie Collective or Haddaway, I had gone to big school and I was now listening to music for grown-ups.

By the summer, Blur and Oasis had become hated rivals, with both groups due to release the first singles from their next albums in the same week. 'Country House' would go head-to-head with 'Roll With It', the excitement not dimmed by the fact that these were by far the bands' worst two singles up until this point. According to everyone paid to offer an opinion it was the biggest chart battle since The Beatles v The Rolling Stones. A real slap in the face for Take That v Mr Blobby.

The footage of John Humphrys being forced to cover Blur v Oasis on the BBC News is still hilarious to watch 25 years later. 'Two of Britain's most popular pop groups have begun the biggest chart war in 30 years,' he announces, articulating the phrase 'pop groups' like he has never heard the two words paired together before in his life. I imagine Humphrys didn't join me in spending his Sunday afternoon listening to Radio 1 to hear that Blur were victorious[59] or watching *Top of the Pops* the following Thursday as they performed 'Country House' with bass player Alex James wearing an Oasis T-shirt on a show hosted by the impartial third party of Britpop, Pulp lead singer Jarvis Cocker.

By this point I had come to convince myself with no little help from the media that this was my Swinging Sixties. Oasis were The Beatles, Blur were The Stones and I was, well, I'm not sure . . . Harold Wilson? Twiggy? That wasn't

---

[59] This win was in huge part due to the fact that they released two CDs with different B-sides while Oasis released just one. And there it is: the most boring thing I know finally being given an outlet. Thank you to everyone involved in this book for giving me a platform.

important. Around this time ITV screened *The Beatles Anthology*, a documentary series about The Beatles which mainly involved Paul McCartney sitting by a campfire in the woods saying things like, 'We were just a really tight band.' It didn't make me investigate my dad's Beatles albums – I wasn't that square – but it gave me a backdrop to my belief that the time I was living through was almost an exact rerun of the greatest period in the history of British pop.

This was the strange thing about the battle between Oasis and Blur – for me, it wasn't a battle at all. As far as I could see Oasis and Blur fans weren't two rival factions like mods and rockers, they were the same people enjoying the same music. It was two indie bands who had taken over the mainstream on the same wave, not Cliff Richard vs. N.W.A. The only real reason to like one and hate the other would have been if you were blinded by the north/south divide, but that didn't apply to us in Devon as everywhere was the north.

Swiftly my love for Blur, Oasis and Pulp spread to any band that was even vaguely close to being labelled Britpop. Which was lucky because these bands were everywhere. I was able to add to my record collection of two CDs brilliant albums by Supergrass, Ash and Elastica and albums that haven't aged as well by Ocean Colour Scene and The Bluetones. Britpop was inescapable, two years earlier it would have been out of the question for someone like Blur to be on *Live & Kicking*, now you could turn on the TV and see Menswe@r performing 'Daydreamer' on CBBC's *Fully Booked* and not bat an eyelid.[60]

But while if you turned on the TV the message was that Britpop had taken over the minds of the nation's youth, this was not borne out at South Dartmoor Community College. Such was the lack of interest in Britpop beyond my small group of friends that I can still picture the one sixth-former I would see walking around school with an adidas tracksuit top and a Damon Albarn haircut, the coolest man I had ever seen in the flesh up until this point. Perhaps the greatest example of Britpop's lack of sway with my classmates came in the final art lesson of the year when Mr Harron allowed us to listen to music while we painted, leading to a stand-off between a tiny pocket of Britpop fans and the rest of the class. Attempting to find some middle ground,

---

[60] Menswe@r had by far the most bizarre career of all the Britpop bands. They formed after Camden scenesters Chris Gentry and Johnny Dean told *Select* magazine that the top unsigned band in the country were an act called Menswe@r, despite the fact no such group existed. When *Select* published this, Gentry and Dean saw their chance and formed the band. After five gigs and with just seven songs they were signed to a £500,000 publishing contract and they went on to became the first ever band to play *Top of the Pops* before they had released a single. Their second single 'Daydreamer' is, to my knowledge, the only Top 40 single ever to use just one chord throughout the whole song; sadly this was to be their main career achievement, except predicting the popularity of the @ symbol way before everyone else was using it.

Mr Harron eventually put on the Mike Flowers Pops version of 'Wonderwall', pleasing no one.

Perhaps there was nothing in the '90s that made Devon feel further away from the action than Britpop, the county's solitary link to the scene being the band Reef, who were both probably not Britpop and actually from Somerset (but apart from that a perfect in). This meant my experience of Britpop, like most things, was absorbed through the television, getting a huge vicarious thrill by watching the 1996 Brit Awards and imagining what it was like to be there – something I have just done again before writing this, with shamefully similar results.

Watching it now the whole event feels like a celebration of a group of people that cannot believe they have taken over; one of the great debauched nights out. It is one of those atmospheres that I see and the drinker in me can't imagine anything better than being hammered in that room (although it must said, I cannot imagine a fate worse than being in that room sober). When Oasis win the Best Album award, Liam leads the band on to the stage, swaggering ahead in a huge brown leather and sheepskin coat holding a can of Red Stripe, like a cartoon of himself. Holding the award upside down, Liam points at the crowd. 'I'd like to thank all the people . . .' he says before stopping and breaking into the chorus of Blur's *Parklife*. 'All the people, so many people and they all go hand in hand, hand in hand to their . . . Shitelife!' As wordplay goes it is quite weak, but I probably wouldn't tell him that to his face.

This was merely the warm-up to the night's most exciting moment, however. When Michael Jackson's performance of his pompous single 'Earth Song' presented him as the messiah, Jarvis Cocker decided to show his distaste by jumping onstage, walking about a bit, leaning over and poking his bum out to the crowd before lifting up his zip-up cardigan and running off. This may not sound like much but in 1996 pissing off the King of Pop was basically a crime and Cocker would end the evening being questioned by the police. In awful news for John Humphrys this meant that the BBC were again forced to cover Britpop as if it was proper news. The main take-home from the coverage being Jackson's statement, which said that he was 'sickened, saddened, shocked, upset, cheated, angry', because seemingly he had just purchased a thesaurus.

Three days after The Brits I watched *TFI Friday* as Chris Evans interviewed Cocker from backstage at a gig in Manchester. Cocker tells Evans that he had been kept in a police station until 3am before being released without charge, adding that he had been represented for the evening by Bob Mortimer, who had volunteered because he had previously been a solicitor for Peckham Council. 'I was sat there watching it and feeling a bit ill because he is doing his Jesus act,' Cocker says of Jackson. 'Once I was there I didn't know what to do so I thought I may as well bend over and show my bum.' 'What were they questioning you about for two hours?' asks Evans. 'Where did you get your zip-up top?' replies Cocker. He was everything that

Michael Jackson wasn't: funny, self-deprecating and in touch with reality.

It is tempting to see this week as the high point for Britpop. The moment when it felt like the outsiders of five years earlier had now taken over the music industry and were being lauded on trendy TV shows for ruining performances by the world's biggest pop star. But if Cocker was celebrated as a hero for being self-effacing and bumbling, the album that was to mark the end of the era the following summer was the complete opposite.

Such was the excitement of the nation for the release of Oasis's third album, *Be Here Now*, that the night before its release the BBC screened a special documentary. *Oasis: Right Here, Right Now* showed the band playing songs off the new album, having a kickabout on the pitch of a deserted Maine Road and playing pool in the pub, a scene in which Noel is holding a bottle that looks suspiciously like a Bacardi Breezer. The best scene, however, saw Noel and Liam driven around the terraced streets of south Manchester where they grew up, with Noel pointing out where he had been caught shoplifting and Liam showing us the alleyway where he had first taken acid. It was both the most rock 'n' roll thing I had ever seen and a real snapshot of quite how different their childhoods had been to mine. Perhaps the perfect example of this difference being that while Liam had taken acid as a teenager, at a similar age I had asked my gran to tape a documentary about him as I was on a family camping holiday in Pembrokeshire.

Knowing the release of *Be Here Now* was a historic day, my brother Henry and I demanded we skip the beach so we could go into town to buy the album on its first day on the shelves. When I recently admitted defeat and got rid of my CDs, I found that copy of *Be Here Now* with a pristine receipt from Slipped Discs, Pembroke still in the inlay. To repeat, I was a very different teenager to Liam. However, if you think that makes me a dweeb and that no proper rock 'n' rollers would queue to buy a CD on the day of release I would direct you to MTV's coverage of fans queuing up outside HMV on Oxford Street that day in which they interview a precocious, baby-faced Pete Doherty about his views on the Gallaghers: 'I subscribe to the Umberto Eco view that Noel Gallagher's a poet and Liam's a town crier,' he says. It would be easy at this point for me to accuse Doherty of being pretentious and showy but I am fully aware that I'm just a couple of chapters past comparing Mr Blobby to the Norse god Loki, so I'll pick my battles.

On its first day *Be Here Now* sold 424,000 copies, making it the fastest-selling British album in history, which was more bad news for John Humphrys. However, sadly for me, my brother and Pete Doherty, it soon became clear that the album wasn't in fact our generation's *Revolver* but a 71-minute long advert for the terrible creative impacts of Class A drugs (although it has to be said I'm not sure Doherty took this lesson on board). The album's producer Owen Morris has since described the mood of the recording sessions by saying: 'In the first week, someone tried to score an ounce of weed, but instead got an ounce of cocaine. Which kind of summed it up.' If you wonder how that kind of mix-up sounds, the track 'My Big Mouth' has an estimated 30 different guitar tracks layered on it, while third single 'All Around the World' had a 36-piece orchestra, three key changes, backing vocals from Noel and Liam's partners, Meg Mathews and Patsy Kensit, and holds the record for the longest song ever to be a UK number one at 9 minutes 38 seconds. Just say no, kids.

While on the first few listens people like me had tried to convince themselves that we were experiencing the greatest musical achievement since *Abbey Road*, soon we began to wonder if we'd been had and before we knew it we were watching *TFI Friday* and laughing as Chris Evans used a defibrillator to try to resuscitate a copy of the album before declaring it dead. By 1999 a *Melody Maker* survey found that *Be Here Now* was the album most often found in the UK's second-hand shops and even Britain's most self-confident man, Noel Gallagher, eventually lost faith in it, saying: 'Just because you sell lots of records, it doesn't mean to say you're any good. Look at Phil Collins.'

It wasn't that *Be Here Now* killed Britpop, it just helped people notice that it had been running on fumes for quite a while. By the following year's Brit Awards the party was over. The main point of interest that night being Chumbawamba's guitarist Danbert Nobacon (underwhelming real name: Nigel Hunter) emptying an ice bucket over Deputy Prime Minister John Prescott. Could there be a bigger downgrade in the space of two years than Jarvis Cocker v Michael Jackson to Danbert Nobacon v John Prescott?

Popular history has come to record Britpop as the soundtrack to the '90s in the UK. In reality it was a scene that only peaked for a couple of years in the middle of the decade before people went back out and started buying far too many Westlife CDs. In fact, only two of the 20 biggest-selling albums of the '90s in the UK could be considered to be under the umbrella of Britpop: *(What's the Story) Morning Glory?* and The Verve's *Urban Hymns* (which is marginal, so let's say one and a half). The truth is, were you to walk into someone's house in 1999 you were far less likely to see *Parklife* or *Definitely Maybe* in their record collection than you were to see Simply Red's *Stars*, *Talk on Corners* by The Corrs or the sixth bestselling album of the decade, *Robson & Jerome* by Robson and Jerome.

But despite this, Britpop defined my teenage years. It was the first time I felt like I had found music that was made directly for me, a feeling I had never really got from Snow's 'Informer'. More importantly, for a brief window it allowed me to convince myself that my generation had a music scene to rival the one my dad had grown up with. Sadly, 25 years on, it's hard to argue that time has proved this to be the case. Beyond a few great albums – *Different Class* by Pulp, *Parklife* and *Modern Life is Rubbish* by Blur – that Britpop was as much about the excitement of the time as the music that was produced. That doesn't mean that it isn't still thrilling for me to revisit, but when I listen back to Menswe@r's 'Daydreamer' now the joy I get is far more a Proustian rush than an appreciation that this was a high watermark for British pop creativity.

At the height of Britpop I could watch *The Beatles Anthology* and have no doubt about their brilliance. I'm not sure my daughter will get the same feeling when she's 12 and I play her the best of Echobelly. Maybe the thing with Britpop is you really had to be there. Or at least in Devon, watching it on TV.

'The truth is out there'
The X-Files
BBC1, 9:30pm, 27 February 1996

I like to think I'm a pretty normal guy but when I was 13
I believed that the Earth was regularly being visited by
astral beings from another planet and the government were
keeping this information from the people. While this may
seem like a big turn in the road at this point in the book, I
should be clear that this belief didn't mark me out as some
oddball outsider but was in fact the general consensus at my
school. The truth is at South Dartmoor Community College
in 1996 you would have been mocked as a weirdo for not
thinking aliens lived among us. We all knew it to be true
and our primary proof for this was the fictional TV drama
The X-Files.

If you are unaware of *The X-Files* – or the government
has wiped your mind of it as part of a bigger conspiracy – it
told the story of agents Fox Mulder (David Duchovny) and
Dana Scully (Gillian Anderson) and their work in a special
FBI department tasked with investigating cases of the paranormal. While Scully was a sceptic, Mulder, whose sister

had been abducted by aliens when he was 12, was a believer. To illustrate this, in his office at the FBI he had a poster of a UFO with the caption 'I want to believe', making the room feel less like the FBI and more like a stoner's bedroom. In hindsight it was weird that the FBI didn't just fire Fox Mulder, not because he was too close to the truth but simply because if someone in your office spent their day talking about aliens rather than doing any proper work, surely HR would get involved.

Each week Mulder and Scully would investigate a different paranormal going-on, Mulder buying into it wholeheartedly and saying, 'The truth is out there,' and Scully remaining a sceptic for far longer than someone who sees a ghost/alien/time traveller every week has any right to. In many ways you felt these other-worldly experiences were slightly wasted on a cynic like Scully, like when I went to Flambards when I was eight and was too scared to go on any of the rides.

Most *X-Files* episodes were based around some general paranormal going-on, like people being killed by robotic cockroaches or a time-travelling ship that disappeared in the Bermuda Triangle. However, for me the show wasn't about the monsters, it was about the long-running story arc about an FBI cover-up of alien life. Maybe I had been stung by *Ghostwatch* but horror and scary didn't appeal to me nearly as much as a shifty man in a suit smoking cigarettes and quietly disposing of a file of grainy photos. As I say, I was the kind of kid who was too scared to go on the rides at Flambards. Such was the influence of *The X-Files* on me, had you asked me in my early teens what the FBI's activities involved, I would have said 10 per cent tracking down the world's most wanted criminals and 90 per cent suppressing knowledge of alien life forms from the masses. A job they were seemingly doing so badly that a 13-year-old boy on Dartmoor was on to them.

The X-Files had arrived in the UK in 1992 but it took until the third or fourth series for me to become aware of it. By this time it had become the biggest American television import of the decade, moving from BBC2 to BBC1 and at its height getting 10 million viewers, although of course cynics like me weren't naive enough to believe these kinds of government-endorsed figures. In a rather more regressive sign of the show's mainstream popularity, in 1996 Gillian Anderson was voted the world's sexiest woman by readers of *FHM* magazine. When *Buffy the Vampire Slayer* star Sarah Michelle Gellar achieved that moniker three years later, I began to suspect that *FHM* was actually being read by dweebs rather than the cool metropolitan males they claimed.

The success of *The X-Files* was superb news for me – finally here was a show that could replace 999 as the main conversation of my peers. No longer was lunch spent discussing 'man with hole in throat falls in river' over a can of Mountain Dew, now we could meet on the far less divisive ground of whether we were alone in the universe. Presented with a show that I didn't just love but which provided a common ground with my peers, I fully committed to *The X-Files*, showing my support by buying the tie-in book featuring the real stories behind the mysteries in the show (as if they weren't real) and 'The X-Files Theme' by Mark Snow on CD single, a song that you would never have a need to put on. More shamefully than this, I also bought the Catatonia single 'Mulder and Scully', presuming it to be about *The X-Files*, only to be disappointed to find out on first listen that it was actually about a tricky relationship. I have no idea if the number of people making this mistake is what led to it being such a hit, but it did chart surprisingly high.

The paranormal wasn't just a fad at my school, it was mainstream entertainment. In the cinema for consecutive summers the big blockbusters were *Independence Day* and *Men in Black*. Both combined the two coolest things in culture at the time: alien life coming to Earth and *The Fresh Prince of Bel-Air*. Even ITV, the most mainstream of all channels, got aboard the extraterrestrial bandwagon with a show called *Strange But True?*, in which Michael Aspel narrated stories of people's 'real-life' paranormal experiences, like 999 but with more headless Victorian ghosts and less clogged airways.

The show would open with Aspel walking through a low-lit library, like a baddie from *Scooby-Doo* about to reveal his real identity. From here he would link together filmed reconstructions of people's claims, such as a couple who went back in time to 19th-century France or the story of some ghost children singing 'Ring a Ring o' Roses' on the construction site for a new bypass in Yorkshire. 'While it may have made the town quieter, some believe the bypass disturbed something that should have been left alone,' says Aspel, implying the planner had weighed up knocking 20 minutes off the journey from Nottingham to Huddersfield against the consequences of disturbing the spirit world and come to the conclusion it was definitely worth it.

Most excitingly for paranormal fans around this time Channel 4 screened *The Roswell Incident*, a documentary showing grainy footage of a supposed alien autopsy from the 40's. While I of course totally bought into the video of the dead alien on the operating table, some weren't so sure and pointed out that the coiled wire on the phone in the background wasn't invented in 1947, as if that rather than the huge fake alien in the foreground was the main reason to dispute the veracity of the tape. Maybe this phone line did mean it was faked or maybe there was an even bigger conspiracy – had the US government been sitting on the invention of the coiled phone wire for years before the public got their hands on it? Sadly we got our answer in 2006 when, in a documentary hosted by Eamonn Holmes, the man behind the alien autopsy video, Ray Santilli, admitted he had faked it. Apparently he had seen real footage of the alien autopsy but the film was too faded to use so he had remade it. Which was convenient. Turns out the truth was out there, it just needed Eamonn Holmes to find it.

Going back to this now, I do have to wonder if anything shows how much lighter the world felt 25 years ago more than the change in the role of the conspiracy theorist. In the 1990s, conspiracy theories were a basis for PG-rated Hollywood blockbusters and a way for schoolchildren to bond over curly phone cords. In the year I write this conspiracy theories have led to an invasion of the Capitol Building by rioters who believed the American election had been rigged and people refusing to take a vaccine for coronavirus because they think Bill Gates is trying to take over the world. Worst of all, often the people spreading these conspiracies are figures from the '90s gone rogue, with Matt Le Tissier and Right Said Fred leading the Twitter charge against the 'plandemic' and all the brainwashed 'sheeple' – their fear that the world is being controlled by a totalitarian regime not letting them miss out on the opportunity to enjoy some lovely wordplay.

The greatest footballer of the '90s and the writers of 'Deeply Dippy' telling us not to take a vaccine during a global pandemic – this isn't what I signed up for when I was watching *The X-Files* all those year ago. I hate to get maudlin and nostalgic but weren't conspiracy theories just a lot more fun when we were young?

'You've obviously heard there is a football match on tonight.'
England v Germany, Euro 96 Semi-Final[61]
BBC1, 7pm, 26 June 1996

When coronavirus put paid to the European Championship in the summer of 2020, the BBC made the correct decision to fill the huge gap in their schedule with some classic matches from Euros gone by. Along with the odd nod to tedious tournaments like Euro 2012 and 'that great Spain team' (no, thanks), it gave me the chance to spend my daughter's nap time one Saturday afternoon rewatching England's historic 4-1 victory over Holland at Euro 96.

---

[61] NOTE TO READER: For people in Scotland, Wales or Northern Ireland, I would like to apologise for the pro-England sentiment of this chapter. I know for many of you Euro 96 wasn't a highlight of your '90s and in fact the only bit of it you enjoyed was England's defeat to Germany. I totally understand that and can only apologise in advance for what you are about to read, or skip over.

To transport us back to that time, the coverage opened with a montage of the summer of 1996, soundtracked by 'Morning Glory' by Oasis. It's all there for us to see, 1996 distilled to its constituent parts: cheering England fans, the Red Arrows, Princess Diana, John Major addressing the Tory Party Conference and someone putting some ketchup on a cone of chips. For those not around at the time, Gabby Logan's voiceover fills in the gaps: 'Britpop was taking over the world, Blur and Oasis were at the height of their powers. Music and sport are entwined, anything seemed possible,' she says, supporting the agreed history of the tournament as the moment of peak '90s in the UK, when everything great about the era came together in one football tournament, from Gazza to Supergrass to putting ketchup on chips. In reality I know this isn't really how life was, but there is something about Euro 96 that makes me quite happy to bathe in this false history.

Doomed relationships are an overused analogy but I don't think there is a better way of describing what it is like to support England at a major football tournament. The hope that this is going to be the one, the feeling that while you have been stung before this time it will be different and then, of course, the inevitable heartbreak of the end from which you think you will never recover. Then, before you know it, your hope returns for the next one. Like relationships, the international tournaments that hurt and define you the most are the ones from your youth. The '90s was the peak of English football heartbreak: Italia 90, Euro 96 and France 98 – I was spoiled.

Italia 90, with its penalty shoot-out defeat to West Germany in a time before we knew we were bad at penalties, had been an utterly heartbreaking introduction to being an England fan, but at the age of seven that can only have so much impact. I assumed getting to the semi-finals of a World Cup was something that happened all the time and anyway, how disappointed can you be when you didn't even know what a World Cup was a month before it started? That's why Euro 96 was the one that hurt the most. I had by this point become obsessed by football. There had been two years of increasingly rabid build-up across the country and – because it was our first tournament on home soil since winning the World Cup in 1966 and my heroes Baddiel and Skinner had written the official England song 'Three Lions' – England winning the tournament felt part of an inevitable narrative I had constructed in my head.

The nation's hopes had been raised two years earlier when Terry Venables had taken over as England manager after we had failed to qualify for the 1994 World Cup. A charismatic and persistently tanned cockney, Venables was a popular figure, having previously managed Barcelona, Spurs and co-created an ITV detective drama called *Hazell*. He would have all his business meetings in his West End club Scribes and is the kind of character who has a Wikipedia section headed 'business interests' that should really be headed 'controversies'. But that is half the picture. Venables was an empathic man manager and a far more progressive

Continental tactician than we were used to. More importantly, he felt like the perfect manager to get the most out of a generation of brilliant players and, in particular, potentially the greatest England player of them all, Paul Gascoigne.

It is easy to forget this now, but in the months before Euro 96 a lot of England fans thought it was going to be a disaster, with Gascoigne considered by most to be a liability rather than our greatest hope. Gazza had become a strange figure for England at this point, by far the most talented player of his generation but for the last six years, either injured, playing but clearly unfit, or releasing his own version of 'Fog on the Tyne'. None were ideal. Then a pre-tournament trip to Hong Kong for a couple of easy friendlies turned into a tabloid front-page story of a drunken night out featuring Gazza strapped into a dentist's chair drinking tequila. It was, as Gabby Logan's voiceover tried to put kindly in the England v Holland rerun, 'less than ideal pre-tournament build-up'.

Despite all this, in the first game of the tournament England started well, with Alan Shearer scoring his first goal for his country in 12 games – it all felt like it was going to be OK. Then Switzerland equalised with a penalty in the second half. Oh dear. The next day Des Lynam opened coverage of another, less nationally important, match with some headlines from the back pages: 'England held in opening game', 'England disappoint in curtain-raiser', etc. Then, like a magician delighting in revealing his trick, he told us these weren't today's headlines but the headlines after the first game of the 1966 World Cup, which England also drew before going on to win the tournament. The desperate football fan's last hope: omens.

In the week that followed, the press increased their attacks on England and in particular Gascoigne, who had done very little against Switzerland and was now public enemy number 1 (if you exclude that bloke who framed Deirdre Rachid for credit card fraud in *Coronation Street*). The following Saturday, England simply had to win in their second group game against Scotland.

In the first half England were bad and lucky to keep the score to 0-0. Then at half-time Venables brought on my favourite England player, Jamie Redknapp – a man who was 50% elegant midfielder and 50% the second-best-looking member of a boy band – and the game changed; suddenly for the first time in the tournament England were a team. The domination paid off when Gary Neville crossed and Alan Shearer headed us 1-0 ahead. It was clear we were going to go on and win this. And then Tony Adams gave away a penalty, for the second time in two games.

The story of England's Euro 96 can be split into two, pivoting on one moment: Gary McAllister's penalty for Scotland. Had that gone in then in all likelihood England would have drawn (at best), the press would have destroyed them and, well, they would surely never have recovered. As it was, he shot to David Seaman's right and the ball cannoned off the goalkeeper's elbow and out for a corner. In surely the strangest piece of Euro 96 folklore, spoon bender Uri Geller claimed he had been in a helicopter over the stadium at the time and used his mind power to move the ball just before McAllister hit it. On the one hand, if you watch the footage the ball does indeed move just before it is struck. On the other, it is Uri Geller making this claim so it is obviously bollocks.

Either way, 60 seconds later the ball was played up to Gascoigne, who nonchalantly flicked it over Scottish defender Colin Hendry with his first touch and smashed it home with his second. It was a moment of pure impossible skill that no one else in the England squad would have even considered. Gazza celebrated the goal by lying on the ground and replicating the dentist's chair from the night out in Hong Kong, sadly with Lucozade rather than tequila, which would have really added an edge to the final 20 minutes. Either way the whole thing was glorious.

The following Monday, the *Mirror* published an apology:

Over the last two weeks the *Daily Mirror* may have created the impression that England soccer star Paul Gascoigne is a fat, drunken, loutish imbecile who should have been kicked out of the team before the start of Euro 96.

It has now come to our attention that he is in fact a football wizard capable of winning the tournament single-handedly.

We would like to apologise therefore to Mr Gascoigne for any distress our earlier reports may have caused him and send the following message from everyone at the *Daily Mirror*:

Go get 'em Gazza, you little Geordie genius!

I think we can all agree that is absolutely pathetic stuff from the *Mirror* but it kind of summed up the mood of the nation.

From the moment Gazza scored that goal it was the Euro 96 people remember. In the next game I witnessed perhaps the greatest performance by an England team of my lifetime, destroying Holland 4-1 at Wembley, and in the following game against Spain in the quarter-finals we were terrible but still got through on penalties, so who cares? This left us with a semi-final against Germany, who we were bound to beat, right?

In the 1990s big football matches were the biggest television moments. These days for big World Cup games people gather in pubs or fan parks to soak each other with official tournament lager if England score a goal, but at the end of the 20th century people were still watching at home. We knew this because every big game led to the same news story: the National Grid worrying about the electricity surge from everyone putting the kettle on at half-time.

If England[62] got to the semi-finals of major football tournaments, the choice wasn't home or pub, it was BBC or ITV.

---

[62] Or Scotland, Wales or Northern Ireland.

Anyone in their right mind picked the BBC.[63] BBC1 was the national channel, it didn't have adverts and, most importantly, it had Des Lynam. For the semi-final of Euro 96 one of the BBC's pundits was Jimmy Hill wearing a St George's Cross bow tie, but we still didn't consider watching ITV – that's how much better we wanted to watch the match with Des. And we were right to do so, because after four days of tense build-up, here was the biggest match on British soil in 30 years and Des began the broadcast by simply raising an eyebrow and saying: 'You've obviously heard there's a football match on tonight.' I want to hear no more about Noel Gallagher or Damon Albarn – Des Lynam was the coolest man of the '90s.

An hour later when the game finally began, the impossible happened. It took just four minutes for Alan Shearer to head England 1-0 up from a corner. If I could stop my life as a football fan at one moment it would be that. To be honest, you probably don't need the phrase 'as a football

---

[63] Beyond sport I never understood channel loyalty; surely you should just choose what you want to watch and not care about which channel is showing it? I had one set of friends at primary school whose family would spend their evenings simply watching whatever was on ITV, starting with *Emmerdale*, ending with the *News at Ten* and taking in everything in between, be it *Coronation Street*, *The Cook Report* or *At Home with the Braithwaites*. Such was their loyalty to ITV they retuned the channels on their TV so that ITV was number one and BBC1 was number three. They didn't even need to go to the effort of changing channel any more. Turn TV on, watch ITV, turn it off, go to bed. Absolute madness.

fan' in that last sentence. The biggest game of my life, the chance for England to win the European Championship in England, and now I knew it was going to happen. We were going to win Euro 96.

Then, after 18 minutes Stefan Kuntz equalised. Into extra time and, look, you presumably know we didn't win. I don't blame Gareth Southgate for missing the penalty; we were never going to win on penalties against Germany. What I can't get over is extra time: Gascoigne sliding in a centimetre away from connecting with the ball, an open goal beckoning, and Darren Anderton hitting the post from six yards out. WE WERE SO CLOSE TO WINNING, IT'S JUST NOT FAIR. (Obviously, in saying that I overlook the fact that Spain hit the woodwork twice and had a goal wrongly disallowed when we beat them in the quarter-finals, but that is a completely different matter.)

Professionally, I should rewatch this as I write about it, but I genuinely can't face it. Unbelievably, it was one of the games the BBC reran in full in 2020. Who is putting themselves through that? I don't need to see it again. I already know that if Gazza had just got to that ball in extra time we would have won that semi-final and then we would have gone on to win the final. It was the same in 1990; we would have won the final there too (England always win hypothetical finals).

People think that the defining moment of English football was winning the World Cup in 1966. They couldn't be more wrong. Euro 96 was the defining summer of the England football team. The 1966 World Cup was an anomaly, one victory in over a century of defeat. I don't care about 1966; in fact, if anything, I find it quite annoying to hear that England won the World Cup and I wasn't around to see it. It's like being shown photos of a party you couldn't go to. Don't talk to me about 1966, supporting England is all about painful but occasionally glorious defeat and nothing says that more than Euro 96.

I read a re-evaluation of Euro 96 recently that argued that we shouldn't celebrate the tournament in the way we do as the quality of the football was often quite low and England fluked their way through against Scotland and Spain. This showed a complete misunderstanding of why people my age loved the tournament. I don't love Euro 96 because of the standard of football or because England got the most out of their wing-backs, I love it because I was a 13-year-old England fan and for a summer I thought I was about to watch us win the European Championship in our own country. As a football fan I can think of nothing as exciting as that. Who cares if we deserved it or if the football was good? Loving something isn't about its definable quality, or reasoning it out; sometimes it can just be about the point it intercepted your life. In the same way you can love an album from your youth even though you know in your heart, when it comes to it, it is shit.[64]

The other stick occasionally used to beat Euro 96 is its associations with Cool Britannia. In the years that have

---

[64] Finley Quaye – *Maverick a Strike*

followed Euro 96, it has taken on mythic qualities as a symbol of the second half of the '90s in Britain, the Gabby Logan-approved myth of the long hot summer of 1996 when football came home and sport, culture and politics combined to change the country and give it a new confidence. A time when Liam Gallagher appeared under a Union Jack bedspread on the cover of *Rolling Stone*, Tony Blair did head-ups with Kevin Keegan and Mark Morrison released 'Return of the Mack'. While at the time this felt exciting, to some it now seems a time of hollow over-confidence – Britpop didn't take over the world, New Labour didn't put us on course for decades of prosperity and Mark Morrison was arrested for being in possession of a stun gun. But I am not sure this is the fault of Euro 96: so let's not damn a football tournament with the problems of New Labour's foreign policy or the first Cast album's inability to stand the test of time.

In my heart I know that Euro 96 is as much about the myth as the facts. The myth that we strode past every team put in front of us and were unlucky not to win the tournament, when in actual fact we only played well twice. The myth that it summed up a time when a new British confidence produced great music and a change in the political landscape, when in fact Britpop was already more than a year beyond all its best albums and Labour were still a year from coming into power. The myth that David Baddiel could sing.

Perhaps the biggest myth though was what that summer of 1996 was really like. In our minds it was the long hot summer of endless happiness and glory when football came home; in reality that period of excitement and joy wasn't even a fortnight. Euro 96 was a three-week tournament and England were eliminated after two and a half weeks. The days after that weren't a glorious summer – they were torture as we awaited Germany lifting the trophy. Then work back through England's fixtures: on the first day of the tournament we drew with Switzerland and didn't play again for another week, that week after the draw with Switzerland (the easiest game in the group on paper!) wasn't part of a glorious festival of football, it was a week of thinking: 'Oh God, here we go again, this is going to be a let-down like all the other times.' The following Saturday England beat Scotland and then it all got exciting. That was when the summer we remember started – St George's flags on cars, 'Three Lions' booming from windows, etc. Eleven days later, we lost to Germany and we were out. In reality the long hot summer of football coming home lasted 11 days. And halfway through that we should have lost to Spain.

There is an episode of *The Simpsons* in which the residents of Springfield are due to celebrate the town's bicentennial with Jebediah Springfield Day, named in honour of their town founder. However, Lisa does some digging into Jebediah's past and finds he is not the person people think. Rather than being the benevolent and loyal hero recorded in local history, he was a murderous pirate who hated the people of Springfield. Feeling the people of the town need to know this, Lisa decides to announce the news to them as they celebrate. However, as she is about to speak she has a realisation: the myth of Jebediah Springfield and the joy it brings is worth far more to the town than knowing the truth. That's how I feel about Euro 96. In reality the football may have been bad, England may have got lucky and it may have been fun for less than a fortnight, but I don't want to know about that. I much prefer to wallow in the myth of Euro 96 to the cold hard facts.

My life as an England fan since Euro 96 has always been seen through the prism of that tournament, every Euros and World Cup failing to live up to that summer. Then, in 2021 it happened again, in the rescheduled European Championship, England went one better than I had ever seen before and made it to the final at Wembley. It was glorious. Having stumbled through a group that again contained Scotland, in the second round we beat Germany, of all people. Then, after beating Ukraine 4-0, in the semi-final with the score at 1-1 with Denmark we got a penalty. It was too much for me – I had seen this car crash one too many times. Before Harry Kane took the penalty I just left the room, put my headphones in so I couldn't hear what happened and, bizarrely, listened to 'Three Lions'. I couldn't take it and somehow my safe place was listening to a song that I associated with defeat in the '90s.

It turned out I couldn't live through Euro 2020 without seeing it as a tribute act to those '90s tournaments. Throughout the month as the excitement grew my friends and I weren't discussing that this was the best tournament ever, we were comparing it to previous years. 'This is what it was like during Euro 96,' or 'This is what being a fan during Italia 90 must have been like if you were old enough to go to the pub.' In the final against Italy, after two minutes Luke Shaw put us 1-0 up with a perfect left-foot finish. Like 30 years previously, if I could stop my adult life as a football fan at one moment it would be that. The biggest game of my life, the chance for England to win the Euros and now I knew we were going to do it.[65]

You are meant to learn lessons as you grow up, turn into a more mature character who is able to cope with pain, having suffered before. I fear I learned nothing from those England defeats. The other day I found myself pondering on if it was actually a good thing England didn't win those tournaments in the '90s, that I didn't top out too early – this way I still have the experience of England winning a World Cup to come. I'm an idiot.

---

[65] We didn't.

'I, for one, welcome our insect overlords'
The Simpsons
BBC1, 5:30pm, 23 November 1996

It is the late '80s and cartoonist Matt Groening is waiting to go into the office of Hollywood producer James L. Brooks to discuss turning his 'Life in Hell' comic strip into a series of sketches for Fox's new *Tracey Ullman Show*. Worried about losing the rights to his characters to a television company, Groening decides to pitch something else entirely and quickly draws a family of characters named after his father Homer, mother Marge and sister Lisa (plus a son named from an anagram of 'brat'). Not to be too simplistic about things but three decades later – according to a quick Google search – Matt Groening now has a fortune of $600 million. Often it only takes one good idea: this was Groening's Reggae Reggae Sauce.

When I first heard about *The Simpsons* at the start of the decade, it seemed to me just to be a cartoon about a badly behaved boy, a Dennis the Menace for the Super Soaker generation. Despite having no way of watching the show to confirm it, this didn't stop me being strangely enthralled by it. As a small boy with spiky blond hair I saw myself in Bart, in the same way I also identified with the Milky Bar Kid, presumably believing that all blond children had a natural affinity, like Beetle drivers. To show my loyalty for the next two years I lived in an oversized Bart Simpson T-shirt I had received as a hand-me-down from my older brother Henry, which sported the slogan 'I Didn't Do It, Nobody Saw Me Do It, You Can't Prove Anything'.[66] Considering what a well-behaved dweeb I was, this slogan could have easily stopped after the first sentence. But it wasn't just the t-shirt, I also briefly collected *The Simpsons* bubblegum cards, after coming into a job lot when my friend's mum got hold of a box and sold them at a primary school fund-raising barn dance. The fact my life at this point involved primary school fundraising barn dances perhaps illustrated why *The Simpsons*' American marketing machine felt so exciting to me.

After this period of strange loyalty to a show I had never seen, I forgot about *The Simpsons* for a few years, filing it next to the *Teenage Mutant Hero Turtles* and *Ghostbusters* in my catalogue of childish cartoons I was now too grown-up

---

[66] This was by far the best item in a childhood of disappointing hand-me-downs from my older brother. The low points featuring a shell suit years after they had gone out of fashion, those stonewashed jeans with an elastic waistband and numerous pants, an item that I am sure we can all agree should never be handed down. (Also, thanks for the Air Jordan T-shirt if you're reading, Henry.)

for. Then when I was 13 the show arrived on BBC2 and it turned out it wasn't a silly animation for American kids but in fact the greatest sitcom of all time. It had the best characters, the best jokes and, despite being a cartoon about yellow people with four fingers on each hand, had a sharper satirical edge, stronger moral compass and more heart than any other comedy on TV. In fact it turned out that the worst thing about it was Bart Simpson. There, I've said it, what we've all been thinking for years.

I instantly became the kind of *Simpsons* fan that wouldn't just watch the show but would bring up the episodes at every opportunity, for example, levering them into a chapter about Euro 96 when writing a book. You want to talk to me about doomed romance? I'll talk to you about Ralph Wiggum telling Lisa 'I choo choo choose you'. You want to understand the majesty of parenthood? I'll point you towards 'And Maggie Makes Three'. You want to know about the fickle nature of celebrity? I'll tell you to watch Milhouse being cast in the *Radioactive Man* movie. To be honest, I'm not really someone to come to if you have a problem in your personal life.

What elevated *The Simpsons* above every other scripted comedy was the huge ensemble cast of characters that populated the town of Springfield, a town presented to us as run by self-interest, in thrall to vapid culture and hilariously corrupt at every level. From arch-capitalist Montgomery Burns ('Family, religion, friendship. These are the three demons you must slay if you wish to succeed in business'), to self-interested vicar Reverend Lovejoy ('Once something has been approved by the government, it's no longer immoral') to Kent Brockman, the vain newsreader who, when thinking that a spacecraft has been taken over by giant ants, uses his news report to try to save himself: 'I, for one, welcome our new insect overlords. I'd like to remind them as a trusted TV personality, I can be helpful in rounding up others to toil in their underground sugar caves.' If *The Simpsons* taught us anything it is that people in positions of authority were not to be trusted, be they religious, political or – say it ain't so – TV personalities.

Perhaps the reason I loved *The Simpsons* is that it represented America as I perceived it. I have it on good authority that in the '80s, America was the place that young Brits wanted to be: the home of MTV, Coca-Cola and an alien called ALF, a land where fizzy drinks were served by the ounce and men with big hair played soft rock guitar solos in stadiums, this apparently being a good thing. Maybe for some the '90s was a time when this Americanisation continued its takeover of the UK, be it through the multiplying branches of McDonald's on the high street or half-time cheerleaders on the pitch at Plymouth Argyle (a disastrous and mercifully short-lived experiment). However, this isn't how it felt to me and by the time I was a teenager I saw America not as the land of freedom and infinite music videos but as a bigger, crasser place that we in Blighty were a bit above (I'm not just saying this because they slagged off Mr Blobby).

Top of their list of crimes was the USA 94 World Cup, which began with Diana Ross missing a penalty in the opening ceremony and was soundtracked by stories about the Americans wanting to make the goals bigger so teams scored more. Not for me – I preferred my football low-scoring and without Motown legends, thank you very much. (Also, England didn't qualify for USA 94, but that was definitely nothing to do with my dislike of the tournament.) In all likelihood I developed my distrust of the USA from my immediate environment. In the Widdicombe household American culture was talked about with deep cynicism, my parents fearing if we didn't stand firm we would all be forced to live on Pepsi and Happy Meals, and Gin worrying that we were starting to pronounce the word 'schedule' the wrong way. We didn't want to be American; after all, the USA was a country whose greatest source of entertainment was televising the OJ Simpson trial.

I only really knew OJ Simpson as the bloke from the *Naked Gun* films; I hadn't realised he was a famous American footballer. Then suddenly he wasn't famous for either of those things. He was famous for going on the run after being accused of the murder of his ex-wife Nicole Brown and her friend Ron Goldman. What followed was a low-speed car chase in which Simpson was driven in a white Ford Bronco[67] down an LA freeway, with people gathering on bridges to cheer him on.

The chase, like the following trial and everything surrounding it, was shown live on television in America.

---

[67] A car I have only ever heard mentioned in the context of the Simpson chase, maybe because it clearly couldn't go above 40mph.

It turned it from a murder investigation into, if we are honest, a reality TV series and one of the culturally defining events of the decade. To us in the UK the fact the trial was televised felt like a mad zenith of American culture – after all, we had only allowed television cameras into the Houses of Parliament in 1989. Of course this comparison conveniently ignored the fact that BBC2 had bought the rights to the Simpson trial and were showing edited high-lights each Sunday night, like *Match of the Day 2* but for a horrific tragedy. Maybe the fact the BBC show included clips of how America was covering this circus allowed us to tell ourselves that we weren't watching the trial as viewers, we were observing this as a strange cultural phenomenon. Telling ourselves it was despicable that they felt the need to televise this kind of thing but if it was on we might as well watch it: it's good to be across the news.

The televising of the OJ Simpson trial felt like the America that *The Simpsons* satirised. In the show the television was central to the Simpsons' lives – the children watching *Itchy & Scratchy* cartoons entranced, Grandpa Simpson agreeing to vote for Sideshow Bob after he says he will name an expressway after his favourite TV show, *Matlock*. The show depicted television as facile, without morals and totally led by profit, often enjoying the contradiction of doing this from a prime-time slot on Fox. Troy McClure even ended the show's 138th Episode Spectacular by saying, 'Who knows what adventures the family will get up to between now and when they become unprofitable?'

The irony is that while this was America as I perceived it, the American TV shows I watched were almost uniformly brilliant. The '90s was the decade in which American sitcoms became a huge part of UK television. The decade began with *Roseanne* – which centred on a working-class family from Illinois and struggled to chime with me as a seven-year-old from Devon – and ended with *Frasier*, a show whose genius was to hide being a traditional, silly farce under the idea that it was highbrow because it mentioned sherry and opera (consequently getting a huge audience of both people who love the theatre and people with a sense of humour). Then there was *Friends*, a show so big that it has come to transcend the '90s and simply become part of our continuing popular culture, still more popular on Netflix than modern shows in which characters live in realistically-sized apartments.

Better than all of these though was *The Simpsons*. I have just picked a book off my shelf that I have had since I was a teenager called *The Simpsons: A Complete Guide to Our Favourite Family*. It contains a precis of every episode of the first eight series of the show and the spine has been destroyed by constant re-reading over the years. Despite pages falling out of the book as I flick through it, seeing all those episodes together in one place I have no doubt that throughout the '90s *The Simpsons* gave us over 100 of the most perfect episodes of television ever made.

One of the main reasons that these American sitcoms were so good was simple economics. They weren't written by two people sitting in a room like in the UK but they had teams of the best Hollywood writers who could keep the quality up over 25 episodes a year. If in the Widdicombe household we associated America with a fast-food culture and a lack of class in other areas, you could never say this about their television comedy – it had become their highest-quality export. *The Simpsons* gave us television that could only be created in America and then joined us in mocking the country which produced it. Although it still didn't make up for the USA World Cup.

'Girl Power!'
This Is 5!
Channel 5, 6pm, 30 March 1997

Promising great shows, free toons, sports, movies, and all the TV you've ever wanted, the lyrics for the Spice Girls' reworking of Manfred Mann's '5-4-3-2-1' for the launch night of Channel 5 could be argued to have set sights a little high for what was to follow in the next few years on the station. It would take a brave advocate of the channel to say it provided all the TV we had ever wanted, particularly as you couldn't even get the signal on Dartmoor.

Obviously I was livid about this. Until this point I hadn't really felt like I was missing out by growing up in Devon. I was quite happy to watch Euro 96 on television and follow the ups and downs of Britpop through *The O-Zone*, but not being able to watch a new fifth TV channel? A step too far. In the build-up to launch night, I had heard talk that Channel 5 were sending people door to door in areas that could receive it to retune people's video recorders.[68] I waited but we never received the knock. Worst of all, my brothers and sisters in Cornwall had perfect reception; how did that work? Surely Cornwall was further away from civilisation. What kind of signal covers London and Cornwall but not the space in between? What a life.

And so it was that watching the opening night of Channel 5 on my computer in 2021 wasn't an exercise in nostalgia but in finally finding out what I had missed. As it happens, not a huge amount.

While the Spice Girls offered unrivalled charisma and pop hits, the rest of the evening involved a documentary about John Major's and Tony Blair's childhoods and a drama about the abduction of Stephanie Slater, neither hugely my scene. From what people said at the time this was as good as it got, my main memory of Channel 5 in the months that followed was that its primary selling point was newsreader Kirsty Young reading the headlines while perching on the edge of her desk, like she wasn't a newsreader at all but just some cool cat who had wandered into the studio to chew the fat about the Good Friday Agreement. This may not sound hugely exciting but you have to remember on Dartmoor we still had to suffer the indignity of receiving our news from Peter Sissons sitting on a chair.

It is a sign of the channel's lack of initial success that the most famous show of its early years was Keith Chegwin's

---

[68] A mission that channel head Greg Dyke described as 'a burglar's paradise'.

Naked Jungle, a one-off programme screened to commem-orate the fiftieth anniversary of naturism in the UK in which Keith and a team of contestants took on a jungle-themed assault course – you're ahead of me here – in the nude. Perhaps the most extraordinary thing about the show – apart from the obvious fact that Cheggers had his dick out – was that it was made by the same people who made the CITV game show *Jungle Run*, which followed almost exactly the same format and, worst of all, was filmed on the same set. I can only imagine how much disinfectant they'd have needed to clean it up afterwards.

The show ended up with 2 million viewers, Channel 5's biggest audience to date, and while there was talk of people being shocked, it transpired Channel 5 only received 50 phone calls about the show and they were split between complaints and praise, with one woman saying it was so funny that it cured her postnatal depression. In fact, the ITC only ever received one direct complaint about it and that was from someone who just didn't like Keith Chegwin. Which seems a little unfair.

The show's notoriety meant that it was one of the few game shows ever to be released on VHS, receiving a 15 certificate. On the cover is a quote from Chegwin saying 'It's a great crack!', which is a perfectly good cheeky joke about his bum, but works less well in a show when you can also see his cock and balls. Most worryingly, the VHS also boasts that it 'Contains Previously Unseen Footage', which I can only assume must be some kind of internal examination of Cheggers.

The fact the Spice Girls agreed to be the star attraction of Channel 5's launch now seems incongruous, like finding out that Madonna was the first person to ride in a Sinclair C5. The Spice Girls' fame in 1997 was such that it actually feels less bizarre to revisit their photocall with Nelson Mandela that autumn rather than the Easter Sunday when they sang about how we could finally get our toons for free.

While it was impossible for me to get Channel 5, the Spice Girls were unavoidable. In the summer of 1996 their first single 'Wannabe' had gone straight in at Number 1 and it felt instantly that the five Spice Girls and their individually assigned two-dimensional personalities were the most famous people in the world. 'Wannabe' went to Number 1 in 37 countries, their next five singles also went to Number 1, debut album *Spice* sold 19 million copies worldwide, becoming the biggest-selling album of 1997, and 500,000 people saw them turn on the Christmas lights on Oxford Street, which you are right to think sounds like a completely made-up statistic, but what am I going to do, start questioning the accuracy of Wikipedia? I don't think so.[69]

The main question in 1997 was what kind of wanker didn't like the Spice Girls? The answer, of course, was me. While I had been the perfect age for the beginning of

---

[69] I am aware you shouldn't judge a band's impact by numbers. It is a fool's errand that never tells the full story and somehow always ends up with the revelation that the biggest band to ever walk the earth was in fact Westlife.

Britpop, I was now exactly the wrong age for the launch of a brilliant all-female pop band, considering myself too clever (cynical) and grown-up (teenage) to do anything other than hate them (except in the obvious secret way teenage boys were fans of them, but let's leave that here and move on). Three years after buying *Parklife*, I was now one of those tiresome 14-year-old boys who thought that people who didn't know how to play the guitar shouldn't legally be allowed a recording contract. It felt obvious to me that bands like Gomez and The Verve, who wrote their own songs and didn't waste their time on things like smiling or enjoying their success, were by definition superior to a pop band like the Spice Girls and history would eventually back me up. This has not proven to be the case.

Nearly a quarter of a century later I am willing to admit I was wrong. While others regret shoplifting or that house party that ended with the police being called, the sad truth is one of my few teenage regrets is living through the glory period of the greatest pop band of all time with a surliness that didn't allow me to admit to myself that 'Say You'll Be There' was a banger. As you get older you are meant to grow out of pop music but I seem to have gone the other way – the pop music I dismissed in the '90s I can now finally appreciate. I look forward to my forties when I can fully explore the back catalogue of Scatman John. (It won't be a huge job.)

The truth is of all of the cultural highs of the '90s, the one I refused to be a part of is perhaps the one that has best stood the test of time. Rewatching the Spice Girls' first performance of 'Wannabe' on *Top of the Pops*, you remember just how different and exciting they felt when they arrived in the mid-'90s. They have a giddiness and energy to which no other group came close. Other pop bands of the time would dance and emote in sync, but the Spices bounce and run around the stage like they're on an impromptu night out, not making a career-defining TV appearance. Like all the greatest bands they feel like a gang: it is no coincidence that their first single, 'Wannabe', is based on the idea of friends coming first (at the time I also operated the policy of friends before lovers, but this was mainly due to my lack of options in the second column).

The Spice Girls had been put together by audition but they didn't feel like that. While American pop bands graduated through the Disney Club, there was something endearingly amateur about the Spices, a band who had spent the two years before global fame practising their dance moves in a house share in Maidenhead. They felt like they were people who would never be told what to say, that at any moment Geri could blurt out something that would end their career. Let's not forget the first time she met Prince Charles; she pinched his arse. We can only be relieved she didn't meet the Queen Mum.

Before the Spice Girls, pop music seemed to be just a string of tedious boy bands. Beyond Robbie, Take That weren't exciting personalities; Jason Orange was never going to goose the heir to the throne. The only boy band who brought any level of excitement were East 17, who at least had the edge of being four quite hard lads from Walthamstow. Sadly they proved to have a little too much edge when singer Brian Harvey killed their career dead by saying he had taken 12 ecstasy tablets in one night and then driven.[70]

The Spice Girls weren't just fun but they had a core message: Girl Power! To the more cynical bores among the population (for instance, me as a 14-year-old), this may have seemed a little reductive, but really it was a positive message about female empowerment and friendship, which can only be a good thing, right? Before this there was a huge lack of female performers in the charts – it felt like Annie Lennox had won Best Female at The Brits 15 years on the bounce – but here were the Spice Girls bringing an essentially feminist message to a young audience. They celebrated female empowerment and they celebrated individuality – if you believed in yourself you could be anything you wanted, from scary to sporty.

The Spice Girls dominated every area of life: one day they were being interviewed in *The Spectator* about how Margaret Thatcher was a pioneer of the ideology

---

[70] This wouldn't be the end of Harvey's driving controversies. He later ran himself over when leaning out of a car door to throw up, having eaten too many baked potatoes. The DVLA really should have reviewed his licence by this point.

of Girl Power,[71] the next day they were recording the almost instantly forgotten official song of the England team at France 98, '(How Does it Feel to Be) On Top of the World'. A song that contained the clumsiest use of brackets in the history of pop and was recorded by the strangest supergroup of all time: England United featuring the Spice Girls, Echo and the Bunnymen, Space and Ocean Colour Scene.

But recording a bad football song wasn't a problem, because the Spice Girls had the personality to carry them through any situation. Even the footage of them meeting Nelson Mandela still feels completely natural. What stands out is that the five Spice Girls are completely fearless. At one point Mandela mentions his old age and Geri replies, 'You're only as young as the woman you feel and I'm 25!' Then, when the journalists ask Mandela what he thinks of the Spice Girls, before he can answer Mel B turns to him and says, 'Watch it, you're stood next to me!' like he is a best man about to embarrass her with a story of a drunken night out rather than one of the great political figures of the 20th century. She needn't have worried. 'You know, these are my heroes,' Mandela says. 'I don't want to be emotional, but it's

---

[71] I have just read it and it's a great interview. They also discuss their worries about the slide towards the single currency, Geri compliments Tony Blair's hair but worries he isn't a safe pair of hands on the economy and Victoria says John Major is a 'boring pillock' but that she would never vote Labour.

one of the greatest moments in my life.' I'm sure it must be a joke, but he doesn't deliver it as a one.

Beyond all of this though, what mattered most is that the Spice Girls had great songs. There is a *South Bank Show* episode about Blur from 1999 which ends with Alex James discussing why the band maintained their success through constant reinventions. 'Basically it all comes down to good songs,' he says. 'It doesn't matter how you present good songs, you don't care what a pretty girl is wearing do you?' While it is a very un-Girl Power way of putting it, he's right. You can dress up songs how you like but in the end the right personality and right attitude is worth nothing without the tunes – when that happens you aren't the Spice Girls, you are Menswe@r. The Spice Girls had the attitude, the message and the personality, but really what they had were the best songs. If there's a better Spotify Top 5 than 'Wannabe', 'Stop', '2 Become 1', 'Say You'll Be There' and 'Spice Up Your Life' then I haven't heard it.

Perhaps what is most impressive about the Spice Girls, however, is just how brief it all was; how much they fitted in. Their fame and cultural domination had been so all-encompassing that in my head they had been at the top for years. In fact in May 1998 when Geri announced through her solicitor that she had left the band, it was less than two years since their first single. At the time, being a teenage idiot, I was delighted. Now, I'm gutted that we didn't get another couple of years of perfect hits and suggestible exchanges with respected world leaders.

The four remaining members carried on without Geri but it wasn't the same; it wasn't that original gang. So in 2000 they also went their own separate ways following that inevitably disappointing phase of all '90s pop bands – the move towards a more grown-up R&B sound. Of course by this point Keith Chegwin was on TV running around an assault course in the nip, so the nation had bigger problems.

'A new dawn has broken, has it not?'
Election 97[72]
BBC1, 9:55pm, 1 May 1997

It is still unbelievably exciting to watch it all unfold again in real time. Michael Portillo – then a poster boy of uncaring Thatcherism rather than a charming railway enthusiast with a collection of colourful jackets – losing his seat to a man called Twigg at three in the morning. John Prescott and Robin Cook bobbing their heads self-consciously to 'Things Can Only Get Better' at the Labour victory party. Tony Blair telling the cheering crowd, 'A new dawn has broken, has it not?', the three words at the end of the sentence a slightly worrying caveat.

---

[72] NOTE TO READER: For readers who voted for the Conservatives, Liberal Democrats or James Goldsmith's Referendum Party, I would like to apologise for the pro-Labour sentiment of this chapter. I know for many of you the 1997 General Election wasn't a great moment of your decade. I totally understand your point of view (actually, I don't understand voting for two of these) and can only apologise in advance for what you are about to read, or skip over.

Beyond that it's just fun to witness the sheer amount of filler in a broadcast that the Widdicombe family had waited 18 years to witness. David Dimbleby crosses to war correspondent John Simpson – for one night only in Sedgefield rather than Sarajevo – minutes after the polls close. He has nothing to report. Behind him people count votes on trestle tables arranged on a floor marked out for various indoor sports. One of the great things about British election nights is the juxtaposition of these huge moments in history happening in municipal facilities and repurposed sports halls, seeing cabinet ministers put out of work in a space usually reserved for retirees to play badminton doubles.

My parents didn't let themselves believe Labour would actually win, even when all the evidence told them it was inevitable. The reason for this was 1992, a pain they felt like I felt Euro 96. Labour led solidly in the polls just over a week before election day but – be it due to the *Sun*'s front page showing Neil Kinnock photoshopped as a light bulb or a reason that gives the British electorate more credit – the Tories came home with a majority of 21. The feeling in my house was that Britain was going to have a Conservative government for the rest of time. In fact, with grim circularity, that is also the feeling in my house as I write this.

Far more than any other opinion, I took my politics from my parents. My other tastes as I grew up – music, clothes, marbles – were defined against those old squares, but for some reason I trusted my mum and dad were correct on how to run a country of 60 million people. I accepted my dad knew what he was talking about on income tax and law and order, as strongly as I rejected his views on Captain Beefheart and the comfort of wearing Birkenstocks.

As a 14-year-old I didn't really understand politics but my parents had distilled it for me in simplistic terms: Labour want to help the poor and the Conservatives want to help the rich. Twenty years later, I now know there is a little more nuance to things (OR IS THERE?!) but for me at the time it was as simple as goodies and baddies. Labour were Blur, Kevin McCallister and the Hurricanes. The Tories were Manchester United, Boyzone and the guy at the FBI who tried to stop Mulder finding out about UFOs (which I bet they also knew about, bloody Tories).

I assumed everyone disliked the Tories, which was odd because they kept winning. Had the election purely taken place in my house, however, it would have been a Labour landslide. There was no one my parents had hated more than Margaret Thatcher (with the possible exception for my dad of Mike Scott at pigeon club), while Gin – as you would expect from an old luvvie who could get angry at someone as inoffensive as Angela Rippon[73] – also had no time for the milk snatcher. She would tell the story of one election in the '80s when rather than putting up a Vote Labour poster outside her house she had made her own sign that simply said 'A vote for Thatcher is a vote against

---

[73] 'Her face is too wide, darling.'

humanity'. While I don't dispute her point, I fear the sign's main message to passers-by actually proved to be 'local mad woman lives here'.

It is now traditional to remember New Labour as the defining political party of the '90s, in the same way Oasis were the defining band or Pipes was the defining paedophile ghost. However, growing up it didn't feel like this; after all, for most of the decade Labour weren't even in charge. My first exposure to British politics in the '90s was as much about the implosion of a party that at one time felt invincible as the rise of a shiny new party based around a suspiciously charming and charismatic leader.

In their final years the Tories had become little more than a long-running joke, a bunch of bungling idiots who had no idea how to get through a week without another disaster. It was like a country was being run by a team from *The Apprentice* but without amusing cutaways to Claude making a funny face. In 1993, John Major launched the 'Back to Basics' campaign at the Conservative Party Conference in Blackpool, his big sell to the nation being 'a world that sometimes seems to be changing too fast for comfort' and a return to 'the old values – neighbourliness, decency, courtesy'. Yes, his big idea was slowing down the progress of humanity. Sadly for Major, despite refusing to get an email address, he failed in this aim and all this speech did was provide a perfect backdrop to four years of news stories about the corruption and sexual exploits of his MPs.

It was all there: affairs, illegitimate children and an MP who shared a bed with a male friend on a rugby tour. Then there was Neil and Christine Hamilton – who came a cropper through the cash for questions scandal – and Jonathan Aitken, who sued the *Guardian* and *World In Action* over their investigation into his links with Saudi businessmen and announced his case by proclaiming: 'If it falls to me to start a fight to cut out the cancer of bent and twisted journalism in our country with the simple sword of truth and the trusty shield of British fair play, so be it.' The libel trial collapsed after it transpired that Aitkin had lied under oath and he was imprisoned for 18 months for perjury. Which, of course, was hilarious.

Every week I would follow the fall of the government by sitting down with my parents to watch the fresh young panel show *Have I Got News For You*,[74] in which Ian Hislop would destroy the government for their latest failed attempt to keep within John Major's old school values. It was clear for everyone to see – the Tories were a joke; in fact they

---

[74] In one of the strangest impacts of TV on my childhood brain, I watched so much *Have I Got News for You* as a young child that at one point I began to have nightmares about Mirror Group pension stealer Robert Maxwell. Despite having absolutely no understanding of his crimes, due to his role as a hate figure on *Have I Got News for You* I assumed Maxwell was the scariest man in the world and he occupied a part of my brain that other children reserved for Pennywise or the Demon Headmaster.

became such an easy target of satire that even my own father got in on the act.

A couple of years before the General Election my dad began a new hobby: writing satirical letters to the local newspaper in which he mocked the government by pretending to be an unquestioning old school Tory voter. As the election got nearer, the *Mid-Devon Advertiser*[75] received a string of increasingly absurd letters from Tom Widdicombe backing up the government on unpopular policies such as privatising the water supply and launching the Traffic Cones Hotline, a phone number you could ring if you wanted to know why there were traffic cones on a stretch of road (bafflingly, this was one of John Major's most famous policies). As a teenager these letters were mortifying, but as an adult they are one of my proudest childhood memories.

As the letters went on, constructing the world view of a Tory left behind by the changing social attitudes and almost always ending with the phrase 'I blame The Beatles', they got more surreal, my dad claiming to be the chairman of The Haytor Traffic Group, a pressure group concerned with alleviating traffic congestion on Dartmoor by building a six-lane

---

[75] To give you an idea of the usual fare printed in the *Mid-Devon Advertiser*, at the age of eight I made it into the paper when I won second prize at the village flower show in the category 'animal made from vegetables'. It is with a heavy heart that I must admit that in fact I didn't make this animal alone but the potato and gooseberry beetle was as much my dad's work as my own.

motorway from Drumbridges Roundabout to Widecombe-in-the-Moor. Locals who didn't get the joke would angrily reply on the letters page and even to our actual address, my dad finding it more hilarious the more people he wound up. One morning he went down to get the post only to find a hand-delivered note that simply read:

You and your pathetic sense of humour are the kind of thing that undermines our society.

You may not like our country but a lot of people do.

Do yourself and everyone else a favour and just shut up and go away.

A true patriot

Even at this point it didn't cross his mind to get a key so that we could lock our front door. Instead he focused his time on self-publishing these letters in a book called *I Blame the Beatles*. Reading it now it acts as the perfect time capsule of those last, embarrassing days of the Tory government and one man's dream of a six-lane motorway alleviating congestion outside Moretonhampstead.

While the Tories felt like relics of a bygone era, the Labour Party felt, and it seems strange to write this now, young and exciting. In 1994 they had elected a new leader called Tony Blair, the former lead singer of Ugly Rumours, son-in-law to actor Tony Booth and a man more than any other in this book who must feel like his reputation was much stronger in the '90s (possibly excluding Mr Blobby).

Blair took heed of Marathon's recent success in becoming Snickers and rebranded the party as the more centrist New Labour, something which betrayed everything the party stood for or finally made them palatable to the wider electorate, depending on your viewpoint.

To me as a teenager, Tony Blair felt like no political figure I had seen before. Throughout my life the politicians in charge had been grey middle-aged men (and one woman) who bore no relation to my existence. As meaningless as this may be, the fact that Tony Blair was 44, had been in a band and supported Newcastle United felt like a huge deal. He was the first political leader I felt would have been able to tell me what was Number 1 without looking like he was taking the piss. New Labour felt different from the Tories in every way. They were the party of the cool celebrities, from Noel Gallagher to Ross Kemp to Richard Wilson from *One Foot in the Grave*. They had a card with five election pledges you could keep in your wallet (not that I had a wallet). They even had a pop song as their election anthem, even if it was a pop song by D:Ream.

Labour's popularity with celebrities was hammered home in their party election broadcasts. While the Tories had John Major droning on in a suit and tie, Labour had Pete Postlethwaite playing a ghost cab driver who can transport a voter forward in time to see how his vote will impact the NHS. Yes please. Watching the election broadcasts now, they capture perfectly how different these two potential governments felt. In another Labour broadcast we see Tony Blair going about his day-to-day life shot on a handheld camcorder to show how real he is, from drinking a cup of tea while leaning against the kitchen sideboard to playing football wearing an adidas coat which, shamefully, I also owned.[76] In comparison, the Conservatives fill their four minutes with some men in jackets with the words 'New Labour' written on them attempting to plant a tree that doesn't have any roots on a hill. Weak, weak, weak.

Perhaps the greatest snapshot of that spring though is Labour's 'Do It 1997' election broadcast. It follows a man on his way to vote on Election Day, from picking up his voting slip from his doormat to the polling booth. As he walks through a happy, sunny London, we never see his face, just his impossibly pressed blue shirt and box-fresh cream chinos. All we know is that everywhere he goes, people smile and cheer and, most bizarrely at one point, a man on rollerblades hands him a balloon. As he arrives at the polling booth and drops his vote for Labour in the box, the camera pans up and we finally get to see his face. It is, of course, weatherman John Kettley. No, it's not. It's Tony Blair.

It is an absurd advert that now seems hilarious in its sentiment and presentation of Blair (and, more to the point,

---

[76] Point of reference: this was one of those coats that you initially thought had no hood but then you realised it was actually folded up and zipped into the collar. Were it ever to rain, the hood was so thin it had absolutely no ability to keep you dry.

rollerblading), but it sums up the mood in my house on the evening of that election.[77] I am aware of what followed for the New Labour government: good (peace in Northern Ireland, investment in education, introduction of the minimum wage) and bad (Iraq, Gordon Brown calling that woman a bigot), but on that night in May 1997 it did feel that a new dawn had broken, had it not? We had replaced the tired and corrupt government with a man young enough and with-it enough to still wear an adidas coat.

I suppose the problem with revisiting any hopeful political moment is seeing your own naivety about the world reflected back at you. It is to realise that to an extent you fell for it, because Tony Blair or Barack Obama or Theresa May (delete as appropriate) didn't save the world and make everything better as you believed they would. Rewatching a prime minister deliver their first speech outside Number 10 is like finding an old teenage diary entry about how you are going to become a footballer and marry Nicole Appleton; life never quite goes how you imagine.

It is easy to be cynical about New Labour years later, but that is the issue with winning an election; you are left with the impossible job of running a country. Who knew being in charge of the UK was actually much more complicated than

---

[77] Full disclosure. My dad would now consider Blair's takeover of the Labour Party one of the great political crimes of the last 100 years and would choose Jeremy Corbyn as their greatest leader. Funny how you get more left wing as you get older.

saying the word education three times or doing headers with Kevin Keegan on the campaign trail? The cliché that all political careers end in failure may be too extreme, but they very rarely end walking down the street in pressed chinos taking balloons from rollerbladers.

To so many people reading this now I may seem an idiot, a nostalgist or, at a push, a war criminal, but I can only write genuinely about how excited I felt about politics in 1997. I was 14 and everything felt so hopeful. My older siblings had grown up during the Cold War in the '80s worrying about the world being destroyed by an atomic bomb, my main political worry was whether the new ban on fox hunting was enforceable on a practical level. I just assumed this was what happened – history moved in the right direction and life got better. I'm not sure if this makes it a naive and embarrassing moment in time or one I wish I could turn the clock back to. Can it be both?

'She was the People's Princess'
BBC News
BBC1, 31 August 1997

I was staying at my friend Tom Hyde's house having been up late playing *GoldenEye* on his N64. In my mind we woke up and his mum told us what had happened but I have no idea if that is true. I don't really have many personal recollections about that day; for some reason the most shocking event of the decade is the one in this book I remember in least detail.

Maybe it is because the week has been relived so many times since through documentaries and movies that I struggle to separate what I actually remember from the public record of it, like a childhood holiday you have reconstructed in your mind from photos in a family album. All I can really tell you about the day is that we watched the coverage when we got up and then in the early afternoon turned over to Channel 4, the only channel not covering it, and watched an Inter Milan match on *Football Italia*. It feels slightly insensitive that we did that now but then I don't really know what you were meant to do; pay your respects by watching the news for three more hours?

The footage from the night is still unbelievably shocking, as only confused and hastily assembled rolling news from the time before 24-hour news channels can be. With a jaw-droppingly bleak prescience, on BBC1 the initial report interrupts a funeral scene in the French film *Borsalino*, the mourners fading out to black and being replaced by the BBC1 logo and the simple words 'News Report'. Knowing what we know now, it feels horribly uncomfortable to watch it unfold, Martyn Lewis telling us of reports on French radio that Diana, Princess of Wales has been badly injured and her partner Dodi Fayed and driver Henri Paul have been killed in a car crash in Paris. Lewis ends the newsflash by saying sternly, 'I repeat, these reports are unconfirmed,' and the channel goes back to the movie.

As the night goes on, the channel is given over to rolling news of the accident until the moment at 4:41am when they stop everything to tell us that the Press Association have announced that Diana, Princess of Wales has died. The newsreader – who I don't recognise, of course, he's the one given the overnight Sunday morning cover shift – seems in utter shock, taking a breath as if he can't quite believe the words he is saying. He goes on to fill in the details of the accident, which are now as familiar to us as anything in the decade.

Perhaps the most telling detail isn't the moment they announce that Diana has died but the minutes just before it when the BBC are filling their through-the-night coverage with a discussion of who would pay for the photos of the crash if the paparazzi have got them. It is a perfect symbol of what Diana's life had become, a world where the idea of photos of her in a car crash being printed by a newspaper wasn't something dismissed out of hand but something discussed in a matter-of-fact tone on the BBC.

Princess Diana had been by far the most recognisable person in the world throughout my lifetime. Her life made up of hundreds of iconic images and moments. The bashful first footage of Lady Diana Spencer getting into her Mini Metro when she first became linked to Charles, Charles saying, 'Whatever in love means,' in their engagement interview, *the* Royal wedding, her barrier-breaking visit to an AIDS hospice, sitting alone in front of the Taj Mahal, the tell-all Andrew Morton biography, separation, divorce, telling Martin Bashir, 'There were three of us in this marriage,' the modern mum at a theme park with William and Harry and the landmines walk just months before her death. The soap opera of the Royals didn't mean much to me growing up, but I still probably saw Diana's image most days of my life. Such was her all-pervading fame that when we went to the newsagent near Tom's house on the day of the accident and saw the papers that had been printed before the news came through, she was still on the front of them, a long lens shot of her on Dodi's yacht.

In the week that followed we had a special assembly at school in which a middle-aged biology teacher played acoustic guitar and sang a song, possibly 'Blowin' in the Wind'. It would not come to be the defining musical performance of the week. It all felt other-worldly and sad, but if I am honest with myself, I didn't feel caught up in the collective mourning of the nation as we now remember it. If anything, the grieving crowds outside the palaces pushed me away from being a part of it. I found these people mourning a woman they had never met like she was their own parent so strange and incongruous that I struggled to identify with what was going on. I didn't feel it was the week I had learned how to cry for the first time. I had cried plenty of times, often at far less tragic events than this, it has to be said.

Watching the footage of the mourners in London that week now feels completely surreal. As people stand silently watching him, a policeman tells the reporter: 'People have come from Newcastle or Liverpool. They've got no reason but they felt they had to come down.' I think he means it as a credit to them, although it is open to interpretation. Later, an ITN reporter tells us that outside the three palaces more than a million bouquets have been laid. The shot from above – like all shots from the sky in those days, jiggling around uncontrollably and soundtracked by helicopter rotor blades – shows the gates of Kensington Palace separated from the crowds by a seemingly infinite carpet of flowers. Outside the palace as people stand silently in thought, one man suddenly snaps at the camera crew: 'It's you that killed her, the press that killed her; just here to pick over the bones.' The crowd around him applaud with three parts anger and one part awkwardness. Next to the man a woman wipes away a tear with one hand, her other hand holding a copy of the *Daily Express* with the simple headline 'Diana is Dead'.

The most unnerving footage from outside the palace, and something I never knew had happened, shows Prince Charles taking William and Harry to see the floral tributes on the day before the funeral. As they get out of their car the crowd applauds them. Someone calls William over to give him a bouquet, others shout, 'William, we love you.' They walk along the front of the crowd, forced to smile as people shake their hands like they are turning up for the premiere of *Notting Hill* rather than attempting to deal with the death of their mother. It feels unreal. Were you to look at the footage not knowing what had happened you would never guess they were the two who had lost their mother, as opposed to the people on the other side of the fence who seem in far more distress. Never have two sets of people grieved more differently than the Royals and the public outside Buckingham Palace in 1997.

I didn't watch the funeral, which considering the things I did watch seems baffling now; turns out I saw every TV show of the '90s except the most-watched event of the decade. I don't know if this was part of some sort of teenage rebellion or just that I felt watching a funeral on television wasn't the way I wanted to spend my Saturday afternoon. Tom Hyde was at my house (it was one of those friendships that burns brightly for about a year and then disappears once you have both got bored of the N64) and while my mum watched the funeral inside, we instead played Frisbee in the garden. If it was teenage rebellion it was a strange kind, considering ourselves too opposed to the norms of society to take part in this big communal moment, but instead spending our time playing the traditional family game of Frisbee. Maybe Tom felt he had missed out. The following week he bought 'Candle in the Wind' on CD single. He claimed this wasn't because he liked the song but because it was a shrewd business decision, one day it would be a collector's item. This reasoning overlooked the fact that for something to be a collector's item it needs to be rare and difficult to find rather than the most-owned CD in the world.

In the weeks that followed, people began to question the mood that had taken hold of Britain. My parents, unsurprisingly, fell into this camp and managed to get hold of that week's issue of *Private Eye*, a magazine that had been withdrawn from a number of shops due to its cover. Under the headline 'Media to Blame', a photo showed the public outside Buckingham Palace with three speech bubbles:

'The papers are a disgrace'
'Yes, I couldn't get one anywhere'
'Borrow mine, it's got a picture of the car'

Inside the magazine ran an article apologising on behalf of the press for having portrayed Diana as: 'A neurotic, irresponsible and manipulative troublemaker' when in fact she was 'the most saintly woman who has ever lived'. They added that they expressed the British press's 'sincere and deepest hypocrisy'. This kind of humour felt hugely dangerous and exciting to me, particularly from a magazine that usually sat by our toilet full of impenetrable articles about the ownership of News International.

In reality, though, it is a week that shouldn't be remembered for our feelings towards *Private Eye* or the mourning crowds outside the palace. It should be remembered as what it was: the tragic death of three people in a car crash, one a mother of two young sons. The footage from that week that remains the most affecting is not the infinite piles of flowers or the first shock announcement of Diana's death but William and Harry – aged 15 and 12 – walking behind their mother's coffin, two boys forced to somehow publicly put on a brave face just six days after their mother had died.

Watching it reminds me of another image from that library of iconic moments in Diana's public life – the clip so often used to present Diana the normal mother, the day she took her boys to a theme park. Such was the closed-off reputation of the Royals before this, the fact they were giggling and joking on a family day out – and not hunting or skiing but at Thorpe Park, where normal people go to queue for rides and get their photo put on a key ring – felt absolutely astonishing in its own way. Diana – in a Hard Rock Cafe bomber jacket – and her two sons laugh uncontrollably as they career down the log flume, getting soaked at the bottom. As they swing past the camera they are lost in the moment and you can just hear Prince Harry say to his mother, 'Can we do it again?' In the back of the cart sits a fourth person, a middle-aged man in a suit, whose training as a bodyguard has led to him sitting on a log flume trying not to be noticed. That was as close as Diana's life got to normality.

'Aha!'
I'm Alan Partridge
BBC2, 10pm, 3 November 1997

My dad was born in 1950 and, in the words only a hippy can get away with, 'caught the '60s just right'. He was 12 when The Beatles released their first single 'Please, Please Me' and was a teenager as they and the Rolling Stones changed British music and society forever. Sixties music defined his tastes and world view for the rest of his life, and more importantly, influenced his decisions on greenhouse horticulture. Being born in the early '80s I had a comparative experience, but while my dad's teenage years ran parallel to the greatest years in British pop history, mine ran parallel to the peak of British television comedy.

When people think of the Cool Britannia boom in British culture in the '90s, they immediately reach for the bands, artists or (two or three) films. However, in reality, throughout the decade none of these areas came close to being as consistently brilliant, original and exciting as British comedy. Let's be clear about this: the best place to be in the '90s wasn't the Groucho Club or Knebworth, it was at home watching BBC2 and Channel 4 on a Friday night. Or at least that is what I had to tell myself, the other two options weren't really on the table.

Television had been transformed in the '80s by the rise of alternative comedy. Beginning in London clubs like The Comedy Store in the late '70s and early '80s, alternative comedy had swiftly moved on to TV with shows like *The Young Ones* and *The Comic Strip Presents* introducing the nation to Jennifer Saunders, Dawn French, Ben Elton, Rik Mayall and Adrian Edmondson. It changed what comedy on television could be. No longer was it Mike Yarwood doing an impression of a trade unionist or Bernard Manning telling racist jokes. Suddenly it was being made by and for young people; comedy that wasn't just right-on (which let's be clear is a good thing, no matter what Jim Davidson may tell you) but quirky, inter-esting and, most importantly, far funnier than anything that had gone before. These were the comedians that my parents and Gin watched and talked about in the house and that I was exposed to from a (worryingly) young age.

At the age of six and seven I would be sitting on the sofa as the TV showed *French and Saunders*, Ben Elton's *The Man From Auntie*, *The Alexei Sayle Show* and, in a sign of ultra-progressive/ultra-lax parenting, *Bottom*. For those too young to remember *Bottom* or with parents who didn't want to traumatise their offspring, it was a sitcom written by and starring Rik Mayall and Adrian Edmondson as Richie Richard and Eddie Hitler, two alcoholic, ultra-violent, sexually frus-trated, down-and-out flatmates. Episodes would involve acts of cartoon violence with frying pans and staple guns and plots would see Richie and Eddie sellotaping a burglar to the ceiling, or being stuck at the top of a Ferris wheel that was due to be blown up the next day. If watching this while still in primary school didn't make me decide that comedy was the most exciting thing in the world, nothing would.[78]

While alternative comedy in the '80s had started on the outside, by the '90s the leading names were the biggest stars in the country. Ben Elton was a bestselling novelist, *Bottom: Live* was touring to huge theatres and Dawn French and Jennifer Saunders were separately starring in *The Vicar of Dibley* and *Absolutely Fabulous*, two of the greatest British sitcoms of all time. However, only a total square would exclusively watch the comedy their parents had introduced them to so it was lucky for me the '90s saw a second wave of alternative comedy, performers and writers who had been raised on *The Young Ones* and *Blackadder* and were now getting their own chance on television. If French and Saunders were my parents' comics, these were mine. (Although my parents did also watch all this comedy too. It was hard to rebel in my house.)

One of the best things about the comedy of the '90s was just how endless it felt. This chapter could have been about

---

[78] In my parents' defence, I am pretty sure I wasn't the only child watching this stuff. There is footage on YouTube of Ade Edmondson promoting *Bottom*'s carnival of violence to a generation of children on *Going Live!* while his daughter Beattie sits on his lap and makes faces at the camera. No wonder we all turned out to have such exquisite taste.

one of at least 30 shows that I loved and can still recite jokes from 25 years later. Such was the breadth of amazing comedy I was watching growing up that in any week I could find myself in front of brand new episodes of three or four of the following brilliant shows: *Father Ted, The Mrs Merton Show, The League of Gentlemen, I'm Alan Partridge, Harry Enfield and Chums, Fist of Fun, The Friday Night Armistice, Marion and Geoff, Big Train, So Graham Norton, The Fast Show, Coogan's Run, Goodness Gracious Me, The Day Today, The Jack Dee Show, The Royle Family, The Harry Hill Show, Trigger Happy TV, Fantasy Football League, Smack the Pony, Red Dwarf, People Like Us, The Adam and Joe Show, The Mark Thomas Comedy Product, They Think It's All Over, Stella Street, Shooting Stars* and *Spaced*.

I adored every one of these shows and many others I have almost certainly forgotten to add to the list (sorry). With each title I write down, I worry I should be writing more about them to let you know why they all in their own way offered a different but perfect comic view on the world and had moments or scenes that I still think about on a daily basis. But I've checked and were this book to be a 250-page list of other people's jokes, I would be in breach of contract. So let's just say they were all brilliant and you should watch them in full if you have any interest in us forming a long-term friendship.

Around this time there was a show on BBC2 called *Rock Family Trees* that traced the interconnections between legendary bands across various scenes using the rather un-rock 'n' roll visual aid of the family tree. It was as dry as it sounds, unless you were after an hour of revelations about how the Yardbirds and Manfred Mann had once shared the same session bass player. However, if you were forced to watch it as your dad caught the '60s just right, you saw how it painted pictures of thriving scenes of creativity in which brilliant art was created by a group of people working in various rotating combinations. To me from my sofa, this is how the British comedy scene of the '90s felt, as interlinked as the Los Angeles folk scene of the '60s and the London punk scene of the '70s but with far fewer anecdotes about someone playing their acoustic guitar with an open tuning.

Every show felt as if it was linked to another like the six degrees of Kevin Bacon. *The Mrs Merton Show* was linked by Caroline Aherne to *The Fast Show*, John Thomson from *The Fast Show* was in *Knowing Me, Knowing You with Alan Partridge*, which was produced by Armando Iannucci, who also produced *The Day Today*, which had additional material from Arthur Matthews who co-wrote *Big Train*, which featured Simon Pegg who was in *Spaced* with Jessica Hynes who played Cheryl in *The Royle Family*, which takes us back to Caroline Aherne.

These comedy shows felt like a separate world away from the rest of television. Dare I say it, a cooler world (although considering the last paragraph I'm not sure how much cool I was bringing to the table). The performers all seemed to be in their twenties and the jokes and subject matter were often surreal or risky in ways no other TV shows were. This –

combined with the fact that most of the best alternative comedy shows were found on the two less mainstream channels BBC2 and Channel 4 – made me think the stuff I was watching was far closer to the indie music I was listening to than it was to other TV shows on major channels (that admittedly I watched as well). I have since played enough provincial arts centres with a rider of a packet of Quavers and tea-making facilities to know that comedy isn't the new rock 'n' roll, but as a teenager it certainly felt to me like a parallel world to that of Damon Albarn and Jarvis Cocker.

To underline the crossover around this time, *Top of the Pops* would occasionally be presented by one of these alternative comedians, the music being overshadowed by that week's presenter Harry Hill having an increasing amount of cotton wool in his ears every time they returned to him. Most brilliantly, in the boardroom at my agents' offices among the National Television Awards and BAFTAs (none mine) sits a *Smash Hits* award. It isn't there because they once managed East 17 but because it had been won by Jack Dee, whose late-night Channel 4 stand-up show – shot in a smoky basement and the coolest stand-up has ever looked – had led to him being crowned the country's most popular comedian with teen pop fans. It brings me great joy to imagine how much he would have hated that.

This feeling of comedy being the music industry without the guitars was hammered home each Christmas when I would watch the annual British Comedy Awards, a far funnier but just as debauched version of the Brits. Here I would see all my heroes in one room, laughing, drinking and occasionally damaging their careers with jokes about fisting Norman Lamont. The whole thing was kept together by a brilliant host called Jonathan Ross, who spent the evening making brutal jokes about the comedy stars' careers while somehow keeping their respect by being by far the funniest person in the room. I couldn't for the life of me understand why this guy wasn't on TV more, he needed his own show. Sadly his career never really took off and he was never heard of again.

I would love to be able to tell you that at this point in my life everything crystallised in my mind and I just knew that I had to be a comedian, but that would be a lie. I didn't for a minute assume this was something I would go on to do with my life any more than five years earlier I had imagined I would become a Gladiator. Were I to re-examine the time and attempt to reverse-engineer evidence of an interest in being a comedian, perhaps I would point to my decision to do GCSE drama, but really this was simply because I was so shit at art and music that I had no other choice. Plus, I had it on good authority that GCSE drama involved a school trip to Plymouth Theatre Royal to see Russ Abbot in panto – the kind of golden ticket music students could only dream of.[79]

I showed absolutely no flair for drama, despite the fact my teacher Mr Sutton was the perfect stereotype of an

---

[79] My main memory of that trip is that in the middle of the panto, Abbot did a bit where he spoke really fast for ages and it felt like the funniest thing I had ever seen in my life. Turns out my comedy tastes weren't that refined after all.

eccentric inspiring role model in the *Dead Poets Society* mould; spoke Klingon, lived in a tent by a river, performed martial arts with a long stick as we walked into lessons. My group's final drama performance was a terrible self-written play about a blinded soldier in a First World War hospital who kept his spirits up by listening to stories other soldiers told him about an imaginary woman. As they always say, write about what you know.

The script for the piece was penned by the group's most confident actor Harry, although he proved to be more adept as a performer than a writer. My main memory of it being that at one point, when describing how beautiful my dream woman was, I had to say 'her back, looking like it is supported by unbreakable iron rods'. While I don't expect a 15-year-old boy to be Barbara Cartland, I am sure we can all agree this sounds less like a heartbroken soldier and more like I was helping the police construct a photofit of 400-metre runner Michael Johnson.[80] I was lucky to get a C.

I had been struggling through GCSE drama for a couple of months when the first episode of *I'm Alan Partridge* was screened in 1997. I had first become aware of Alan Partridge on *The Day Today*, a show created by Armando Iannucci – who has gone on to be perhaps the most important figure in UK comedy in the last 25 years – and Chris Morris, whose previous career in radio had seen him falsely announcing

---

[80] Harry has since gone on to have a successful acting career, although his IMDb doesn't say if he used the 'unbreakable iron rods' line in his work in the National Theatre or, far more excitingly to me, on ITV's *Doc Martin*.

the deaths of Michael Heseltine and Jimmy Savile, and filling someone else's recording studio with helium.[81]

The Day Today was primarily a spoof news show but was far better than that studenty description implies; in fact, I would go as far as saying it was such a perfect satire of TV news coverage that it is still impossible to watch the news 25 years later without thinking about it. Behind Morris as the main news anchor was a brilliant ensemble cast from Patrick Marber as inept reporter Peter O'Hanraha-hanrahan to David Schneider as Brant, the physical cartoonist from the *Daily Telegraph,* who would act out terrible stretched metaphors like Bill Clinton as Icarus flying too close to the political heat.

In fact, I hardly even noticed Steve Coogan playing a sports reporter named Alan Partridge, thinking there were far better characters on the show, which shows what I know. For what started out as a fairly straight pastiche of the sports

---

[81] Morris would take this seam of comedy further later in the decade with *Brass Eye*, which in its most memorable moments saw him prank celebrities into talking about non-existent news stories and scandals. John McCririck condemned a new Peter Sutcliffe musical in which Sutcliffe himself appeared onstage to apologise for his crimes, Phil Collins delivered a message that paedophiles have more in common with crabs than humans before telling us that he is talking 'Nonce Sense' and Noel Edmonds warned today's youth about a new drug called Cake that affected the part of the brain called Shatner's Bassoon. You would presume Edmonds would have found being pranked amusing, having built a career and theme park out of it, but of course he didn't.

reporters of the '90s has since stretched to nearly three decades of sitcoms, live shows, books, podcasts and a film as Partridge went on to become a perfect three-dimensional caricature of a vain, ambitious and deluded C-list celebrity.

Partridge's first step outside the sports desk a year after *The Day Today* was *Knowing Me, Knowing You with Alan Partridge*, in which he was given his own light entertainment chat show complete with house band, Glenn Ponder and Chalet, and lame catchphrase 'Knowing me Alan Partridge, knowing you [insert name of guest] Aha!'. However, after his chat show ended with him shooting a guest dead live on TV, we would next see Partridge in his greatest incarnation, the sitcom *I'm Alan Partridge*, which followed him as he moved into local radio and, worse still, a hotel equidistant between London and Norwich. Over six episodes we saw Partridge smuggle a bigger dinner plate to the all-you-can-eat breakfast, piss off some local farmers so much they dropped a cow on him and pitch a variety of terrible programme ideas for BBC Director-General Tony Hayers with such prescience that it is difficult to look at the TV schedules now and not see echoes of *Youth Hostelling with Chris Eubank* or *Arm Wrestling with Chas and Dave*.

Partridge's desperation, ego and obsession with petty victories felt like they captured a type of person that we had seen on TV but never understood until that moment. He became a byword for the light entertainment personalities that made the comedy I watched seem so cool in comparison. Even now the Twitter account Accidental Partridge tweets daily real-life clips and quotes that could come direct from Alan, from journalist Christopher Hope tweeting 'Why do owls get a right to a commemorative stamp but Brexit doesn't?' to a clip of Richard Madeley interviewing some squatters and asking, 'What is your supermarket skip of choice? I mean, I personally like shopping at Waitrose.'

Over the decades Alan Partridge tapped into a depth and truth that made him perhaps the greatest character in the history of British comedy, but in the '90s he was one of hundreds of comic creations I loved. From Ted and Ralph on *The Fast Show*, to Mrs Merton, to the most-loved character of them all, Blind Horny Soldier in South Dartmoor Community College's Year 11 GCSE drama showcase.

'Papa?' 'Nicole?'
Commercial Break
ITV, 7:45pm, 29 May 1998

One Monday evening in May 1998 I sat down to watch my first ever episode of *Coronation Street*, which, according to the listings was based mainly around Les Battersby pretending to have a bad back so that he didn't have to give someone a lift in his car. While no one can deny that sounds like superb entertainment, sadly I have no real memory of it; the reason I was watching was purely for the commercial break. After eight long years the final instalment of the Papa and Nicole Renault Clio saga would finally be premiered to the nation.

The Papa and Nicole story began in 1991 as a single advert for the new Renault Clio, a 30-second story about French girl-about-town Nicole sneaking out to meet her lover while her father, Papa, slept in a deckchair. What Nicole didn't know was that the moment she had gone, silver fox Papa also set off for his own secret liaison, the dirty dog. The advert was such a success that the adventures continued for nearly a decade for Papa, Nicole and their life of clandestine relationships and slowly improving Renault Clios, with each advert seeing Papa and Nicole courting different partners before crossing paths and offering their immortal catchphrase: 'Papa?' 'Nicole?' In doing so they presented a perfect snapshot of all the things we knew the French did best – high fashion, bistros and kissing.

The final instalment of the Nicole and Papa saga was rumoured to see Nicole getting married, but the question was to whom? On the day of broadcast it was speculated over in the morning's papers, discussed by Zoe Ball on the *Radio 1 Breakfast Show* and replaced Johnny Vaughan and Denise Van Outen as the main topic of conversation for 15-year-olds at my school. But despite everyone's best efforts it was impossible to guess the identity of the groom – the only other regular character was Papa and that would have been a hugely shocking twist. In the end, in a brilliantly unlikely choice, the advert deserted the usual fare and instead featured Vic Reeves and Bob Mortimer with Nicole jilting Vic at the altar to marry Bob in a pastiche of *The Graduate*. You could get away with anything in adverts in the '90s.

Rewatching the full eight-part Renault Clio series (all four minutes of it) may be the most Proustian trip back to my childhood I have had in writing this book. Not because I am about to reveal to you that I spent my teenage years in a series of secret liaisons with a French girl in a compact car, but simply because it turns out that more than almost anything else an old television advert has the ability to transport you back in time.

All the best television from your childhood has been repeated, the best clips have been popped on to YouTube or, in the case of Euro 96, the pain is there every night when you close your eyes. Seeing Tubbs and Edward ask a customer if they are local doesn't take you back to the first time you saw it, because you have seen it 50 times since. On the other side of the coin, no one ever has a reason to revisit an advert they watched absent-mindedly 100 times in 1994, which means when they then do that (because, for instance, they have committed to write a book that they are starting to worry is too niche for a mass market) it transports them straight back to that year. Like the smell of sun cream taking you back to a Cornish beach holiday, it only takes one Crisp 'n Dry advert and suddenly you are in your school uniform on the sofa waiting for *Home and Away* to start.

Adverts occupy the same place in the mind as the songs that you used to hear every day on the radio as a child, but you haven't listened to or thought about since. No one is taken back to 1997 when they hear 'Let Me Entertain You' by Robbie Williams because they have heard it thousands of times since on the radio or TV or at some terrible karaoke night. No, the songs that take you back are the minor hits of the day that haven't had any airplay in the years that followed, to go back to 1997, just listen to 'Arms Around the World' by Louise.[82]

If you want to test this for yourself there are YouTube videos with names like 'UK TV adverts from 1993–94' that last for two hours and consist entirely of adverts that you haven't thought about in over 25 years but will remember instantly. They are almost impossible to stop watching once you start, the excitement of which advert will come next keeping you hooked like some kind of terrible Dan Brown thriller. It turns out if you want to be transported back to your childhood, you don't need to look at old school photos or visit your childhood home, just pop on the Carling Black Label advert where a squirrel does an assault course to the *Mission Impossible* theme tune.

The power of these adverts to take me back partly comes from how central they were to the experience of watching TV in the '90s. Not because they were in some way superior to the lesser-watched adverts of the 21st century, it is simply that they were impossible to avoid. It is hugely unlikely that you would actively watch an advert today. On the rare occasions you are watching TV live and so can't fast-forward through the adverts, you will instinctively pick up your phone the moment you see the words 'sponsored by Foster's'. In the '90s the choice was between a Crunchie advert or just looking at a wall – only an idiot wouldn't

---

[82] I've just listened to it and there is a reason it was left there.

choose the Crunchie advert (particularly because it gave you that Friday feeling every time you saw it).

In comparison such is my inbuilt aversion to watching adverts these days, there is no point in my life when I am more alert than when waiting for the 'Skip Ads' button to come up on the advert before a YouTube video, clicking it the moment it appears so I don't have to watch a sixth second of a completely inoffensive sales pitch from Domino's.[83] I now find adverts such an imposition on my life that if I stream a show that has unskippable adverts at the start, I have to talk myself out of quitting on it there and then, questioning if any show is good enough to sit and wait patiently for a full minute.

My dad was ahead of the curve, even in the 1990s he had a 2020s aversion to watching the adverts. If in control of the remote he would insist on muting the breaks so we could talk as a family (usually a discussion about why we couldn't just watch the adverts like everybody else). It was his fightback against capitalism, getting to watch an episode of *The Darling Buds of May* without being tricked into buying a box of Kellogg's Crunchy Nut Cornflakes. Luckily for Kellogg's he was a lone soldier in this battle, for the '90s

---

[83] It was a strange moment when I found myself waiting impatiently to skip the advert before the YouTube compilation of adverts from 1993–94. My mind thinking, 'Hurry up with this pointless advert for something I might need; I want to watch some adverts for products that don't exist any more.'

was a time when adverts were treated with a strange level of respect. Like they were important pieces of culture in their own right, rather than just a way to convince people that stringy cheese was a perfectly natural product to put in their mouth. In the year 2000, Channel 4 ran a series of Top 100s, from TV moments to characters to Number 1s. Such was people's love of commercial breaks adverts were chosen as the topic for the second countdown of the series.[84] This was a world in which adverts were being discussed in the same way as great songs or films. (And quite average songs, in fact, I've just checked and 'Groovejet' by Spiller feat. Sophie Ellis-Bextor came in as the ninth best Number 1 of all time. Surely it's top 30, max).

In fact, adverts were so loved they had the ability to not just sell the products they were advertising. Having your song used on an advert became a legitimate way of getting a Number 1 single. I've just done some rudimentary research and it turns out that across the '90s, Levi's adverts had more Number 1 singles than Blur – turns out Noel's main threat

---

[84] The number-one advert was one of the most annoying of the decade, Surfer by Guinness, which featured black-and-white footage of surfers attempting to ride waves that had taken on the form of rearing white horses while a pompous voiceover says things like: 'Ahab says, "I don't care who you are, here's to your dream,"' like that meant something. I'm not saying it doesn't look beautiful, I'm not saying it is forgettable; what I am saying is do you really think this is better than a squirrel on an assault course?

to world domination wasn't Damon but Mr Oizo. I myself fell for the trick of the Levi's advert soundtrack, buying the single 'Inside' by Stiltskin after it was used on an advert in 1994. While I assumed the soundtrack was a cool new track by an edgy rock act, I have since found out that Stiltskin was just some guy who had been commissioned to write a song for an advert and the men in plaid shirts I saw rocking out on *Top of the Pops* were just blokes they had got to play the part. Who knew the world of advertising could be so cynical and money-driven?

At their '90s peak, adverts had transcended their primary aim of selling us stuff. The biggest adverts were great hits, as iconic as the TV shows they delayed us seeing. I enjoyed John Barnes' Lucozade Sport advert as much as I enjoyed seeing him actually play football and I can remember the words to the Milky Way 'Red Car and Blue Car' song far more clearly than those from 'Champagne Supernova'.

When this book was announced a friend texted me and said, 'I hope you'll be talking about the Tango adverts.' Somehow that was his main touchpoint of '90s television. While this may seem mad to anyone who wasn't there, it was actually a pretty fair response. The 'You Know When You've Been Tango'd' advert series – which saw people in the street slapped in the face with a giant orange glove – was one of the most recognisable things on the television at the end of the 20th century. It was an advert so influential that it has been credited with pioneering guerrilla marketing;

an advert so popular it had to be withdrawn and replaced with something less violent due to a spate of children being injured by copycat Tangoings. And when it comes down to it, surely that is the ultimate sign of success, apart from people buying more Tango.

'I turned on Ceefax and read that I had been sacked'
Ceefax
Throughout the '90s

It's the late '90s and England manager Glenn Hoddle is about to be sacked after telling a newspaper he believes disabled people are paying for sins of a previous life. After Prime Minister Tony Blair uses an appearance on *This Morning with Richard and Judy* to say that Hoddle should go, his daughter Zara decides to fight for her dad's job and writes to the press to put their side of the story: 'I am Zara Hoddle and I would just like to say that I am very supportive of disabled people, so is my dad,' her statement begins. She doesn't send it to the *Sun*, *Daily Mail* or *Daily Mirror* – she faxes it directly to Ceefax. And why not? Ceefax has 20 million weekly readers, far more than any newspaper.

I feel it would be a dereliction of duty to write a book about TV in the '90s and not take a brief stop to discuss teletext.[85] In doing this, let's begin with some honesty. More

_____

[85] A brief note about the terms teletext and Ceefax. Teletext was what the service was called across all channels and Ceefax was the BBC's

than anything else I talk about in this book (perhaps with the exception of John Fashanu), teletext was appalling at what it did. In fact, its huge popularity and staying power is perhaps the most baffling and unjust success story of the '90s across the whole cultural landscape. A decade, let's not forget, in which Wet Wet Wet spent 15 consecutive weeks at Number 1.

Describing TV shows to people who haven't seen them is easy: you have other reference points from a lifetime of television. *SMTV* was *Saturday Night Takeaway* for kids; *Blind Date* was a frigid *Take Me Out*; *Soccer AM* was a crap *Fantasy Football League*. Describing teletext to someone lucky enough to have never spent a day following a live Test match on Ceefax page 341 is close to impossible. Teletext existed in its own universe, a rudimentary internet in a decade when the internet was the rudimentary internet. An electronic newspaper on your TV screen, allowing you to check the latest headlines, sport and weather, or just play Bamboozle, a quiz that was so slow that by the time you got to the end of it, a lot of the answers were no longer factually correct.

Most of all teletext was basic. Its iconic look was made up of a black background, a single font for everything and

version of it. ITV's version was called Oracle, but no one cares about that. Referring to teletext as a whole as Ceefax is like calling all vacuum cleaners Hoovers, in that if someone picks you up on it being wrong, you can safely assume they are a bellend.

headings like 'Sport' drawn in huge blocky pixels. It was like getting your news from the title screen of a Commodore 64 game. Occasionally – particularly on the more tabloid commercial channels – it would try its hand at pictures. The weather page making a vain attempt to capture a map of the UK despite having to represent Cornwall with just one huge pixel; the holiday page[86] accompanying its menu with a rendering of the world's most crudely drawn palm tree. It was like you were there, lying on a sun lounger in the Caribbean under a completely square coconut.

I recently watched a documentary on *Rolling Stone* magazine in which legendary gonzo writer Hunter S Thompson argued that all reporting is subjective and there can be no such thing as objective journalism. He had clearly never been on teletext,[87] a medium with such a tight word count it was written completely without editorialising or literary flourish. News stories would be stripped to the bare minimum of words to fit on to each page, huge events that would get five pages in a newspaper boiled down to three paragraphs. Mainly this would be achieved with the rampant use of brackets. In football team news pages you would read 'Newcastle will be without Steve Howey (knee)' and be forced to use your imagination to fill in the blanks on

---

[86] After Googling this it turns out that astonishingly Teletext Holidays still exists as a brand and they have a website on the Information Superhighway; give it up, lads.

[87] I'm pretty confident of this.

what had happened to his knee or even if he still had one. If we currently live in an age of too much information then the days of teletext were surely an age of not quite enough information. There must have been a middle-ground moment in the early 2000s when people had just the right amount of information but I don't remember it specifically.

Teletext wasn't just sparse, it was difficult to use. You would have to wait minutes for pages to load and then when they did, they would flip over to a new page before you had even finished reading it. Even the cool extra functions just made teletext worse. In the mid-'90s we were excited to upgrade to a TV with the teletext function MIX, which allowed you to lose the black background and watch the TV at the same time as reading. It was the worst of both worlds, my mum too distracted by the writing to enjoy *Goodnight Sweetheart* while I was unable to make out the Liverpool score against a backdrop of Nicholas Lyndhurst's face.

Considering all this, I would like to pose the following questions. If teletext was so bad, how come no show I have discussed in this book comes close in viewing time to the hours I spent looking at teletext growing up? How come the writing on the teletext button was the first to wear off on our remote control? And how come I can still find the numbers to teletext pages in my brain quicker than I can find my current internet passwords?

The answer is simply that I, like everyone, loved teletext because it was our only source of continuous news, sport or TV listings. This was a time when the internet was still rubbish, you didn't have rolling news channels on TV and my parents refused to buy the *Radio Times*. Ceefax was how everybody found out about the news, even when they were involved in it. When Ruud Gullit was sacked as manager of Newcastle in 1999, he told the press he had found out via Ceefax. Yes, even Ruud Gullit, the cosmopolitan Dutchman and king of sexy football, spent his days checking teletext. Lower down the food chain, in 1997 QPR assistant manager Bruce Rioch had the same experience when he was fired, his description of the incident being perhaps the most '90s sentence ever put on record: 'I was at home watching the Louise Woodward case on television when I turned on Ceefax and read that I had been sacked.'

It turned out everyone in football read Ceefax, sometimes with far more positive results than Ruud Gullit. When third-tier Wycombe Wanderers faced an FA Cup quarter-final against Premier League Leicester in the middle of an injury crisis, they sent Ceefax a press release asking any interested strikers to contact them. Roy Essandoh got in touch, passed the trial and was named as a substitute. With 20 minutes to go, he was brought off the bench and scored the winning goal. The real sadness was that Ceefax only had space for 100 words in which to tell this astonishing story.

There is a reason why football and teletext went hand in hand – it was often the only way of following live matches. Throughout the '90s I, along with millions of other football fans around the country, would spend Saturday afternoons and weekday evenings watching the games unfold on Ceefax. By that, I don't mean we watched some pixelated representation of what the game looked like[88] or even the kind of minute-by-minute update that you get now on the BBC website. I mean I would sit and stare at the score for 90 minutes, begging for it to change in my favour, trying to imagine what was happening behind the simple fact of:

Oldham 0-0 Plymouth

As if this image isn't bleak enough, living on Dartmoor with a dodgy TV signal meant there was often the added issue that teletext would not be transmitted perfectly and there would be rogue letters sent through, meaning we would be presented with:

Oldham   1-%   Ply$$$th
Littlejohn 43   %%%

---

[88] Apparently in the '80s Ceefax tried covering the boat race by drawing the map of the Thames in pixels and then having two different pixels slowly move down it to represent the Oxford and Cambridge boats. My main issue with this is not that I can't imagine following a sporting event this way – I can – but that the boat race was shown live on BBC1, you would have had to actively close down the picture of the actual race to watch it on Ceefax.

Were those percentage symbols a sign the score had changed? Were they a bugged version of the name of the player who had scored our equaliser? There was little as tense in sport as trying to follow an evening kick-off via teletext during a storm on Dartmoor. Clinging on to the hope of some rogue pound signs before they suddenly disappeared back to:

Oldham 1-0 Plymouth
Littlejohn 43

The goal taken away like it had never happened in the first place. It was VAR 25 years before VAR.

Perhaps the most surreal aspect of the bizarre world of Ceefax came at night when the BBC wouldn't close like in the olden days but instead would just show Ceefax pages set to music for hours on end. I would like to think this was because people loved Ceefax and couldn't get enough of it, but it was almost certainly because it was cheap. Either way, it was a dark day for that girl playing noughts and crosses with the clown.

If you want to relive the halcyon days of Ceefax you can still watch long videos of these overnight Ceefax marathons on YouTube, often hours in length. They have tens of thousands of views so clearly there's a market for them. Maybe that is how some people like to relax, reading brief snippets of news stories from 20 years ago set to chilled-out beats. I won't lie, I've just wasted half an hour on it.

It's an eclectic mix. From 1987, you get a tune that sounds like a quirky '70s sitcom soundtracking the news that an army has seized control of Fiji in a coup while from 1990, you get swelling strings reminiscent of the Golden Age of Hollywood backing a story headlined 'Radar contract awarded to UK company'. In the corner the clock ticks over to 4:08am. It takes a special type of insomniac to have watched that live.

While this may seem like something from the distant past, there are videos that show it was still going in the mid 2000s, although by then they were opting for sexier music: a duelling saxophone and Spanish guitar providing a lustful backdrop to the headline 'Diabetes issues at record high'. It doesn't feel right for Ceefax. It's the kind of music you imagine Jay Kay from Jamiroquai would pop on to seduce a lady back at his Thames-side flat, but I suppose by this time Ceefax knew it was on the way out and was trying anything to stay relevant, like Bruce Forsyth doing a rap.

And so it was that on 12 October 2012 the BBC turned off its analogue transmitters and with it went Ceefax. It was like when a celebrity dies and your first reaction is, 'Really? I assumed he had been dead for years.'

A string of odes to Ceefax were written in the papers, mourned like a dependable companion rather than a great technological advance. Nothing captures a moment like the technology of the time. We can listen to music or watch films from 30 years ago and still get the same joy from them as we did the first time we saw them, but outdated technology is left in the past, its only role being to provide a nostalgic rush. You would have to be a spectacularly insistent Luddite to claim you wish you were still using Ceefax to get your football scores in the days of the internet and football actually being on television every single day.

Perhaps the best tribute on Ceefax's final day was a spoof suicide note that the comedy writers Joel Morris and Jason Hazeley put on Twitter, made to look like a page from everyone's favourite moribund news service:

> By the time you read this, I will be dead.
>
> When I first started out in 1974, I was the future – TV's first robot newsreader. But what once seemed cutting-edge is now regarded as hopelessly old-fashioned, and I have been frozen out by the powers that be, yet another victim of BBC ageism.
>
> I can't take it any more. It's a struggle to get up for the night shift, and my poor pixels are tired. My friend Oracle said it would end like this.
> Goodbye cruel world.

If anything it had a little too much personality. Surely the real voice of Ceefax would have just gone with 'Teletext to no longer exist (internet)'.

'This is the place to be at 6pm'
TFI Friday
Channel 4, 6pm, 4 September 1998

In the space of a couple of hours one Tuesday morning last winter, I was sent the same news story in four separate WhatsApp groups. Clicking on the link, I read that a six-bedroom house in east London had gone on the market for £5.75 million, the cost per bedroom of property in east London astonishingly not the reason the *Mirror* considered this a news story. The reason this had made the news was because the property for sale was Lockkeeper's Cottages on Old Ford Lock, or as those in the know referred to it, the *Big Breakfast* house.

Breakfast television had launched in the UK a couple of months before I was born in 1983. I know this because my mum has told me that her main memory of her early mornings when I was a baby was watching Roland Rat on *TV-am*, delighted that I had been born in an age when there was TV on at this time to offer her some company. I'm confident this isn't where my addiction to TV began, but let's not rule it out.

Unlike my exhausted mum in 1983, by the time I was watching TV in the '90s I had little interest in breakfast television. From what I could tell it consisted almost entirely of middle-aged men and women sitting on beige sofas behind bowls of fruit discussing the news of the day – even I struggled to find an in. It didn't feel like anyone watched breakfast TV because they actually enjoyed it. At best it felt like TV you put on because you didn't yet feel ready to have a conversation with another human. No one was popping on a video so they could watch the last hour of *BBC Breakfast News* when they got back from work.[89]

Then in 1992 Channel 4 launched *The Big Breakfast*. As far as I could tell this was the first time someone had the idea to make breakfast TV that was as good as the stuff they put on at other times of the day. In fact, if anything, it was better. I can still remember the almost visceral experience of the first time I turned on the TV to kill time before school and didn't see a middle-aged man in a suit but primary colours, the camera swinging round to show the cheering crew and a ginger-haired co-host with a magnetic manic energy. That day I went to school and talked to my best friend Thomas, not about *Neighbours* or *Knightmare*,

---

[89] I have just checked and for some reason *BBC Breakfast* is available on iPlayer. I find it hard to believe anyone is taking them up on the option to watch it later in the day, unless Dan Walker goes home to review footage of his performance each day like Pep Guardiola after a poor display by Manchester City.

but about how the following morning he needed to turn on Channel 4 as soon as he woke up. It is a memory that is particularly vivid because I know exactly where I was having this conversation – eating lunch in the car park of B&Q.

I now know that what I had seen the first time I watched *The Big Breakfast* was channelling the ramshackle energy and irreverent approach of late night Channel 4 shows like *The Word* and Jonathan Ross's *The Last Resort*, but I had no idea of this at the time. It just felt to me that Channel 4 had decided to completely reinvent television and had made the strange decision to do so at 7 o'clock in the morning. Everything about it felt like nothing I had seen before: the presenters would run around and fall off chairs, the crew and production team would shout out catchphrases like 'Don't phone, it's just for fun!' and the whole thing had the air of a student house party that was going to end up costing the tenants their deposit.

The fact it came from a house in east London felt perfect, it was the opposite of those other shows in TV studios with their boring newspaper reviews and fake backdrops of the London skyline. On *The Big Breakfast* you didn't have Dr Hilary discussing the menopause on a sofa, you had Paula Yates interviewing Robin Williams while lying on a double bed. You had Zig and Zag, aliens from the planet Zog, puppets that were so cool they dressed in trendy '90s jackets and, in the case of Zag, had a Mark Owen-style curtains haircut. In 37 years of life I am yet to find a better way to use my time at 7:30am than watching Zig and Zag interview Louise Wener from Sleeper squashed into a tiny bathroom, wondering if there was also another bathroom in the house or if this is where the crew had to go for a piss during the adverts.[90]

The only thing that felt familiar about *The Big Breakfast* was co-host Gaby Roslin, who I already loved from her time on *Motormouth*, ITV's version of *Going Live!*. I had no idea who the other bloke presenting with Roslin was but it turned out to be a seemingly unhinged man with ginger hair and thick-rimmed glasses called Chris Evans. He was as funny as a comedian, as unpredictable as a rock star and had the ability to make even the most mundane phone-in competition feel like the most exciting TV you had ever seen. While I would hate to be accused of exaggerating, it was clear to me that Chris Evans was the greatest presenter of live television in the history of the world.

Evans, with his trusty clipboard in hand, would banter with newsreader Peter Smith before handing over to him or take charge of features like 'One Lump or Two?', a game in which a blindfolded guest would lie on an inflatable made to look like a teabag in a swimming pool made to look like a huge teacup. Viewers would then phone in and direct them around the cup, attempting to find floating sugar lumps to

---

[90] Zig and Zag proved so popular they actually became bigger pop stars than a lot of their guests, having a Top 5 hit with the raga pastiche 'Them Girls, Them Girls', one of Simon Cowell's first hits (and let's be honest, best).

win a cash prize. It was both as brilliant and terrible as it sounds, and hilarious for that very reason.

While 'One Lump Or Two?' would involve viewers winning the tedious prize of money, a couple of years in, the show launched 'Housey Housey', giving away perhaps the most audacious prize in the history of TV: a newly built exact replica of the *Big Breakfast* house. Like anyone in their right mind, I got hold of a game card and watched *The Big Breakfast* for the next six weeks, playing what seemed like a very drawn-out game of bingo and imagining how amazing it would be for us to move into the newly built *Big Breakfast* house 'somewhere in the UK'. As the competition reached its climax, it was revealed that the location was . . . Telford. In hindsight it was probably for the best that I didn't win as my parents would have been against the move and I would have struggled to balance my schoolwork with being the 11-year-old landlord of a house in the West Midlands.

By the time of 'Housey Housey', Evans was in the process of leaving *The Big Breakfast* to host his own prime-time Saturday night game show *Don't Forget Your Toothbrush*, which involved celebs, games and, most excitingly, every audience member bringing a passport and packed suitcase in the hope of winning a holiday for which they would leave immediately after the show. It was a programme that showed that Evans's brand of entertainment wasn't just funny compared to GMTV. Whatever the time of day, who doesn't want to see people throwing ten items out of the windows of their house in a minute to win money on live TV?

It was Evans's next show, however, which would be the defining peak for British television in the '90s. The first episode of *TFI Friday* began with a sketch showing him going to collect a death certificate from a coroner (played by the soon-to-be-famous producer of the show, Will Macdonald). 'What is the name of the deceased?' Macdonald asks Evans as he sits down. '*Top of the Pops*,' he replies. 'What was the exact time of death?' 'Well, just very slowly over the last ten years,' says Evans before he is asked to identify the deceased and a TV is revealed, showing The Outhere Brothers singing 'Boom Boom Boom'. 'Sorry, I realise these things can be very distressing,' says Macdonald. It was a sketch that told you everything you needed to know about *TFI Friday*: it was exciting, funny and it didn't seem to give a fuck.

The show was presented by Evans from a desk at the end of the *TFI Friday* bar, a real working pub full of attractive pissed people in their twenties standing around holding pints and wearing Suede T-shirts. The best comedy entertainment shows feel like you are listening to conversations that would happen anyway if the cameras were not there, *TFI Friday* felt like you were watching a piss-up that would probably continue for the following six hours after the cameras were gone. As a teenage boy that bar felt like the only place I wanted to be in the world.

After the *Top of the Pops*-baiting sketch, the first episode began with Evans walking backstage, passing the dressing rooms at Riverside Studios, greeting the viewers by saying:

'Good evening and welcome to Friday nights live on Channel 4. From now on this is the place to be at 6pm.' That was exactly how it felt. *TFI* seemed to me to combine everything that I cared about in the second half of the '90s: all the comedy, music and sport that I loved had come together in one place. In the space of one hour on Friday night we could watch a performance by Pulp, be introduced to a comedian called Harry Hill, hear Ewan McGregor slag off the Tories and – strangely – see an interview with Rangers striker Ally McCoist. Cool Britannia, that nebulous idea of everything in the country heading in the same confident and positive direction in the late '90s, only really felt real in the *TFI Friday* bar.

But it wasn't just celebrities. *TFI Friday* was populated by characters from Evans's day-to-day life. Links would feature a man called Cedric who ran the cafe across the road, while the bar was run by a man called Andrew who owned Evans's local: 'He's a real barman, he's not an actor . . . as you are about to find out,' Evans says before having a conversation with him in the first episode. It felt like he was opening up his life to you. When *TFI* started, he was also hosting the Radio 1 breakfast show and they felt like two companion pieces that I couldn't miss out on. I would listen to and watch both religiously to keep track of the people and jokes variously crossing between the two shows. Somehow in a small way Evans made you feel that just by watching you were part of his inner circle.

The greatest of these breakout stars was Will Macdonald, a baby-faced producer who first popped up sitting in the corner of the bar in his headphones, prompting Evans with what is coming next and ended up with his own catch-phrase, which involved people pointing at him and saying the word 'Wiiiiiiiiiiiiill' with as many i's in it as possible.[91] Before long, Wiiiiiiiiiiiiill had his own feature on the show, 'Pub Genius', in which he would show off tricks you could do in the pub, the crowd cheering him on as he attempted to get an olive over a hurdle without touching it. Considering the other sports Channel 4 had shown over the decade, this was actually pretty high-end stuff.

If at times it felt like the show's running order had been devised by mates talking in the pub, that was because often it was. In his book *Going on the Turn*, Evans's co-writer Danny Baker tells of how the final script meetings before the show would take place in one of the nearby pubs with panicking members of the team sent to find them when they were nowhere to be seen half an hour before being due on air. Opposite Riverside Studios where it was filmed there is a pub called Channings. It would be unremarkable but for two things. Firstly, I once went in for a pint and they were giving out free cheese sandwiches cut into small trian-gles. Secondly, the walls are covered in photos of Evans, his team and superstars drinking in there in the late '90s. The

---

[91] Macdonald is now a hugely successful TV producer and a very nice man. I once bumped into him in the street and the friend I was with simply pointed in his face and said 'Wiiiiiiiill.' It was one of the worst moments of my life.

pictures sum up what made *TFI* so unique – the clash of huge superstars with boozy mundanity.

This feeling of the show just being a trip to the pub with a Hollywood or rock A-lister was reflected in the fact that Evans would never just do a straight interview. When Paul McCartney appeared as a guest, Evans began by saying he had been thinking for weeks about his opening question and had the perfect one: 'What about all this rain?' When Samuel L Jackson was booked for the show, he simply appeared in a feature called 'The Hollywood Star We Didn't Have Time For'. This involved him just walking on looking pissed off, saying a few facts about himself and walking off again while Evans sat in the background checking his watch.

Unlike some other Channel 4 shows that tried hard to constantly feel anarchic to win over the precious youth market, *TFI Friday* managed to marry left-field ideas with a genuine mainstream entertainment sensibility. Between Hollywood superstars would be surreal features like 'Baby Left, Baby Right' where people would be asked to guess which way a toddler would fall – and 'Ugly Bloke' in which a very unattractive man would be cheered into the bar and then be given the opportunity to turn down the advances of a model with the line, 'Sorry love, you're just not my type.' It was a show that didn't just celebrate the famous but also celebrated the man in the street. As long as he was ugly.

TFI Friday was the show everyone wanted to be cool enough to be invited on. So it was only logical that when the greatest pop star of the 20th century, David Bowie, had a new album to promote in the late '90s, he flew overnight from New York to appear on a show at 6pm on Channel 4. It is an astonishing interview that couldn't happen anywhere else. As Bowie appears for the traditional walk on through the crowd to Ocean Colour Scene's 'Riverboat Song', you can feel the excitement in the room that he is actually there, even if he is wearing a bright pink shirt over a neon yellow T-shirt and baggy cargo trousers, like a man dressed for decorating the spare room rather than pop's greatest stylist. Then, before Bowie even gets to sit down, Evans instead makes him measure his height and mark it on the door like you do with small children, proving he is taller than previous guest Ben Elton.

Once he is sitting down, Bowie takes over, launching into a surreal shaggy dog story about his recent gastroenteritis. He is an unbelievable guest – funny, engaging – and just when you think a story is going nowhere, it has a brilliant pay-off. When he goes on another flight of fancy about the seating on the plane over and how he has been up for 29 hours, Evans says: 'We can tell.' 'This is me straight, buddy, you're lucky you didn't know me 25 years ago,' replies Bowie.

For 15 minutes you see one of the most untouchable men of the late 20th century speaking without any mask or inhibition. But then it would be impossible for an interview to go any other way in the *TFI* bar. I can only imagine how much fun it was in Channings after the show.

'Sex, drink, football and less serious matters'
Men Behaving Badly
BBC1, 9pm, 28 December 1998

Of all the exciting symbols that Christmas was coming – purchase of the advent calendar, decorating the tree, my dad saying he wasn't really into consumerism – none compared to the arrival of the special double issue of the *Radio Times*. For the rest of the year we were happy to keep track of what was on TV through Ceefax or just flicking between channels, but in tribute to God giving his only son to mankind to save us from our sins, for two weeks we would read what was on in a glossy magazine (also featuring a heads-up on which *EastEnders* character would be brutally killed on Christmas Day). It was in this double-issue *Radio Times* that I would find out which show the BBC had deemed big enough to be the main Christmas special of the year.

In 1996 the final episode of that most '80s of sitcoms *Only Fools and Horses* was the big headliner and became the most-watched show of the '90s outside of news and sport. Two years later the BBC's big Christmas event was again the climax of a hit sitcom. And again it was a show that had come to represent the social trends of a decade, this time the unrefined, lager-drinking lad culture of the '90s. Some shows can be repeated years later and feel like they still make perfect sense, other shows feel like a time capsule of their era. *Men Behaving Badly* falls into the second category.

Men Behaving Badly revolved around Gary and Tony (Martin Clunes and Neil Morrissey) and their blokey London flat share. Episodes would involve them getting drunk, struggling to understand women and invariably end with them on the sofa drinking more lager and putting the world to rights. Despite my inadequate description, it was in fact one of the funniest shows of the decade. Clunes and Morrissey gave Gary and Tony a huge likeability, Caroline Quentin and Leslie Ash made up a great ensemble cast and it was full of great drunk acting and brilliant writing:

Tony: Why does Dorothy still live with her parents?
Gary: Her mother keeps threatening to kill herself if she moves out. I think she should risk it.

For me, *Men Behaving Badly* was more than a comedy show, it was aspirational television. When people talk about television in this way you usually imagine *Dallas* or that bit in Jamie Oliver shows where his mates come round for lunch and they listen to Toploader, but for me at the age of 15 the TV lifestyle I wanted more than any was shown on *Men Behaving Badly* – I had downgraded my heroes from Baddiel and Skinner to a far lower rent pair of flatmates. Yes, I could see that Gary was trapped in a soul-sapping office job and Tony was variously unemployed and unable to get the woman of his dreams, but as a teenage boy with no sign of progress with the opposite sex and very little social life outside of school, Gary and Tony's laddy existence of alcohol, friendship and occasional sex was as aspirational as it got.

There are few things to come from the '90s as ugly as lad culture – a celebration of bone-headedness, sexism and mass-produced beer, couched with the occasional justification of irony. Coming about as a response to the rise of the new man, laddism kicked against such terrible character traits as being in touch with your emotions and respecting women. As a 15-year-old boy torn between the liberal values instilled in me by my parents and the undeniable thrill of a hypothetical life of beer and shagging, my feeling towards the new lad was an excited but guilty confusion.

So far the closest I had got to living the life of a lad was purchasing that bible of the '90s bloke, the lads' mag. It would be easy to dismiss lads' mags simply as a way for teenage boys to access pictures of semi-naked women under the alibi of wanting to read an article about the Columbian drug trade, and that is because for the most part that is exactly what they were.

If I associate one emotion with lads' mags it is shame. The terrible awkwardness of buying them, unsure if a 14-year-old boy was legally allowed to exchange money for some pictures of Emma Noble in a bra. The grim ritual of hiding them in my pile of *FourFourTwo* magazines to avoid an awkward discussion with my mum. The interminable attempts to read articles about off-roading in the Alps in an attempt to convince myself that I wasn't just in it for the photos of Melanie Sykes.

The first lads' mag I bought was an issue of *Loaded* that set out its appeal to me with a free double-sided gatefold poster featuring supermodel Lisa Snowdon on one side and Blackburn Rovers manager Kenny Dalglish on the other. Something for everyone. While I know time has not been kind to them, I struggle to stop myself from having a soft spot for those early issues of *Loaded*, a magazine influenced as much by *Viz* as it was by *Playboy* and edited by a hard-drinking, brilliant loudmouth called James Brown, who described the audience as '50% *Sun* readers and 50% *Guardian* readers'. I have just re-read his editorial for the first issue and, pathetically, I still find it utterly thrilling: '*Loaded* is a new magazine dedicated to life, liberty and the pursuit of sex, drink, football and less serious matters. *Loaded* is music, film, relationships, humour, travel, sport, hard news and popular culture. *Loaded* is clubbing, drinking, eating, playing and eating. *Loaded* is for the man who believes he can do anything, if only he wasn't hung-over.' I had to admit, it wasn't a perfect snapshot of my life.

Since kissing Sophie at Marble Mania at the age of 11, it had been pretty slim pickings on the girlfriend front for Widdicombe. And by slim pickings I mean zero pickings. Looking at the negatives, I had yet to come close to kissing a girl at secondary school. Looking at the positives, my friend Ian and I had spent an English lesson working out the probability that one day one of us would date Sarah Michelle Gellar, coming up with the relatively short odds of 75,000-1. So who was the real loser? (For those interested in our method, this task involved us starting at the global population of 6 billion and slowly narrowing it down with factors that would prevent people dating SMG. For instance, half the world were women, cut 50%, cut 25% as they are too old, etc. The sad truth was that we had missed one key factor: we had just spent our English lesson working out the probabilities of us having a relationship with Buffy the Vampire Slayer; we had zero chance even with girls in our school).

If you worry I spent my whole secondary education inside my own head considering impossible fantasy relationships with Hollywood actresses, do not despair; I also did this for girls in my class. For the final two years of secondary school I was in love with a girl in my year called Emma; she was funny, intelligent and had a back that was supported by unbreakable iron rods. Obviously Emma didn't know I was in love with her and I wasn't about to tell her as that would have involved drawing attention to myself. Instead I made the wise decision to hide these feelings from everyone and concentrate on going public about my statistical chance of dating Buffy the Vampire Slayer. I would love to say I regret this and learned a lesson about always being true to your heart, but I bumped into Emma years later and it turned out she is someone who, in conversation, would repeatedly refer to her partner as her 'lover', which I am sure we can all agree is totally unacceptable. A close escape.

While my romantic life was at a standstill, the late '90s offered a greater opportunity in that other great pillar of laddism, drinking. On television the benefits of alcohol were there for everyone to see, from Gary and Tony and their fridge full of lager to the excitement of the *TFI Friday* bar. Watching these shows, how could you not want to experience what it was like to spend your Friday night drinking in a bar, with or without Chris Evans asking risqué questions of Anna Friel at one end of it? The rise of the lads and the ladettes made drinking not just normalised but, somehow, the must-have lifestyle. Suddenly drunken celebrities weren't middle-aged embarrassments like Oliver Reed and George Best, they were the life and soul of the party, like Liam Gallagher or Zoe Ball. If you drank beer you weren't ruining a chat show, you were living your best life (something I still tell myself regularly when filming *The Last Leg*).

On top of this, as I reached my teens a new invention had arrived: the alcopop. Gone were the days of training yourself to like the rancid taste of beer, now we lived in a world where alcoholic drinks could taste like a normal glass of lemonade or orange juice (that was on the turn).

What now seems clear is that the stars had aligned and my teenage years had become the perfect opportunity for a life of rebellious debauchery. What is even clearer is I failed to make this happen. It isn't that I didn't want to go out and get drunk, it was simply a case of logistics. It turned out that no-holds-barred hedonism was very difficult to organise in the middle of Dartmoor.

I have friends who grew up in 24-carat party towns like Reading or Bromley and they will tell stories of the evenings they spent as teenagers lurking in bus stops or outside local newsagent's asking passers-by to go in and buy them a cheap bottle of 20/20. This wasn't an option for me. We didn't have a bus stop to lurk in, and my nearest licensed shop was three miles away in Bovey Tracey. Had I wanted to loiter outside it, asking strangers to grab me a bottle of Hooch, I would have had to get my dad to drop me there and back in his car, hugely damaging the illicit nature of the whole experience.

Even when I got to sixth form and my friends and I started going out in the nearest student city of Exeter, for our first proper nights out we were still heavily lift-dependent. With Exeter 15 miles away and no public transport, the night out would depend on our ability to convince a parent to drive us there and back. This would mean that in the hugely unlikely scenario that our NUS cards (without date of birth) were taken as proof we were 18 and we could get pissed, we would still have a hard deadline of 10:30pm to finish our hellraising before meeting at the agreed pick-up point.

And at that time we would still need to be sober enough to hold a conversation with a friend's parent on the 45-minute journey home.

For a while it felt like the freedom that teenage drinking brought would forever be paired with the slightly less exciting bedfellow of transport administration. Then, in the downtime between sitting my GCSEs and getting the results, I got a call from my sister Kate who was working at Glastonbury Festival. Perhaps feeling sorry for her younger brother and his staid countryside existence, she announced that were I to head up to Somerset three days before the festival started, she had the sway to get me and a friend on to the site. Finally my life was turning into a *Loaded* editorial.

I had of course watched the Glastonbury Festival on television throughout my childhood, a time in which it transformed from an anarchic hippy paradise with inadequate fencing into a Radio 1-friendly, commercial juggernaut with inadequate fencing. While it represented the only weekend of the year when the West Country was considered the place to be, it hadn't initially appealed to me. Channel 4's coverage of the event could best be summed up as having a title sequence of bongo drums over footage of a huge dragon puppet and some unicyclists shot through a psychedelic filter. Combined with the other fact I knew about Glastonbury – that my dad had been to the first festival – it left me with little doubt that attending was not for me. I could do without a weekend being forced to take hallucinogenic drugs or, worse, being taught how to juggle.[92]

However, throughout the '90s, with the rise into the mainstream of the indie music that Glastonbury had often supported, the festival slowly had the edges smoothed off and became a more mainstream event, making it far more palatable to a straight like me. Coverage even moved to the BBC – where they made the bizarre choice to focus on showing the bands rather than the unicyclists – and it somehow become part of the summer calendar alongside Wimbledon and the Boat Race. In short, it seemed to now have the exact level of anarchy and debauchery for me to handle.

I had decided to give the second place on the train to Castle Cary station to my friend Robin, deeming him the person I knew with a brand closest to the Glastonbury spirit I was looking for. Robin had always been excitingly alternative – his dad's house didn't have a TV, he somehow got away with wearing a hoodie rather than a school jumper and for his GCSE art coursework he submitted a picture of Mother Teresa with a blood-red

---

[92] The largest ever crowd at Glastonbury remains not for Beyoncé in 2011 or the Rolling Stones in 2013 but for the anarchist folk band the Levellers, who reportedly played to 300,000 people on the Pyramid Stage in 1994. This illustrates two things: 1. The type of crowd the festival attracted in the early '90s. 2. Just how bad the fences were – the capacity for the whole site was meant to be 150,000.

tear ('Thought provoking' Mr Harron). Most excitingly, he played drums in a band called Weedle. For those who aren't au fait with drug lingo, Weedle had chosen that name because it contained the word weed, something they smoked occasionally but mentioned with a regularity that only 16-year-old boys who smoke cannabis can. If the name Weedle was too subtle a hint to their passion for the green, they would hammer it home by opening their gigs with a song called 'One Day in Amsterdam'. The fact they had only been to Amsterdam once on a school music trip was not dwelled upon in the lyrics.

Arriving at Castle Cary station we met my sister and it became apparent she had overstated the sway she had on getting us into the festival. In actual fact her plan involved smuggling us on to the site under a tarpaulin in the back of a transit van like we were escaping the Soviet Union rather than, as we believed, entering adulthood. To this day I have no idea why we needed to arrive three days before the festival started for her to execute this plan; I can only presume the tarpaulin was being used from Wednesday as a finishing touch to the Pyramid Stage.

Despite early doubts, the tarpaulin plan went off without a hitch and we found ourselves inside the festival. Once we had got over the fact that, despite it being 1999, the place was still full of jugglers, we found our friends Beanie and Jamie, who had got into the festival by buying tickets (squares!). More importantly, we discovered that Beanie had brought with him the coolest of all the drugs, a home-baked hash brownie. While Robin was of course excited about this, I wasn't as nervous as you would have presumed I would be. My main issue with weed up until this point had been my mild asthma, so the cake felt like an exciting loophole to begin my experiments with Class C substances. So, on our first night at the festival, the four of us made the bold decision to share the whole baking dish (I have no idea why he hadn't decanted it into Tupperware) before heading out to experience the true excitement of a festival three days before any bands were actually due to play.

It soon became apparent that the lack of bands was the least of our problems. Our main issue was that it turned out Beanie had the kind of laissez-faire attitude to measuring ingredients you would expect from a man with the name Beanie and we had consumed a full baking dish of the world's most potent hash brownie. Within minutes we all began to hallucinate. Then, while I was dealing with the realisation that I was seeing the ground as muddy even though it hadn't rained (what a pathetic hallucination), I somehow became split off from the group. Whether for reasons of panic or reaction to the herb, at this point my mouth became the driest it has ever been and rather than sourcing some water to remedy this it felt logical to me that the best thing to do was repeatedly lick the back of my throat. Around this time in the Premier League there had been a spate of footballers being knocked unconscious and swallowing their tongue, only being saved from death by other players pulling their tongue out of their throat. You wouldn't expect this to be the main thing someone would think about on their first drugs trip but suddenly this fear became my sole focus.[93]

For the next hour I walked around the site lost, trying to get moisture into my mouth by licking the back of my throat but at the same time worrying I was about to swallow my tongue and die. Or, worse, swallow my tongue, survive and end up on an episode of 999. After an hour of walking and worrying, I eventually managed to navigate my way into the welfare tent and, preparing for them to kick into to action, explained I was about to swallow my tongue. It didn't cause the panic I had been expecting and, ignoring my explanation of what had happened to John Fashanu when Wimbledon played Spurs, they decided I was just some loser who couldn't take smoking a bit of weed and made me sit down on a chair with a blanket over my legs. A position I slept in for the next 11 hours.

I woke up the next morning and made my way back to camp only to find that while I was in welfare, Robin had arrived back to the campsite, just in time to throw up his portion of the hash cake in our tent porch. As the days

---

[93] A couple of years after this I took magic mushrooms at Glastonbury and the only thing I hallucinated was a cricket pavilion. I fear hallucinogenic drugs really open a window into the fact that I have the boring subconscious of a BBC 5 Live sports reporter.

at the festival passed and the sun shone, the vomit baked and an unforgettably acrid stench permeated into where we slept. It was by a distance the best weekend of my life so far. Who needed to be Gary and Tony sitting at home drinking cans in *Men Behaving Badly* – I had experienced *Loaded*-style hedonism and it was even better than it looked in the magazine.

'Look how dark it is outside'
Total Eclipse: Live
BBC1, 9:45am, 11 August 1999

For the first time in living memory Devon was the place to be. It was purely an accident of astronomical alignment, of course, but we were happy to take it. The first total solar eclipse to hit the UK since 1927 would only be 100 per cent in the West Country. Those losers in London may have Wembley Stadium and a really big HMV but they were only going to see 96% of the sun blocked out by the moon. It would hardly be worth looking for.

Devon and Cornwall, population 1.1 million, was expecting 4 million eclipse chasers. It felt like quite a lot but what did I know? I had never experienced the thrill of it going dark for two minutes in the middle of the morning before. The West Country survives on its tourist industry so you would presume the eclipse would be welcomed by the region. However, alongside excitement at the opportunity to sell out-of-towners eclipse-themed tea towels, the region was gripped by panic. How would we deal with that many people?

In the months leading up to the eclipse the local papers were full of stories about supermarkets worrying they would run out of food, the nation facing up to a shortage of Porta-loos as they were all shipped down to the West Country and fears the region's reservoirs would run dry, leading to that most '90s of things: a hosepipe ban. Really, it had been a mistake for the total eclipse to choose to appear in an area without the infrastructure to cope, but to be fair to the West Country, we had only had 72 years to prepare.

It is hard to pinpoint the most embarrassing moment in the West Country's months of pre-eclipse panic. Perhaps when Devon Police asked for Exeter City, Plymouth Argyle and Torquay United to help out by playing their games away that weekend, greatly overestimating the pull these clubs would have on weekend crowds. Or perhaps when MPs in Cornwall told the government that they were going to have to appoint a Minister for the Eclipse, surely the most under-whelming role in the history of governmental office. Some people are tasked with keeping world peace and trading with international superpowers, others are tasked with seeing that everyone has enough toilets when the moon goes past the sun over Bideford.

While half the West Country worried about the impact of the eclipse, the other half decided they were going to profit from it. And in a surprise to everyone – most of all myself – I found myself in the second camp. By this point my sister Fran had moved to Newquay and got a job in one of its many tourist shops working for a man called

Brian. Brian, whose business up until this point was built on selling shark's-tooth necklaces to teenagers who couldn't afford to go to Ayia Napa, had decided the eclipse would provide his pension and had invested his savings in hundreds of boxes of solar eclipse viewing glasses. If you've never worn a pair of these – and in all likelihood you have only had a window of two minutes in your life to do so – they have cardboard frames like those 3D glasses you get at the cinema but with black lenses, allowing you to look at the sun safely but offering you no help if you want to watch *WALL-E* in three dimensions.

By this point the government had made it clear that you shouldn't look directly at the sun during the solar eclipse for fear of damaging the retinas in your eyes, so it seemed logical everybody would be needing a pair of these glasses. Particularly because the only other option suggested for following the eclipse was something called a pinhole camera. This involved putting a hole in a piece of paper with a pin and using that to project a small circle of sunlight on a different piece of paper, then watching the shadow of the eclipse occur on that piece of paper, never looking up at the once-in-a-generation celestial event occurring in the sky above you. If that is your idea of fun, you can have that thrill anytime you want with a torch and an orange – knock yourself out.

With this kind of competition there was little doubt the solar eclipse viewing glasses were a goldmine; my sister was sure of it. So sure in fact that she made it clear to me that I would be an idiot not to buy myself a box to sell on. Despite having absolutely no means of selling them, anywhere to sell them or any sales experience, I decided this was an opportunity too good to miss and went in three ways with my friends Ben and Jeffrey (not the hippy ice-cream guys) on a box of 100 pairs for £80. At a potential RRP of £4 a pair (*checks calculator watch*) . . . £400 in total! . . . minus £80 investment . . . divided by three . . . £106.66 profit each!

Problem one. Within 48 hours of us handing over the money and receiving the box of glasses, the government made an announcement that they could no longer recommend people using the solar eclipse viewing glasses as a simple scratch to a lens could blind you. This was not the start I needed, Blair and his cronies jumping on the shadow crossing the paper bandwagon. As someone who had backed the New Labour project, this felt like a huge slap in the face, perhaps greater even than the subsequent invasion of Iraq. Maybe Blair wasn't the man I thought he was and I should have believed the Tories' 'New Labour New Danger' poster showing him with demon eyes. Eyes that I can only assume had been turned red when he looked at the sun, having grown tired of his pinhole camera.

Despite being lumbered with a box of 100 potential retina-based lawsuits, we weren't to be beaten and decided we had to try to sell our glasses anyway. For a reason I still can't fathom, our first tactic was to go shop to shop, seeing if they wanted to buy some pairs to sell on, like uninvited travelling salesmen. Even more bizarrely we decided to target this sales pitch at proper high street chains. Simply walking into WHSmith in Newton Abbot and asking the person on the till if the shop would like to purchase some solar eclipse viewing glasses, then watching them look at us with an expression that said, 'Are you aware how shops work? We are meant to sell you stuff.' It was a tough way to learn that the people on the tills in WHSmith didn't wield the power at head office that we thought.

With the wholesale option gone, we next decided to approach the man in the street, or more specifically, people on the beach in Torquay. Going up to holidaymakers like we were selling homemade jewellery on the Copacabana, rather than Government-discredited glasses on the English Riviera. I don't know when you feel you would be most likely to buy eclipse viewing glasses, but I would guess it isn't when approached by a teenager as you come out of the sea soaking wet and without your wallet a week before the eclipse is even about to happen. We ended the day with zero pairs sold. It was an early lesson in the cut and thrust of business and has given me a lot more pity for struggling teams on *The Apprentice* ever since.[94]

With the eclipse approaching and panic setting in, we had one final throw of the dice. A friend of my dad's pulled some strings and got us a pitch on Totnes market the Friday before sundown. To give you an idea of Totnes market, we were sandwiched between a stall selling homemade herbal remedies and one selling healing crystals, so at

---

[94] It hasn't.

least customers were used to products rejected by the mainstream medical community. Finally we had found our market and somehow in the space of a few hours we managed to sell most of the glasses, and by somehow I mean we halved the price. After petrol, parking, stall rent and an ice cream on the beach, I had made a tenner for a week's work. Mainly I felt relief, knowing if I had lost that money it would have made the experience of seeing the sun eclipsed by the moon bittersweet, particularly as I would be doing it through my own unsold stock.

As the eclipse approached, discussion turned away from the dangers of dodgy glasses and on to where people would be watching it. It felt like a big decision. You needed to be somewhere meaningful for such a celestially important matter, be that the meeting point of two ley lines or at the official party on Plymouth Hoe (sponsored by Stella Artois).

Of all the events of the decade, the eclipse felt like the one least suited to television. This is not a criticism of God – he/she can't be blamed for not making it TV-friendly – but really coverage should have simply been a holding card on the screen saying, 'Look out of the window'. Despite this, the build-up to the event on TV had still been huge, the BBC painting itself as the home of the eclipse with special episodes of *Blue Peter* and *The O-Zone,* and, bizarrely, Radio 1 promising to cover the sound of the solar eclipse live. For anyone unfamiliar with astronomy, that is called silence. Most excitingly, *EastEnders* had a special eclipse storyline in which Mel followed Ian down to Devon for the eclipse in an attempt to win him back after they had broken up. The *Radio Times* synopsis for the episode read: 'Can Ian hide his true feelings, and will anyone see the moon eclipse the sun?'; an exciting double cliffhanger presumably based on Ian Beale wrestling with both his emotions and his ability to use a pinhole camera.[95]

Watching the footage of BBC1's coverage of the eclipse now it feels surreal that it was televised at all. It is a hugely staid viewing experience hosted by *999*'s Michael Buerk, presumably with the hope that the moon would fall out of the sky and someone would need to be rescued from a near-death experience. The best bit of the whole thing is the brief moment when the screen goes completely black and Buerk says, 'Look how dark it is outside,' before someone points out to viewers that they have just lost the picture. Sadly, this is as exciting as it gets. I have a friend who claims he remembers the coverage including Noel Edmonds 'chasing the eclipse on Concorde', but there is no mention of this on the show and actually, if I'm honest, I don't fully know what 'chasing the eclipse on Concorde' means. It does, however,

---

[95] I've just checked and *Coronation Street* had a far more unappetising eclipse storyline involving Spider and Toyah setting up a tent in the local park to watch the eclipse, but missing it because they were having sex for the first time instead. I suspect this was meant to be seen as romantic but the idea of the two of them having sex in a tent in a local park at 11am strikes me as borderline illegal, whether it was briefly dark or not.

say a lot about Noel Edmonds that when I was told this I assumed it to be true.

This coverage was all new to me, however, as despite having experienced the last decade of my life through the television, I considered the eclipse a step too far. And so on the day I found myself watching the eclipse from one of the local tors on Dartmoor, a place that had the right amount of poignant relevance without having the wrong amount of out-of-towners. As 100 or so locals stood waiting for the moon to pass the sun, all I could think was that everyone was wearing the glasses. Where had they bought them from? It wasn't just on Dartmoor. Look back at photos of that day now and around the country all you will see is people in the bloody specs. There are thousands of people wearing them on Plymouth Hoe (sponsored by Stella Artois), policemen in London with them on and more than one photo of people putting them on their dogs.[96] Who knew the mistake we made all along was targeting the human market?

Maybe the reason I was so focused on people wearing the glasses was that in the end I didn't even get to see the moon pass the sun. When the moment of the total eclipse came to Devon, we couldn't make out a thing – it had clouded over. British summertime: nature's solar eclipse viewing

---

[96] To be fair, if you have a dog and a spare pair of eclipse shades and don't pop them on him, at least briefly, then you need to question what you are doing with your life.

glasses. Even worse than the cloud in Devon was the news that they had clear skies in London. Somehow even when it was Devon's day, it was not the place to be.

The next total eclipse in the UK will occur on 12 August 2026. One benefit of climate change in the intervening period is that I am confident it'll be a hot day this time. I still have a few pairs of shades kicking around in my parents' shed if anyone needs them.

'Governments shouldn't try to run tourist attractions'
2000 Today
BBC1, 9:15am, 31 December 1999

Like any public panic, from Covid-19 to how to correctly hold a sparkler, the government decided to educate the nation with a TV advertising campaign. At a cost of £10 million they launched Action 2000, a campaign title that was both completely uninformative and a perfect illustration of how adding the number 2000 to anything instantly makes it feel like the naffest thing in the world.[97] Action 2000 would address the greatest fear of our age: the coming dangers of the millennium bug. A dystopian future in which you might have to redo your accounts for the previous tax year. *Tomorrow's World* hadn't warned us about this apocalyptic hell.

With the slogan 'you need to be in the business of getting ready' – a sentence which makes less sense every time you read it – the adverts captured the mood of the nation with

---

[97] The first prize for this goes to an Indian takeaway near where I live called Curry 2000.

futuristic images such as circuit boards and binary numbers interspersed with footage of people looking pensive at work, from Colin Marshall, 'the MD of British Airways', to Edmund O'Donnell, 'Farmer'. As it all drew to a close, a voiceover implored worried viewers to call a phone number for that perfectly '90s of items: a 'free action pack'. Presumably the information wasn't available online as we didn't want the computers to know we were on to them.

The millennium bug was the biggest cloud on the horizon as the end of the 20th century approached. The fear was that computers programmed with just a two-digit year would tick over from 99 to 00 and think they had travelled back in time to 1900, presumably giving up the ghost because they hadn't been invented yet. It was a similar situation to the time my dad bought a second-hand Datsun Sunny that was so old we got to watch the milometer tick round back to zero on the way to school one morning. But while this didn't have much impact on a car that was old enough to be deemed road tax exempt, no one really knew how it would impact the advanced minds of our modern Pentium processor-enabled computers. Mainly I remember the phrase 'planes will fall out of the sky' being bandied around a lot, although why anyone was planning to spend their millennium in a plane that could stop working at the stroke of midnight was anyone's guess. Perhaps Noel Edmonds planning to chase the year 2000 in a Concorde.

The bug played out as a perfect metaphor for the turn of the millennium itself, a breathless and overly important build-up to nothing really changing. In fact, beyond the worries about computers misfiring, the main thing occupying people's minds as the millennium approached was looking back, mainly through the medium of lists and countdowns. In the months leading up to the turn of the century it was impossible to turn on the TV or open a magazine without seeing a poll of the songs, person or train station of fewer than four platforms of the century. And the one thing that united all of these polls was, whatever the topic, you could be sure it would be topped by Robbie Williams. It was as if the previous 2000 years had been bookended by the two most important people that had ever walked the earth, Jesus and Robbie. The main difference being that Jesus went into the desert and was tempted by the Devil, while Robbie Williams went to Glastonbury and drank lager with Liam Gallagher.

The reality was that – putting aside the views of a few exceedingly religious types who thought the world was going to end[98] – the main issue of the millennium was that it was a huge historical event in which nothing was going to actually happen. Nowhere was this problem more apparent than on the BBC's Millennium Eve broadcast, *2000 Today*,[99] a show which (and I can't believe I'm writing

---

[98] Shout out to Argentina's World Cup 1998 goalkeeper Carlos Roa, who retired from football in the summer of 1999 to await the apocalypse on a religious retreat only to re-sign for his former club a year later when it turned out the world hadn't ended.

[99] Another victim of the 2000/naff principle.

this) began its build-up at 9:15am and ran for 28 hours, ending the after-party at 1:30pm the next day, just in time for people to begin the new century by watching *World's Strongest Man*.

Teaming up David Dimbleby and Peter Sissons with Gaby Roslin – to show they had no idea if this was coverage of a breaking news story or a party – the show mainly seemed to be footage of different places around the world hitting midnight, showing it could be a huge non-event wherever you lived. It turns out after 2,000 years of progress, the one uniting factor for humanity across the globe was standing in the dark watching fireworks with cameras flashing for photos that will never be looked at again.

While on the previous couple of New Year's Eves I had gone to friends' houses to inevitably watch *Jools' Annual Hootenanny*, the millennium felt like the first time I needed to celebrate properly. If I had learned anything from Glastonbury and the eclipse it was that not every-thing was best viewed on TV (also on the lessons learned list: always check quantities before making hash brownies and under no circumstances attempt to make money from disposable sunglasses).

Planning in advance I managed to get an invite to the place to be: a night on the piss with my brothers and sisters in Cornwall. Having spent the decade coveting their exciting lives, now I would end it by living like them for one night only. In my head this involved Thailand-style beach parties or crawls around pubs as vibrant as the *TFI Friday* bar. In fact, it meant ringing in the next 1,000 years gathered at the Ferry Lanes in Torpoint. And just to be clear, the Ferry Lanes was not a trendy nightclub in which you might see Wimbledon's Dean Holdsworth, it was the lanes that cars would queue up in to get on the ferry back to Devon from Cornwall. With the ferries stopped for midnight, for some reason this had become the agreed place for locals to gather to bring in the new year. When my children ask me where I was for the millennium, I will have to tell them that I was essentially in a large car park being pummelled by a bitter wind coming off the River Tamar. After years of imagining the life I was missing out on across the Cornish border, the reality was a little disappointing.

Still, it could have been worse. While I was freezing on a riverbank in Cornwall, on TV Tony Blair was belting out 'Auld Lang Syne' while next to him the Queen sported a face that can only be described as absolutely livid. She had every right to be; she had been forced to spend her evening in the Millennium Dome. Surely if one thing symbolised the strange atmosphere of the millennium and people's confusion with what it represented and how to mark the occasion, it was Britain's decision to celebrate the arrival of the year 2000 by erecting a big marquee in south-east London.

My abiding memory of the Dome was that everyone joked that it was going to be shit, and then it was shit. Originally commissioned in 1994 by the Conservative government, the Dome was the kind of project you pitch when you are confident you won't still be in power to have to see it through. However, when New Labour came to office in 1997, Tony Blair decided to double down, seeing the Dome as a symbol of Britain's future, 'a triumph of confidence over cynicism, boldness over blandness, excellence over mediocrity'. After all, this was going to be the world's biggest dome, which it goes without saying is a world record no one has ever wanted to achieve.

Inside the world's biggest dome would be a series of 14 exhibits which would sum up who we were and how we lived, plus two large McDonald's and a cafe called Simply Internet. In one zone they promised the world's largest billboard (another superb record); as tall as a four-storey house, as wide as a Boeing 747, containing a photograph of Richmond Park. Sadly, when the photograph came back from the printers, it became clear that there was a naked man standing in the woods who was only visible once the image was blown up to its record-breaking size. You would be right to think that this is my favourite thing I have discovered when researching this book.

The Dome aimed to bring in 12 million visitors, but in the end attracted 6.5 million people with the bill for the project coming in at a bargain £789 million. It looked like the biggest mark it would leave on culture was that they had to change the map at the start of *EastEnders*. Then a few years later, after rumours it would become the new home to Charlton Athletic, it was transformed into the O2 Arena, a highly profitable tent containing a strip of mid-range high-street restaurants and the UK's most soulless live music venue.

Far from being New Labour's crowning glory, the Dome came to represent the most facile side of the new government, with many believing it was a visual representation of a party that was far more interested in presentation than achievement. Which seems unfair; they had, after all, built a really big dome. 'Hindsight is a wonderful thing,' said Blair, the autumn after it opened. 'If I had my time again I would have listened to those who said governments shouldn't try to run tourist attractions.' Noel Edmonds could have told him that.

While the millennium didn't prove to be the important historical moment or indeed once-in-a-lifetime celebration that everyone had hoped, for me it did arrive at a point when my life was beginning to change. A few months before the new century I had decided not to go to the sixth form of my farmer-heavy secondary school but instead do my A-levels at a big college (!) in Exeter (!!). Maybe eschewing my local school for big college in the Big Smoke (of Devon) was my attempt to leave Dartmoor behind and push my life towards those I had seen on *TFI Friday* or *Men Behaving Badly* or maybe it was just that all my mates were going there and I thought it would be easier to just copy them (it was the second of these). In reality, life at sixth-form college proved to be a frustrating halfway house. Occasionally when we went to Wetherspoons on a Wednesday afternoon I would glimpse the exciting party life, but in reality

I was still living at home with my parents and spending an inordinate amount of time in front of the television in the evenings. The difference was that by now watching television wasn't so much something that I loved, more than just a way for me to kill time. In fact, there would only be one more television show that would take over my life in the way so many had previously.

'Um . . . I've made a mistake'
Big Brother
Channel 4, 10pm, 18 August 2000

Like a lot of shows in this book I hadn't planned to watch *Big Brother*, there was just nothing else on. While putting ten people in a house and filming everything they do now seems a simple and familiar idea that has become the basis for hundreds of other shows, in the year 2000 it felt to me like the least appetising premise for a TV show since Michael Buerk said, 'I'm here at Britain's biggest cattle prod factory, a place you would assume nothing could go wrong . . .'

The closest thing I had seen to *Big Brother* at this point was *Castaway 2000*,[100] a BBC documentary that involved a group of 32 people living on a remote Scottish island to see if they could thrive as a community for a year. Sadly it proved to be a relatively dull experiment, the main achievement of which was not to hold a magnifying glass to the dark heart of human civilisation but to launch the career of Ben Fogle. Still, the whole thing was worth it for the episode

---

[100] Add that to the 2000/naff principle list.

in which the Britpop also-rans Dodgy turned up in a boat and offered to play a gig, only for the islanders to say they would rather they didn't.

Before I turned on the first episode of *Big Brother* all I really knew about it was that it had been a huge hit in Holland. This didn't fill me with hope, my previous experience of European television coming exclusively through *Eurotrash*, a late-night Channel 4 show which painted the Continent and its television as an unfettered hotbed of unhinged and usually sexually explicit goings-on, similar to how I now imagine the dark web.[101] So, it probably didn't help *Big Brother*'s cause over here when in episode one the housemates were given quite a sedate pottery challenge and ended up stripping off, covering themselves in clay and making prints of their naked bodies on the walls. You can claim as much as you want that it is a brave and interesting new TV format, but when a naked builder is getting a laugh by making a clay print of his cock look longer than it should, you are on slightly shaky ground.

Despite (or maybe because of) this start, I found myself being slowly dragged in to *Big Brother*, soon becoming

---

[101] It should be said that understanding the landscape of European culture wasn't the main reason teenage boys watched *Eurotrash*, a show that was the main driving force behind almost all my friends' attempts to talk their parents into letting them have a TV in their bedroom. Full disclosure to any parents reading: it wasn't because we wanted to watch *Rugrats* on a Saturday morning without getting out of bed.

addicted to the thrill of simply watching normal people interacting in a house together. It was a completely fresh television experience and the fact it was shown every night of the week meant it soon came to define the summer of 2000 for me in the way Euro 96 had done four years earlier. The main person Channel 4 had to thank for this success was Nasty Nick Bateman, a posh man in his early thirties who would start the year as a broker in the City and end it releasing a book called *How To Be a Right Bastard*, which I recently bought for 1p on Amazon out of grim curiosity and still feel like I've been had.

The show had all started so well for Nick. In one of the first episodes he had won over the housemates with the heartbreaking story of his fiancée dying in a car crash in the Outback and he had carried on to be the only housemate never to receive a nomination for eviction. However, as the show went on it became apparent to viewers that Nick wasn't the good guy he seemed and in fact he was playing the housemates off against each other to save himself.

What was so intoxicating about it was that because the *Big Brother* house was cut off from the outside world, we were watching this play out in real time but we had no way of stopping it. Even when a member of the public flew a remote control helicopter into the garden with leaflets detailing what Nick was up to, the production team intercepted them before they got to our poor innocent victims. Here was that soap opera the BBC had needed all those years ago. They hadn't needed to build an echoey town in

Spain, they had needed to shove some people in a temporary house on the outskirts of London.

For weeks I wasn't just watching *Big Brother*, I was listening to the radio, buying tabloids and checking teletext for updates. How could I be expected to follow the greatest and most unjust saga of our time through just one hour's television a day? Then, from nowhere, the news broke (on teletext if I remember correctly) that the housemates had rumbled Nasty Nick and he had been removed from the house. It was that moment that never happens in real life: the bully getting their comeuppance and that night at 10pm on Channel 4 we would see it all play out.

The main thing that struck me watching the episode again years later is just how innocent it all feels. So far in this chapter I have implied Nick's actions to be terrible and reprehensible, but for those of you who aren't connoisseurs of the ballad of Nasty Nick, I should just make clear exactly what he was caught doing. Perhaps the most dramatic and shocking moment of television that I can remember watching in the first 18 years of my life can quite simply be boiled down to this: in *Big Brother* you have to nominate other housemates for eviction. You are not allowed to discuss those nominations with other housemates. Nick had been going around doing just that. Worse still, he had been writing down names of people and showing them to the other housemates with a pencil he shouldn't have had.

The nation-gripping drama wasn't about someone cheating on someone and dumping them on *Love Island*;

it wasn't about someone refusing to lie in a coffin of rats on *I'm a Celebrity . . . Get Me Out of Here!*; it was about a man in possession of a contraband pencil. Despite this, even after two decades, the tension and grim fascination of the Nasty Nick confrontation is still utterly compelling. The housemates gather around the kitchen table for a house meeting, Nick sitting opposite Craig, who proves to be a superb cross-examining barrister, in no way undermined by the clay prints of his own penis on the wall behind him. The whole thing is racked by tension and the shot of Nick's unshaven face is so tight you can see him swallow as he is confronted with what he has done. The slow pauses and the feeling out of the accusations and what people know makes it feel like a lower stakes *Tinker Tailor Soldier Spy* or a slightly more accessible version of the Commons Select Committee.

Despite Nick's early denials it soon becomes clear that he has been showing names to the housemates. Darren – a friendly housemate mainly notable for wearing tiny pants and naming one of the chickens Marjorie – has more reason than most to be annoyed as it also transpires that he was the only housemate Nick hadn't shown any names to. 'Where did you get the pencil?' he asks furiously, like Nick has smuggled a can of Coca-Cola into North Korea. Like a master criminal revealing his methods to Hercule Poirot, Nick says he just kept a pencil that was used for one of the tasks. Darren sadly shakes his head and mutters, 'This is sick.'

When the cross-examination is over, Nick goes to the diary room to talk to *Big Brother* about his punishment. He sits down, pauses and, in the high-pitched voice of a ten-year-old trying not to cry, simply says: 'Um . . . I've made a mistake.' Suddenly the evil mastermind that we have spent weeks hating melts away to be replaced by a schoolboy who doesn't want to be in detention. As a viewer it almost makes you feel sorry for him, but not quite. After leaving the diary room Nick sits with Anna as he awaits his fate. 'Was the story about your fiancée true?' she asks, and Nick tells her it wasn't. 'Nick, you're so strange,' she replies.

Eventually it is decided by *Big Brother* that Nick cannot stay in the house and he is ushered out by a side gate. After all the drama, suddenly as the gate opens you see the house for what it is: some barbed wire and prefab buildings just outside Stratford. It is hard to believe that it is the most impenetrable and talked-about building in the country. As Nick gets in his car, Nicola looks out of the gate and mutters, 'Oh my God, there's cameras there,' seemingly forgetting that inside they are being filmed 24 hours a day.

By the end of that summer *Big Brother* had changed British television forever, and along with ITV's *Popstars* it would be the catalyst for the beginning of the age of reality TV. Without these two shows there would have been no *Love Island*, *The X Factor* or *I'm a Celebrity . . . Get Me Out of Here*! (I will leave you to have your own opinion on whether that is a good thing). *Big Brother* marked the beginning of a new century for television and, more importantly to me, the end of the '90s. What better way to finish?

It is irresistible to label decades as having their own unique characteristics, particularly if they were the decade in which you grew up. And while I'm aware that putting a decade into a box involves shortcuts, exceptions and prominence of your own experience of the time, for all the Jim Davidson TV vehicles and penalty shoot-out defeats, it is almost impossible for me not to see the '90s as having a more positive and hopeful character than the decades that have followed. Maybe that optimism for politics, sport, music and the eclipse went unfulfilled, but that doesn't mean that it wasn't fun to, for a few years, live in that bubble, a time when it felt like there was so much for me to be excited about. Or maybe that was just the feeling of being young.

At the time of writing it feels like every year there is a knife-edge election or referendum in which the future of Western democracy is at stake and, at best, people are further divided into two constantly warring political extremes. It is a time when global conspiracy theories are spread from the White House rather than from schoolchildren who have watched too many episodes of *The X-Files*. A time when the richest clubs in football want to form a closed shop Super League rather than play in a Premier League in which the best player eats two McMuffins on the way to training. A time when Gus Honeybun has gone to the great rabbit warren in the sky. In comparison, sandwiched between the fall of the Berlin Wall in 1989 and 9/11 terrorist attacks in 2001 and resultant wars, the '90s feels almost like a self-contained period of naive political and social hope.

Maybe in a way, Tony Blair achieved his aim and the Millennium Dome did act as a perfect symbol of Britain, not a representation of its future as he intended but of the decade we were leaving. For those with a half-empty perspective, the Dome could be seen as the crowning moment of '90s excess: expensive, slightly embarrassing and full of baseless hubris – it was the *Be Here Now* of tourist attractions. For those of us looking from a half-full perspective, perhaps the Dome represented what an optimistic time the '90s was, an era when people could convince themselves that a big dome with an internet cafe would attract 12 million visitors in a year. Only in a time as affluent and carefree as the '90s would it be felt that the biggest news story of the day was government money being wasted on an underwhelming theme park. For the Millennium Dome to be the biggest concern on the front pages of the country's newspapers, well, did we ever have it so good?

No one was thinking this at the time, of course; they were excited for the limitless potential of what was to come. As Big Ben struck midnight on the BBC's millennium coverage, David Dimbleby brought in the next 1,000 years by saying: 'The last year of the last millennium slouches offstage, to make way for the youthful entry of the new.' I think it would be fair to say he couldn't have been more wrong. It was the decade just gone that felt youthful and exciting; the one to follow would be defined by 9/11, the Iraq War and the global financial crash. Still, it would have been a bold prediction from Dimbleby to call that one at midnight on BBC1.

But let's not blame Dimbleby for his prediction; after all, I am a man who spent the '90s believing the internet wouldn't take off. In fact, the following decade would see the launch of Facebook, Twitter, YouTube and the iPhone – I was an idiot. One consequence of this was that it meant the '90s was to be the last decade when the television was the most important piece of furniture in the house (or at least it was in my house). In fact, if you consider that in the '60s and '70s millions of households didn't have TVs, and even the first couple of years of the '80s were lived with only three channels and without the debatable joys of breakfast TV, perhaps the '90s was the only decade that television dominated from start to finish, every hour of every day.

Towards the end of the decade the BBC approached Caroline Aherne and asked her to write a sitcom for her character Mrs Merton. To get the deal across the line they also agreed to let her make a far less obviously commercial idea that she had been desperate to write. *The Royle Family* took a realist approach to the family sitcom dispensing with a laughter track, most elements of plot and usually taking place in one continuous scene. While the sitcoms of the '90s had played to studio audiences for big laughs, *The Royle Family* went in the opposite direction, shot in low light and getting its laughs almost entirely from character and conversational nuance. More than any other show it would set the tone for comedy in the next decade.

The Royle Family's greatest nod to realism, however, was how the Royles spent their time – watching television. As the family came and went in the lounge, the TV was constantly on in the corner. Occasionally referenced but often just babbling away, it showed a family that lived their life around the box. They talked through *TFI Friday*, bet on the *Antiques Roadshow* and answered the questions on *Who Wants to be a Millionaire?*. This was the first programme that showed us ourselves as we watched TV.

The titles for the show began with the TV being switched on and the family framed staring at the screen, soundtracked by the wistful Oasis B-side 'Half the World Away'. Whatever side you were on in the fabricated Britpop war of the mid-'90s, there was no doubt Oasis had become the defining rock band of the decade. Years later, when the band had split after one brotherly argument too many, their story was captured in the film *Supersonic*, a documentary charting their rise from a Manchester council estate to playing at Knebworth to 250,000 people in 1996. As the film comes to an end, we see footage of the band landing by helicopter backstage while over the top Noel talks about what the event represented. 'It was the pre-digital age, things meant more. It was just a great time to be alive, let alone be in Oasis,' he says, before adding with his usual mix of soundbite and hubris, 'It was the last great gathering of the people before the birth of the internet.'

Epilogue

Big Brother was the last TV show I loved with a passion you only can growing up. By the time I reached 18 I had begun to suspect there may be more fun to be had going out with my friends than there was to be found watching *How Do They Do That?*. Just before *Big Brother* had begun, I had returned from my second trip to Glastonbury. I hadn't come as close to death as the first time but I had still loved being in a field with my friends drinking 7% cider and watching the mismatched headliners of David Bowie (returning to the festival having played the first Glastonbury 30 years earlier) and Travis (didn't quite have enough big hits so had to pad the set out with a cover of 'Baby One More Time').

Maybe one of the reasons I loved *Big Brother* was that it was a show I wanted to be a part of. Not because I wanted to be a reality TV star and release my own single like Craig's 'At This Time of Year', but simply because it looked such fun to be living in a house with people of your own age, getting drunk and possibly using a contraband pencil.

The following summer I moved to Manchester to go to university. I would love to say I had chosen to go to Manchester by weighing up the quality of universities and suitability of courses, but the reality was I liked the idea of living in Manchester because that is where Oasis came from. While if I had to pick I had preferred Blur, my loyalty wasn't strong enough for me to choose to go to the University of Colchester, if such a thing existed. While it may seem counter-productive to move to the city that was home to my ultimate kryptonite, Manchester United, I had been assured by shows like *Fantasy Football League* that their fans were from everywhere except Manchester. Real locals like Noel and Liam supported City, so in fact this was another superb reason to go there. On arrival this proved to be complete bollocks, much like in Devon, everyone seemed to support United. It turned out that was a pain I just couldn't escape.

Before leaving for university my parents announced that they wanted to buy me a going away present. I asked for a television. This way I could have one in my room in case I didn't like what people were watching in the shared lounge. Upon arrival, it turned out not only was there no TV provided in the main living area (lounge is a big word it turns out) but no one else had brought one with them so mine was sacrificed to the greater good. It was not a good start.

My halls were in Fallowfield, a south Manchester student district in which anyone who has fully examined the prospectus and written a list of pros and cons would choose to live. While I had been excited to go to university and move away from home, until the day of arrival I hadn't really considered just how different Manchester would be from Dartmoor, as strange as this seems to write now. On that first night there I walked out of my front door – locking it behind me for the first time in my life – and wandered the 20 yards it now took me to get to the main strip on Oxford Road, lit neon by a collage of signs for takeaways and late-licence bars. It felt to my eyes like I had moved to Times Square. That night my housemates and I went out and got drunk on what would now be hugely illegal drinks offers until the last of the bars were closed, got a takeaway and fell asleep. We then repeated this every night for the next week. And most nights for the next year.

Within a couple of months I had sold the telly to a mate. I had found an even better way to waste my life.

Bonus Chapters

'I was pissing by the door, when I heard two shats' *'Allo 'Allo!*
BBC1, 8pm, 9 November 1992

In 2014 I moved to east London. While I told my girlfriend I was excited to move to the area because of the excellent range of independent patisseries and shops selling meaningless slogans masquerading as art, in reality my main reason for excitement was that my local pub would be The Royal Oak. The reason I was buzzing to live near The Royal Oak wasn't because it did an excellent battered halloumi and chips (although it really is excellent), but simply because I had been told that it was the pub from *Goodnight Sweetheart*. No, I couldn't afford to move into the Big Breakfast house or be bothered to travel to Melbourne to visit Ramsay Street but this was (a distant) third best.

To my surprise, once I had moved to the area The Royal Oak didn't prove to be the thrilling local point of interest I had hoped. In fact, my proximity to a key location for a forgotten '90s sitcom had almost no impact on my life, save for the times I would go for a drink with a friend and drop the information into conversation with under-whelming results.

Me: Interestingly this is actually the pub from *Goodnight Sweetheart*.

Friend: Is that that sitcom with Rodney from *Only Fools and Horses* going back in time?

Me: Yes, that's the one.

Friend: Oh, OK. Have you heard the new LCD Sound-system album?

And repeat with every new friend I took there.

While The Royal Oak didn't make me desperate to revisit the show and watch all six series like a modern box set, it did keep it in my mind. So when I finished this book and a few people asked me if there were any programmes that I regretted not being able to include – presumably expecting me to say big hits like *Friends*, *EastEnders* or *Woof!* – the only show I ever thought to mention was *Goodnight Sweet-heart*.[1] I want to be clear this isn't because I think it is one of the great underrated shows of the decade (it very much isn't), or because I feel it needs to be re-evaluated, possibly increasing the value of property in the area surrounding

---

[1] This isn't totally true. I also regret that the book doesn't discuss *The Krypton Factor*, a show that featured contestants trying to slot together a model of a human genome, do an army assault course and land an aeroplane on a flight simulator in the space of half an hour. It's a shame we don't have more time to dig deeper into the sheer madness of that combination of tasks.

The Royal Oak (although that would be nice). It is simply because it was a show with a premise that made *You Bet!* feel as mundane as *Good Morning with Anne and Nick*.

Goodnight Sweetheart followed Gary Sparrow, a TV repair man in modern-day Cricklewood who finds a time portal that takes him back to the East End during the Blitz. On the surface it's a quirky yet pretty standard premise, but what makes the show still strike me as something mad to put on BBC1 at prime family time was the main use Gary had for this time portal. Each episode he travelled back in time not to help the Allies' war efforts or even just to have a bit of an explore of wartime London, but to cheat on his wife with a barmaid from the past. Yes, the BBC were expecting us, the viewers, to sit at home and laugh in support of a man using his modern-day knowledge and access to stockings to sleep with a woman who in the present day would have been in her seventies.

Like Gus Honeybun or a school that couldn't cook its own meals, for some reason it took me years to stop and think, 'What the hell was that all about?' But there was a simple reason for this. *Goodnight Sweetheart* was merely a footnote in a decade of insane primetime sitcoms, a time when being on before 9pm on BBC1 didn't mean that a show had to play it safe, but instead meant that you could find yourself watching two separate family sitcoms about married men shagging around during the Second World War. It is odd to think that *Goodnight Sweetheart* was the more pedestrian of these wartime sex parties, but then it was up against *'Allo 'Allo*.

'*Allo* '*Allo* was set in a cafe in occupied Paris and followed owner René Artois as he attempted to remain on the good side of the Allies, the Nazis and his wife, who – it won't totally surprise you to learn – he was cheating on with a variety of waitresses. Perhaps the most astounding thing about '*Allo* '*Allo* wasn't that again we were being asked to identify with a main character who had no respect for his marriage vows, but just how many main characters featured in the show. While *Friends* had six core characters and *Frasier* had to make do with four, '*Allo* '*Allo* could call on twenty-two regular characters. Twenty-two! To give you some perspective that is more characters than feature in *Great Expectations* (I assume, I've never read it). I've just found a publicity shot for the show, and it features a huge group of soldiers, Nazis and comedy Frenchmen, and feels less like a promo for a sitcom and more like a group shot of a well-attended but badly misjudged fancy-dress party.

While a sitcom with twenty-two regular characters may sound like a lot to take in, in reality it was quite a simple watch because each character came with a ready-made catchphrase (which, due to the amount of other cast members that also needed to speak in the episode, was usually about all they got to say). Let's be clear, these were great catchphrases. Beyond *The Simpsons*, I cannot think of a show that has given us more classic catchphrases across the decade, from the timeless, 'Listen very carefully, I will say this only once', to the brilliant, 'It is I, Leclerc', to the much needed, 'How are the BBC able to afford to pay this many actors?'

Beyond the difficulty of finding enough dressing rooms for the cast, there were two main issues for the producers of *'Allo 'Allo*. Firstly, how do you make Nazis funny? Once they had solved this problem by calling the leader of the Gestapo Herr Flick, they could move on to the second big sticking point. How do you deal with the fact that all these characters are from different countries, and so would have been speaking in different languages? The answer is that they all spoke English, but just in hugely stereotyped national accents. How do you communicate that Captain Alberto Bertorelli is Italian? Simply give him the catchphrase, 'What a mistake-a to make-a'. Genius. On the one hand it all feels a little reductive and offensive, on the other I bet *Eldorado* would have lasted a bit longer if it had taken this approach.

Anyone who has seen an episode of *'Allo 'Allo* will tell you that the character who dealt best with the languages issues was Officer Crabtree, an English policeman who thought he could speak French but was actually terrible at it. Because of the way the show worked, this didn't involve him speaking French badly, but instead meant that he would mangle English words in a French accent with us having to believe he was mangling the French words he couldn't say because he was English (simple). It may sound like a complex comic concept, but really what we are talking about here is endless innuendo. He didn't say, 'You should be grateful that the RAF bombers are still fighting for freedom,' but instead said, 'You should be grateful that the RAF bummers are still farting for freedom.' Instead of, 'I was passing by the door, when I heard two shots,' he would say, 'I was pissing by the door, when I heard two shats.' I loved it. Although I should add that I was nine when the show ended.

While on paper *'Allo 'Allo* was a mess, I, the rest of my family and the nation found it hilarious. In fact, it was a good rule of thumb in the '90s that the madder the family sitcom, the better it was. This was a decade in which *The Vicar of Dibley* featured a character whose main joke was to answer everything by saying, 'No, no, no, no, no, yes.' A decade when *The Brittas Empire* killed off its main character at the end of two separate series and featured a receptionist who kept her three children in cupboards under the desk. In some ways the '90s wasn't a simpler time.

'It Could Be You'
The National Lottery Live
BBC1, 7pm, 19 November 1994

An armoured lorry is led by five motorcycles through the London night, circling Trafalgar Square and Piccadilly Circus. But who could be the driver of this mysterious vehicle and what are they transporting? It's Noel Edmonds of course, driving the prize money for the first ever National Lottery to BBC Television Centre. 'I must say the whole atmosphere surrounding *The National Lottery Live* is really something very special. Within the next hour somebody watching this show is going to be a millionaire,' Edmonds says, before taking his eyes momentarily off the road to look down the camera. 'And it could be you!'

In the cold light of day is there anything more boring to watch on television than the National Lottery draw? Of all the claims made about the lottery in the build-up to its launch, the strangest surely was that it was fun to play. Anyone who has ever bought a lottery ticket knows fun is not an emotion that has ever been associated with watching six numbers you haven't picked come out of a snazzed-up tombola. Far closer to the surface are boredom, disappointment and confusion over why that voiceover man keeps telling us stats about the number 44. However, on the night of the first ever draw we weren't to know that this was what we were in for. We thought we were viewing a huge moment in television history and the start of a must-see event for Saturdays to come.

Noel Edmonds knew as much as he drove his lorry into the studio, gleefully telling the audience, 'On my second lap of Piccadilly Circus I was thinking, bearing in mind the money at stake, I might do a swift left and be off with it . . . but no amount of money would make me not be here this evening for a moment of television history.' At the time this made sense. In hindsight I think Noel made the wrong decision, because it would have been the greatest story of the '90s had TV's most recognisable face absconded with the prize money for the UK's first ever National Lottery.

It is still difficult to comprehend how extraordinary it felt for the BBC to suddenly be giving away millions of pounds on a Saturday night; *Gladiators* gave away £5,000, *Big Break* gave away a television with teletext. The most I had won before the launch of the National Lottery was £16 on the Grand National, and here was the chance to win millions of pounds with the added bonus that a horse wouldn't die in the process (unless the draw went very wrong indeed). In the weeks leading up to the first draw no one talked about anything else. It was the ultimate in water cooler television, ignoring the fact that in Devon in 1994 no one had a water cooler. All we wanted to discuss was how we would spend the money if we won the jackpot. For me it was a simple decision: buy Plymouth Argyle, The House of Marbles and one of those stereos where you can put in 6 CDs at a time (and if I didn't win enough to buy all of them, then just the stereo).

Considering the mood of the nation it is difficult to think of a more perfect advertising slogan in history than 'It Could Be You'. Even Prime Minister John Major was photographed buying a ticket in a local newsagent, smiling thinly as he marked his numbers down with a biro. Papers released in 2019 show that, astonishingly, there was a concern among Major's advisors that he might win (a 14-million-to-one chance) and that it would play badly with the electorate. This is how much lottery fever had now made people lose all perspective, that a key concern for John Major's inner circle was how he was going to explain to the nation that he was a brand-new multimillionaire.[1]

And this was the problem. Due to a mix of the advertising campaign, the excitement of the new and our own stupidity, it isn't an exaggeration to say that before the first draw, every person you spoke to was confident they were going to win. We had heard the odds were 14 million to one, but for some reason had discarded that knowledge

---

[1] In the end it was decided that were Major to win, the money would go to charity. He must have been livid; what a waste of a new biro.

in favour of an advert showing a big hand coming through the night sky to tell us we were the chosen one. For a small period of time, the country was overcome with a baseless confidence towards their own lucky destiny normally only seen in contestants on *Deal or No Deal* (perhaps it was Noel that had done it to us). Consequently, watching the first National Lottery draw would turn out to be an exercise in dealing with the surprise news that, somehow, we weren't now millionaires.

The first episode of *The National Lottery Live* was watched by 22 million people across the UK. (What were the other 38 million people doing? Didn't they want to be millionaires?) A more baffling stat is that the show was an hour long. How long did these balls take to come out of the machine? What else would we be watching? The answer was filler. The main body of the show involved Noel running a competition to see which audience member would get to turn on the machine for the first ever National Lottery draw (the honour!). 'Here we have 49 ordinary souls,' says Noel, announcing those competing like he is the Grim Reaper, before leading us through a string of baffling games, such as a competition to see which team weighs the nearest to 1,000lb. Elsewhere in the show, it doesn't get any more high octane as we join Anthea Turner in a Nottingham shopping centre talking to some people buying tickets. After the draw we return to Turner who is now in a pub chatting to two people who have won a tenner. She asks what they will do with their winnings and they reply, 'Get drunk!' 'You're not gonna get drunk on ten pounds,' Turner replies sternly.

The excitement of this first show seems mad now; in fact it felt mad about two weeks after it aired, by which point everyone had realised quite how rubbish the lottery was. I know my parents carried on doing the lottery for a few years, but I have no memory of anything that happened in the following broadcasts of *The National Lottery Live*, with one simple exception: Mystic Meg, the undeniable high point of The National Lottery coverage.

Each week for around a minute, Meg would offer a description of the people the planets had told her were going to win the jackpot, performing her monologue – in a move that could be described as a little on the nose – surrounded by dry ice and from behind a crystal ball. Part of the popularity of Mystic Meg was that she was such a gearshift to the rest of the show. You would go from Anthea Turner interviewing a woman who had opened a local municipal swimming pool with lottery funding to Mystic Meg telling you, 'An Aquarius who bought their ticket in a shop in which the colour mauve means something is going to win a big prize too.' Like all great astrologers, her tips were vague enough to get people excited but also be totally unverifiable at the same time, from 'a house with number 7 on the door in a town that begins with the letter B' to 'a pet bird and the name Colin are important'. Sadly we didn't know anyone with the name Colin, although Gin did have a mug with it written on.

Mystic Meg was the breakout star of *The National Lottery Live*, achieving such popularity with the nation that for a period she even became the front woman of Oasis.[2] In fact, Meg had become so central to the show that there is a clip online of *Points of View* vox-popping people in a Mecca bingo hall, not about the National Lottery as a whole but simply about their views on Mystic Meg. It remains one of the least illuminating pieces of TV I have ever watched, with quotes ranging from, 'If she says, "someone wearing a yellow jumper" I think, I wish I had a yellow jumper on,' to 'The things she says . . . "it's going to be a bus driver that wins it, somebody who's Capricorn . . ." Half the time none of them win.' I have no idea how this woman knew that half the time it wasn't a bus-driving Capricorn who won, but she seemed very certain.

Meg would be part of the National Lottery coverage from 1994 to 2000, far longer than any of its main presenters lasted and far more popular than any other part of the show, something no one could have predicted (perhaps apart from her). These days she is still going strong. She still has a column in the *Sun* and has even diversified into selling her own jewellery range, The Mystic Meg Collection, so that's Christmas sorted. She is even active on Twitter, her tweets summing up her brand perfectly:

---

[2] Before you get too excited, I should point out that this sentence refers to the mid-nineties' fruit drink Oasis, rather than the band. A shame really – what a show that would have been.

PISCES

Mysterious, deep, capable of intense love and intensely ruthless, very imaginative business deals, too.

Planet Ruler: Neptune

Element: Water

Jewel: Amethyst

Flower: Lily

Colour: Violet

Healing Crystal: Onyx

Or, the slightly more surprising:

#WIN WIN WIN!

RALPH by Ralph Lauren, a magical #fragrance. Crisp apple notes mixed with soft, subtle florals gives the perfect summer scent – reminiscent of sea, sunshine and fresh air.

For your chance to win, head over to the OFFICIAL MYSTIC MEG Facebook page to enter. Good luck!

In many ways, it's Mystic Meg in a nutshell – a mix of astrology and getting people overexcited about winning things.

In the end, seven people matched the numbers of the first National Lottery draw, all winning less than a million pounds. When Noel said that within the next hour somebody was going to be a millionaire, he was wrong, and after all the build-up it turned out it couldn't be you. The reality was that the biggest winner to come out of the first night of the National Lottery was a strange woman with a crystal ball who dreamed of getting a contract promoting a weak fruit drink.

Acknowledgements

I've been looking forward to writing this bit for the past year, but now I come to it I am late getting it in for deadline and exhausted from having a new child, so sorry to people I have forgotten (although there is a chance I didn't forget you but just didn't deem you worthy of thanks, text me and I'll let you know which it was). Anyway, enough delaying, the odds are if you have read this far you think you are in with a chance of making this list. So, let's see ...

Thank you first to my editor Matt for taking a risk on a book that isn't just a normal autobiography but instead has nine pages about kabaddi. I have loved working with you and hugely appreciate that you haven't once told me to take out a reference to a niche part of '90s culture that only I remember, will you live to regret it? And thank you for bearing with me and being polite as I kept making changes far after you would have happily never seen my name appear on your phone again, it must have been very annoying.

Sophie, Ali, Karen and everyone at Bonnier, thank you. You have all been incredibly supportive and worked so brilliantly to help – hopefully – make this book a success. I hugely appreciate it.

Flo – it is genuinely difficult for me to articulate how much I appreciate what you have done for me, you have completely changed my life. You took a chance on me when I had nine minutes of material, and let's be honest, neither of us thought it would end up with me being a published author. Thank you for the advice, reassurance, support and, most of all, gossip. You are the best agent and friend I could wish for.

Lily – thank you for all your support in the last year while Flo was off concentrating on more important things than Last Leg release forms, you are the only person who could talk me into getting a soda stream. And thank you to everyone else at Off the Kerb for all their support over the years, without you I would be nothing. Or worse, I would still be doing gigs for Rick in High Wycombe on a Tuesday evening.

Thank you for those that have given me advice along the way as I wrote this. Nathaniel Metcalf – the only man more obsessed with 90s popular culture than me – for pointing me in the direction of numerous bits of TV I had forgotten about. Phil Jerrod for telling me to loosen up and make the *Ghostwatch* chapter sound less like a G2 article. Matthew Crosby and Isy Suttie for reading it and telling me it mainly wasn't shit but which bits were. James Acaster, Tom Allen and Romesh Ranganathan for picking up the phone/replying to a text and reassuring me that writing a book often makes you feel like shit. Also, thank you to Tom Craine for pointing out to me quite how mad it was that *Neighbours* is screened twice a day, a small but important contribution. You are all amazing, brilliant people and I appreciate you wasting your time on me hugely.

Thank you to Joe Filbee for spending his lunchbreak in the British Library finding the transmission dates of *You Bet!* episodes in old copies of the *Radio Times*. Important work.

Thank you to Leslee Udwin for agreeing to chat to me about the only dodgy moment of an amazing career, I hope it wasn't too painful.

Thank you to Rob for writing a book at the same time I did so that we could talk about it on the podcast in an attempt to sell some units guilt free, although I fear your neck is far too loose to have reached this far into the book.

Thank you to Michael and Chris for helping me test the appeal of my love for the 90s in podcast form, the odds are I would never have done this without that proof that people were interested in jokes about Uri Geller and Gladiators.

And so onto the personal . . .

Thank you to my parents Tom and Sarah for never putting pressure on me to do well at school or indeed do anything. I can't tell you how much I appreciate my upbringing, it is easy to be nostalgic when your childhood was that laid back. To my siblings – Henry, Kate, Fran and Jake – thank you for being role models throughout my youth, I don't know if you realised how much I wanted to be living your cool lives. And to Gin, the funniest, most charismatic, most entertaining person I have ever met. I wish so much that you were here to read this book. Or just sit around and slag people off.

Thanks to The LBs for keeping me sane, nothing relieves the stress of writing alone like looking at a terrible screen grab of Garry. And thank you to the Music Block reunion pint WhatsApp group for reminding my just how strange our school years were. We will always have the night of the three dinners.

Thank you to Sam Hanson for all the cooking and baby-sitting that have allowed me to disappear upstairs, sorry there was no mention of Rainbow.

Finally and most importantly, to the people who have kept me going over the last year as I wrote this. Rose, Pearl and (more recently) Cassius. Waking up in a house with you three is the greatest joy in my life and I can't believe how lucky I am to be a part of this family. Thank you, Rose, for putting up with me waking up at 5 in the morning to say the Euro 96 chapter needs re-ordering and forgiving me for getting in a mood because cooking a Riverford had got in the way of editing a paragraph about John Virgo. You are an amazing brilliant person, the world's greatest interior designer and, crucially, you have been very patient with an idiot pretending to be an author.

Most of all thank you all for reading this, I hope it was not a complete waste of your time. Or worse, a complete waste of mine.

Index

INDEX

I

I'm Alan Partridge 240, 243–4, 247–50
IMDb 62*n*, 247*n*
information technology (IT) 108–16, 261*n*, 301

K

kabaddi 33, 39–40, 117, 118*n*
Kettley, John 229

L

lads' mags 280–1, 285, 290
Lamont, Norman 18, 245
Le Tissier, Matthew 159–61, 188
LGBT+ community 6, 124*n*, 234
Live & Kicking 84, 88–9, 93, 114, 174

M

magazine shows 9, 69, 296
Major, John 108, 115–16, 190, 212, 218*n*, 224–6, 228
Marble Mania 91–3, 149
Men Behaving Badly 278–90, 306
Millennium Dome 57, 57*n*, 304–6, 315
Minogue, Kylie 75
Mr Blobby 43, 135, 136, 138–45, 206, 227
movies 5, 34, 40–1, 51, 57, 62, 62*n*, 71–4, 78, 91, 97, 115, 125*n*, 154, 167–9, 186, 204, 237, 243, 247*n*, 276, 293, 310
music/musical tastes 47, 75, 85–6, 92, 94, 145–6, 172–82, 190, 199, 211, 216, 245, 256–7, 273–7, 279, 291–9, 305, 309, 317, 318–19

N

NatWest 48*n*, 54, 55, 164
Neighbours 9, 23*n*, 52, 73–83, 92, 102–7, 123, 127, 132, 148, 269
New Year programming 301–4, 315
news programming 11, 196*n*, 212, 233, 271, 302
Newton Abbot 8, 28, 31, 89–91, 120, 295
999 147, 152–5, 161, 185, 186, 289, 297
Noel's House Party 43, 135–46, 156

P

panto 99–100, 246, 246*n*
Parkinson, Michael ('Parky') 61, 64, 65, 67, 69, 69*n*, 71
phone-ins 64, 64*n*, 69–71, 88, 145, 187–8, 213, 226, 254, 270–1
pigeon racing 34, 34*n*, 40–1, 222
Plymouth Hoe 296, 298
Portaloo shortage 292
Postlethwaite, Pete 228
puppets 3–12, 16, 26, 30, 135, 248, 268, 270–1, 314

Q

Queen's Speech 74
quiz shows *see* game shows

R

Radio Times 24*n*, 68, 69, 70, 263, 278, 297
reality TV 23, 46–7, 98, 133*n*, 143, 166, 169, 208, 224, 260, 295, 308–17, 318, 318–19
Reith, Lord 1
role models 126, 246
Ross, Jonathan 245, 270
Royal Family 24, 74, 75*n*, 216, 232–9, 304